Closer to Christ

Other books by
EMILY BELLE FREEMAN

Even This: Getting to the Place Where You Can Trust God with Anything
The Christ-Centered Home: Inviting Jesus In
Celebrating a Christ-Centered Easter
Celebrating a Christ-Centered Christmas

Closer to Christ

INCLUDES:

21 Days Closer to Christ

—

Becoming His

EMILY BELLE FREEMAN

DESERET
BOOK

SALT LAKE CITY, UTAH

Background: Beautiful_textures/iStock/Getty Images and traffico/shutterstock.com

Library of Congress Cataloging-in-Publication Data
(CIP data to come)
ISBN 978-1-62972-526-0

Printed in the United States of America
Lake Book Manufacturing, Inc., Melrose Park, IL

10   9   8   7   6   5   4   3   2

*If you have ever wondered if He knows you,
if He understands your need, if He is really there—
this book was written for you.*

Preface

It's been just over ten years since *21 Days Closer to Christ* was released. Over the past decade, I have heard story after story of how the words on these pages have encouraged people to spend more time in their scriptures and prompted them to consider where they currently are in their relationship with Christ, and to ponder where they would like to be. I have been to youth conferences centered around this theme, spoken to groups of women who have studied the scripture stories within these pages over the course of a year, and attended young single adult events where invitations to know Christ better were extended. Yes, my heart is full with the stories of how this book was the beginning of a journey that would lead hearts closer to Christ.

Perhaps it would interest you to know that this book began with a story of its own. It was a late afternoon almost thirteen years ago. I felt a prompting to go visit my brother. It had been a rough couple of months, and this happened to be a particularly hard day. We talked for some time, wrestling through the hard things. He wondered if he would make it through. I remember telling him that with the help of the Savior he would. I was certain of it. I had been in that dark place myself, so I was speaking from experience. "Turn to the Lord," I told him. "Just one day at a time. Day by day. That's how He will get you through."

On my way home, my thoughts filled with memories of the time when I had been in that place. Perhaps you know that place. Sometimes you just need a place to start, a reminder of how near the Lord is, a little bit of hope. So, I sat down and wrote my brother a letter, which I folded up, placed in an envelope, and left on his front porch. It was a Monday. On the next Monday, I wrote another letter. And, a week later, another one. My brother read each letter one after the other, and hope began to return. After a month, he asked if he could share one of the letters with a family he was visiting. Then he called to see about sharing another one. It wasn't long before other people started calling to ask if they could pass the letters along. The letters brought hope. They invited people to turn to verses of scripture, and the scriptures testified of the Savior who heals.

That first letter is chapter six in *21 Days Closer to Christ*, "When Hope Is Gone." In fact, each of the chapters in that book began as a letter I placed on my brother's front porch in an effort to help him turn to Christ during a really dark time.

Each of us will experience moments when we find ourselves seeking healing, hope, and the grace that Christ can bring. Maybe you or someone you love is in that place right now. If so, consider this your own stack of letters meant to help you or your loved one find the peace that comes through Him.

Five years after that first book was published, I wrote a second book—a continuation of the journey to know Christ better—*Becoming His*. It is a book filled with scriptures, stories, and quotes to help us continue our daily journey toward discipleship. The two books were meant to become companion volumes that would help each of us on our journey to come closer to Christ, and now they are. My heart is thrilled about this.

I have a deep and abiding love for Jesus Christ. Throughout my life I have experienced His hope and His healing. I have no other desire than to teach of Him, to testify of His goodness, and to lead others to experience His love. The words on these pages might be simple, but they are my witness of the reality of a Savior who knows us, who loves us, and who wants to walk with us throughout every part of our journey.

"Let us lay aside every weight,
and the sin which doth so easily beset us,
and let us run with patience the race that is set before us,
Looking unto Jesus the author and finisher of our faith; . . .
Consider him."

—Hebrews 12:1–3

21 Days
Closer to
Christ

*"Lift up the hands which hang down,
and strengthen the feeble knees."*

—D&C 81:5

The Invitation

"If with all your hearts ye truly seek me,
Ye shall ever surely find me."

—Children's Songbook, 15

The best invitation I have ever seen came by mail in a large box addressed to my sister. The return address was that of a dear friend. We opened the box and began to lay the contents out on the table. Nestled in beautiful tissue paper, with gold ribbon winding throughout, there was an intricately designed nutcracker, two round-trip airline tickets to San Francisco, and a gift certificate for a three-night stay at a hotel. At the very bottom of the box, on a sheet of fine linen paper, there was an engraved invitation to attend a Christmas party that would last all weekend. It was almost as if she were being invited to Cinderella's ball. Even I was excited for the party, and I wasn't even going. What set this invitation apart from any other was that it came with the promise of a treasure, a journey, and a celebration.

I wish I could have sent this book to you wrapped up in beautiful paper and tied with a gold ribbon, but that would have been a publishing nightmare. Instead, carefully nestled between the covers of this book, you will find an invitation that includes a treasure, a journey, and a celebration.

This is an *invitation* for you to take a journey to come to know and recognize more clearly the hand of the Lord in your life. Scattered throughout this book you will find *treasures* that can make the journey more meaningful to you. The *celebration* will come from the moments and experiences that bring you closer to Christ.

"Behold, and lo, I am with you even unto the end."

—D&C 100:12

Let's begin the journey by quickly unwrapping the book. Most of the chapters include recommended daily scripture study and a reminder to have daily personal prayer. These are two important practices in developing a testimony of Jesus Christ. We can learn much about the Savior as we read of His life and teachings in the scriptures. We can draw closer to Him through prayer. To make these daily moments more meaningful, there are questions at the end of each chapter, which will allow you to assess your own personal journey to know the Lord. Pondering these questions will make the treasure you discover from each day your own. Perhaps these simple moments will become the celebration of your day.

This is your journey, your treasure, and your celebration. Because it is an invitation, you can do with it whatever you like. Maybe you will focus on one chapter every day, or perhaps you would like to read one chapter a week. Choose the way that works the best for you. I hope that what you will receive at the end of your journey is just what you yearn for.

If you begin this process with a humble heart, seeking for a stronger testimony, and come with a desire to truly find the Lord, I believe the Spirit will guide you in the direction you need to travel to find yourself closer to Christ. Remember, these twenty-one days are only the beginning of a journey that will last forever.

May you find joy in the journey, may you have the courage and the commitment to know the Lord, and may His choicest blessings attend you along the way.

"You are embarking on something which is going to take the whole of you."

—C. S. LEWIS, *MERE CHRISTIANITY*, 78

Come and See

Thou shalt see greater things than these.

—John 1:50

Years ago, following a particularly long and furious storm, I walked out the front door to assess the damage. My young son Josh who had been terrified of the flashing lightning and the constant pounding of thunder, clung to the bottom of my shirt and followed me outside. As we stepped onto the front porch we were stunned by the most brilliant rainbow I have ever seen. The colors were so amazingly vivid that you could differentiate the breaks between the purples and blues, the greens and yellows, the oranges and the reds. And above this breathtaking sight was a second bow, almost as brilliant and beautiful as the one mirrored below. We stood still, taking it in, and then we began to call out to the rest of the family who were still sheltered inside, "Come and see! Come and see!" This announcement was not good enough for Josh, who took off running across the street and began to knock on the doors of our neighbors. We all gathered to witness the beautiful event that lasted only moments, as rainbows do, and then we returned to our homes feeling blessed to have beheld such a wondrous sight.

Just over two thousand years ago, a similar invitation was given to two men who were fishing. As Christ walked along the shore of the Sea of Galilee, He saw two brothers, Simon and Andrew, casting their net into the sea, for they were fishermen. They said unto Him, "Rabbi, . . . where dwellest thou?" and He said unto them, "Come and see" (John 1:38, 39; see also Matthew 4:18–19). Several other men were given this same invitation, and one of them, Philip, ran to tell his friend Nathanael, who questioned whether or not Jesus was the real Messiah. Philip answered him, "Come and see" (John 1:46).

This simple invitation summarizes the Master's ministry. His was always an invitation: come and see; come follow me; come unto me. He asked His followers to come, and then He showed them the blessings that followed the simple invitation: water turned to wine; loaves and fishes multiplied; the lame walked; the blind saw; the dead would live again. The invitation was always extended. Acceptance was left to the individual. They could do as did the disciples—who straightway forsook their nets and followed Him—or they could continue the journey alone, completely missing the blessing of the wondrous sights they might have beheld.

Today we are given the same invitation that was extended many years ago to the fishermen of Galilee: set aside your nets and come and see. But, will we leave behind our nets, which are so full of other interests and everyday challenges?

We are pulled at on every side by distractions that entangle us. Time constraints, daily chores, work demands, worldly pursuits, pride, or other

> *"My desire today is for all of us . . . to have more straight-forward personal experience with the Savior's example."*
>
> —JEFFREY R. HOLLAND

pressures may prevent us from developing a relationship with Christ. If we are to be truly happy, if we are to reach our full potential, I believe we must create a place for the Savior in our lives. I testify the sacrifice is worth it. The precious moments that will come as we cast aside our nets will allow us to discover something of much greater worth. As Elder Jeffrey R. Holland said, "My desire today is for *all* of us . . . to have more straightforward personal experience with the Savior's example. Sometimes we seek heaven too obliquely, focusing on programs or history or the experience of others. Those are important but not as important as personal experience, true discipleship, and the strength that comes from experiencing firsthand the majesty of His touch" ("Broken Things to Mend," *Ensign*, May 2006, 70; emphasis in original).

Two thousand years ago, two fishermen left their nets and walked away from everything that would hold them back from coming to know Jesus Christ. Heeding the invitation, they followed the Savior and were blessed to experience incredible events, which burned an undeniable testimony upon their souls. If we are willing, we too can find opportunities that will allow us to come to know the Savior personally.

Learn to listen for the quiet invitation of the Master, the times when He invites you to come and see. Most often this whisper will come as we read the scriptures, visit the temple, attend church meetings, and during the still moments when we sincerely pray. Perhaps you will be led to places in your life where you can come to know Christ more fully. Maybe you will learn how to incorporate His attributes into your character. Hopefully you will come to know and recognize the peace and comfort His Spirit makes possible.

Make this the first day of your twenty-one-day journey. The soft rhythm of sandaled feet might not accompany you, but if you prepare with a prayer in your heart before the experiences of each day, I am confident that the Spirit of the Lord will whisper assurances to your soul that you do not travel alone.

If you want to know who Christ is, come and see. If you need to find answers to deep longings within your soul, come and see. If you are desperate to know the healing power Christ can and will bring, come and see. If you want to become a true follower of the Christ, come and see.

THE INVITATION . . . *Come*

Read the account of the fishermen in Mark 1:16–18 and in John 1:38–39.

THE JOURNEY

• Determine what fills your nets. Are everyday challenges such as time constraints, demands from work or home, or feelings of inadequacy or fear holding you back from developing a relationship with Christ?

• Today try to listen for the quiet invitations from the Lord to *come and see.*

Take His Name

Behold, I will lead thee by my hand, and I will
take thee, to put upon thee my name.

—ABRAHAM 1:18

Every celebration begins with a time of anticipation. Expectation fills the air as guests gather and mingle, waiting for the host to seat them around a table that has been carefully spread. Little can compare with the pleasure of an evening spent with friends.

This feeling of anticipation surely filled the upper-level room on the evening of the Last Supper. After all that had happened previous to that night, the disciples must have looked forward to a quiet evening alone with the Lord. Entering the room from the dusty, crowded streets below, each would have removed his sandals at the door and found a seat around the table. It was at this moment that Christ taught a powerful lesson that was completely unexpected. Just before supper began, Jesus took a bowl and, after girding himself with a towel, knelt in turn beside each guest to wash his feet. This service caught the disciples by surprise because washing the feet of the guest was traditionally deemed a lowly act, one that only a servant would perform. As was His nature, the Savior connected this unexpected act of service with a teaching moment: "To share in this washing, was, as it were, the way to have part in Christ's service of love, to enter into it, and to share it. . . . There was deep symbolical meaning, not only in *that* Christ did it, but also in *what* He did. . . . *What* He did, meant His work and service of love; the constant cleansing of one's walk and life in the love of Christ. . . . it is the daily consecration of our life to the service of love after the example of Christ" (Alfred Edersheim, *Life and Times of Jesus the Messiah* [New York: Longmans, Green, and Co., 1899], Vol. II, 500; hereafter, AE).

After performing this sacred service, Christ introduced the ordinance of the sacrament we are familiar with today. "The weekly opportunity of partaking of the Sacrament of the Lord's Supper is one of the most sacred ordinances of The Church of Jesus Christ of Latter-day Saints. . . . We may fail to recognize the deep spiritual significance this ordinance offers to each of us personally" (David B. Haight, "The Sacrament," *Ensign,* May 1983, 14). Just as the washing of the disciples' feet helped them to remember to follow His footsteps daily, the ordinance we participate in each Sunday is intended to remind us of the covenants we have entered into with the Savior. That relationship should be the focus of our everyday life, for the Lord has instructed that "the members shall manifest before the church, and also before the elders, by a godly *walk* and *conversation,* that they are worthy . . . walking in holiness before the Lord" (D&C 20:69; emphasis added).

By partaking of the sacrament we covenant that we are willing to take upon us the name of His Son, and always remember Him, especially in our daily walk and conversation (see D&C 20:77). Think over some of the situations you encountered during the past week. Were your actions consistent with the covenant you have made? Were you able to always remember Him? How did you represent His name?

Each of my children was named after someone they can look up to. My husband, Greg, and I felt just as Helaman did when he explained to his sons Lehi and Nephi, "Behold, I have given unto you the names of our first parents who came out of the land of Jerusalem; and this I have done that when you remember your names ye may remember them; and when ye remember them ye may remember their works; and when ye remember their works ye may know how that it is said, and also written, that they were good. Therefore, my sons, I would that ye should do that which is good, that it may be said of you, and also written, even as it has been said and written of them" (Hel. 5:6–7). Our children enjoy hearing the stories behind their names and the qualities we admire about the person they were named after.

In our home we have a quote from President Gordon B. Hinckley that hangs just above our front door. It reads, "Be true to who you are, and the family name you bear." Shortly after we hung the quote we talked about what it meant to be true to a name. We wanted our children to be reminded every time they walked out of our door that everything they do outside our home represents the entire family. Their choices determine whether or not they bring honor to our family, and also to the person they were named after. Then we talked of another important name that each of us has been given. This is the name of Jesus Christ. King Benjamin said, "Therefore, I would that ye should take upon you the name of Christ. . . . And it shall come to pass that whosoever doeth this shall be found at the right hand of God, for he shall know the name by which he is called; for he shall be called by the name of Christ" (Mosiah 5:8–9).

Taking the name of Jesus Christ helps each of us to remember Him. As we come to know the Savior through different situations, we might find ourselves remembering Him by different names that endear Him to us. Among others, we may consider Him as a Brother, a Friend, a Healer, or an Advocate. The names of the Savior can become names that we reflect on often, to bring us comfort and calm in times of trial, peace and hope in times of trouble, and courage and strength to always stand as His witnesses. We can concentrate on the meaning of these different names every week as we take the sacrament.

Renewing and keeping this covenant weekly enables us to receive a wonderful blessing. Elder Robert D. Hales explains that when we take "His name

When we take "His name and always remember Him and keep His commandments, He gives us the greatest blessing He can give us: that is to always have His Spirit to be with us."

—ROBERT D. HALES

and always remember Him and keep His commandments, He gives us the greatest blessing He can give us: that is to always have His Spirit to be with us" ("In Remembrance of Jesus," *Ensign,* Nov. 1997, 25).

Just as the disciples did in the time of Christ, we can consecrate our lives to serve the Lord. It might be in the words we speak, the service we render, or the promptings we follow. Today make it a priority to bear burdens, give comfort, and stand as a witness.

Try to remember Him always.

THE INVITATION . . . *Covenant*

Read the account of the Last Supper in John 13:4–15.

THE JOURNEY

- As you go through this day, find ways that you can bring honor to Christ's name by letting the walk of your life exemplify Him. On this day, try to remember Him always.

- This twenty-one-day journey will introduce different names of the Savior. Every chapter contains one name that relates to a scripture story or gospel principle. Take a moment each day to reflect on how each name describes a way that He blesses your life.

A Common Thread

The keeper of the gate is the Holy One of Israel;
and he employeth no servant there.

—2 Nephi 9:41

In my house there is a keeping room. It is the place where I keep everything that is dear to me. Framed treasures, favorite books, and memory-filled trinkets fill the room. One of my dearest possessions is a copy of a journal written by Greg's great-grandma, Susan Marinda Bullock. She was a renowned nurse, a beloved mother, and a devoted wife. Every January the women in my husband's family gather together to study her journal. While sifting through the stories of her life, we have found a common thread that is woven throughout each page. This thread has helped us come to know and understand the strength of Marinda's faith. Page after page testifies of the power of prayer and the importance of listening to the promptings of the Spirit. Because she is no longer with us, the memories she penned are even more priceless.

Through very simple examples, this journal explains how Marinda obtained her testimony of listening and following the promptings of the Holy Ghost. Her success as a nurse came in part because she would pray before visiting her patients and then listen for the direction that she knew the Spirit would send. Marinda learned to rely on this direction. She recorded many examples of when a mother or child's life had been saved because she had followed those whisperings of the Spirit. Many times, after being faced with a complicated decision, she wrote about how she would go off alone and make it a matter of fasting and prayer as she waited for the answer to come. Her life was filled with adversity and trial. During an especially trying period she writes that a voice spoke to her, most true and tender, "You must be tried, to be proven." Shortly thereafter she wrote, "My Heavenly Father was surely mindful of me. And when we know that, we live our lives free and apart without murmuring with life or the part we are called to play."

This is a woman who had learned to rely on the Spirit in her profession, in her marriage, and in her home. In fact, story after story testifies of her relationship with the Holy Ghost and the miracles that filled her life because she learned to rely on the Spirit. The most powerful entry of the entire journal is found on the very last page. Here Marinda left advice that has been passed down in our family from generation to generation:

"To my children and grandchildren.
Learn to listen to the whisperings of the Spirit."

That is wonderful advice. But her counsel is even more convincing because of the many personal stories she recorded in which following the Spirit resulted in wonderful blessings. Now, four generations later, we are learning from the lessons of her life—how to listen to the whisperings of the Spirit.

President Spencer W. Kimball counseled members of the Church in this regard:

> "We renew our appeal for the keeping of individual histories and accounts of sacred experiences in our lives—answered prayers, inspiration from the Lord, administrations in our behalf, a record of the special times and events of our lives. From these records you can also appropriately draw as you relay faith-promoting stories in your family circles and discussions. Stories of inspiration from our own lives and those of our forebears as well as stories from our scriptures and our history are powerful teaching tools. I promise you that if you will keep your journals and records they will indeed be a source of great inspiration to you, each other, your children, your grandchildren, and others throughout the generations" ("Therefore I Was Taught," *Ensign*, Jan. 1982, 4).

What if you were to keep a journal of your relationship with Jesus Christ? The pages could contain attributes you admire in Him, lessons He has taught you, or moments when you have felt His love. The journal could become a keepsake of your testimony. Perhaps you would like to start it on this journey closer to Christ and continue it throughout your life. Nephi recorded a promise the Lord gave to him in this regard, "that these things which I write shall be kept and preserved, and handed down unto my seed, from generation to generation, that the promise may be

> *"For we labor diligently to write, to persuade our children, and also our brethren, to believe in Christ."*
>
> —2 NEPHI 25:23

fulfilled. . . . For we labor diligently to write, to persuade our children, and also our brethren, to believe in Christ" (2 Ne. 25: 21, 23).

Maybe someday, generations from now, someone in your posterity will read through the stories you have recorded and find a common thread, one that will lead them closer to Christ.

THE INVITATION . . . *Keep*

Read 2 Nephi 25:21–26.

THE JOURNEY

- Do you have a written copy of your testimony of Christ? Take time to write one today. You might want to include your belief in Him, your gratitude for Him, or an experience that has strengthened your testimony of Him.

- Obtain and keep a journal of your twenty-one-day journey, recording the treasures and discoveries that come to you as you follow this path.

Come

✦

Covenant

✦

Keep

Never Stopping, Ever Searching

The cultivation of Christlike qualities is a demanding and relentless task—it is not for the seasonal worker or for those who will not stretch themselves, again and again.

—Spencer W. Kimball

Sometimes our search to find the Savior can be complicated. We seek Him for direction and advice, searching through the maze of our everyday life to feel His Spirit. Looking back on my life, I realize that the most demanding and relentless moments of the search have done the most to teach me to treasure His companionship. The scriptures are filled with story after story, telling of man's ongoing search to find the Lord. One of my favorites is the story of Jairus, one of the "rulers of the synagogue," whose only daughter was on the verge of death.

With no time to lose, Jairus traveled through the night, never stopping, ever searching to find the Lord. At the journey's end, the distraught man fell at the Savior's feet, saying, "My little daughter lieth at the point of death: I pray thee, come and lay thy hands on her, that she may be healed; and she shall live" (Mark 5:23).

Immediately, Christ set off with the worried father. I am sure the journey toward home must have been just as nerve-wracking as the father's journey to find the Lord. Having left when his daughter was close to death, Jarius's every thought must have been consumed with the hope that his daughter would be alive when he returned. How discouraging it must have been to realize that the journey home would take him down a street thronged with people. The crowd was dense and probably loud. I am sure Jesus moved down the street surrounded by His disciples, determined, just as Jairus was, to arrive at His destination.

In the commotion one woman sat quietly and watched. Suffering from an illness that had debilitated her for twelve years, she had tried all she could to relieve the suffering. Only one option remained, and so she waited. With faith the only thing prompting her actions, she reached out and touched the hem of the Savior's robe at the precise moment He stood closest to her. "For she said within herself, if I may but touch his garment, I shall be whole. But Jesus turned him about, and when he saw her, he said, Daughter, be of good comfort; thy faith hath made thee whole" (Matt. 9:21–22).

In this brief encounter, I imagine that Jairus learned a great deal. This woman had come to know the Savior and therefore had enough faith to know that He would heal her. In her illness she had tried everything she possibly could on her own to resolve the issue—she had seen physicians, she had done all. Through the process she had reached the point where the only relief she could find would come from her faith in the Lord. In this case, "faith had to be called out, tried, purified, and so perfected . . .

[because] the thing sought for was, humanly speaking, unattainable" (AE Vol. I, 617). What encouragement this must have brought to Jairus's worried heart, for he also sought healing from the Lord. It was but a small moment, but one that must have had a profound effect on his faith.

The scriptures do not tell us what Jairus did as he waited. But we do know that just after the woman was healed, a messenger arrived from Jairus's house, saying, "Thy daughter is dead: why troublest thou the Master any further?" (Mark 5:35). The father must have been heartbroken to hear such news, but "even these dread tidings of certainty failed to destroy the man's faith; he seems to have still looked to the Lord for help" (James E. Talmage, *Jesus the Christ* [Salt Lake City, UT: Deseret Book, 1976], 314). How could Jairus deny that he had just witnessed a miracle? Perhaps what he had thought to be a detour was part of a process he needed to experience before he could exercise the faith required for his own daughter to be made whole. Christ encouraged, "Be not afraid, only believe" (Mark 5:36).

Upon entering the home, they were met with great disbelief, even laughter, as people mocked the Lord. But Jairus's faith remained firm as he and his wife went with Jesus into their daughter's room and watched in gratitude and wonder as Jesus took their daughter's hand and said: "Damsel, I say unto thee, arise." Imagine their amazement and joy when the young girl "arose, and walked" (Mark 5:41–42). I am sure the gratitude that overwhelmed Jairus's heart must have brought him to his knees. The demanding and relentless journey had been worth it—his precious daughter had been restored.

Both Jairus and the woman who touched Christ's robe were steadfast in one desire—to become close enough to Christ that they could obtain the miracle they needed. Both, like many of us, realized the desired out-come was humanly unattainable. But they had come to believe that Christ could provide a healing that could not be provided in any other way.

Jairus was relentless in his search to find the Lord. The woman who touched Christ's robe stretched until she received the miracle she longed for. We too can cultivate a relationship with Christ by applying these same principles. Most likely the answer will not come easily. The woman was plagued by her illness for more than twelve years before the answer came. Imagine how trying it must have been for Jairus when, even though he was with the Savior, his situation became worse before it got better. Joseph Smith said, "Whatever God requires is right, no matter what it is, although we may not see the reason thereof till long after the events transpire" (*History of the Church,* 5:135). No matter how long or hard the search, if it brings us closer to Christ, it is worth it. The intensity of the search will make the treasure priceless, one that we will not ever give up.

Our son, Josh, was diagnosed with diabetes when he was three. Dealing with the disease has made the past eleven years difficult. They have been filled with many ups and downs and a lot of discouraging and trying moments. I have spent countless hours pleading with the Lord to lighten our burden. Although Josh has not been healed, I have felt the Savior strengthening both Josh and me to be equal to the task. This year we were asked to participate in a research study. As part of the study, we both took a six-page self-evaluation test. One of the questions asked if we would choose, given the opportunity, to not have this trial in our life, realizing that we would have to also give up all of the learning that had come. Before responding to the question, I sat for ten minutes and pon-dered all that we have learned, reflecting most on my relationship with

Christ. He has lifted me and strengthened me. When I thought I could not go on, He made up the difference. I have come to know the Savior through this journey—and so has Josh.

In the end I determined I could not give that up—it was too precious. This detour, though demanding and relentless, has made me stretch again and again in my search to know the Savior, and that process has led me closer to Christ.

THE INVITATION . . . *Search*

Read the account of Jairus in Matthew 9:18–26.

THE JOURNEY

- Think back on a time in your life when you had to search for the Savior to find strength beyond your own. Try to remember the process you went through in that search. Was it scripture study, more meaningful prayers, or another avenue that led you to Christ?

- Stretch again. Apply one of those principles today.

Who Is This Jesus?

Whom say ye that I am?

—MATTHEW 16:15

It was a room of discovery tucked inconspicuously behind the door at the foot of the basement stairs. My mother called it a root cellar. As a child, I was fascinated by this room. In the midst of winter you could walk through the door and find yourself surrounded by the smell of the damp earth, fresh dirt, and summer. I spent many late afternoons running my small fingers through the clean, white sand and digging up potatoes for our dinner. On one such afternoon, a small magnet that had been in my pocket fell onto the sand. I bent to pick it up and noticed that a cluster of soft black *fur* had attached to the back. I looked closely at the sand where the magnet had fallen, but I did not see any more of the fur there. So I took the magnet, along with the potatoes for dinner, upstairs to my mother to see what I had discovered.

With research we learned that there were particles of iron scattered throughout the sand. Drawn to the magnetic force, these particles clung to the magnet when it fell. Sometimes, when there was absolutely nothing better to do, my sisters and I would go down to the root cellar like gold diggers with pie tins and all different sizes of magnets to see how much iron we could collect. We would drag the magnets through layers of sand and pick up the tiny black fragments, so small that our naked eye would never have noticed them. Although the reward was small, we loved to sift through the clean, black iron in the bottom of our tins at the end of hours of effort.

Years later I discovered a quote from the American preacher Henry Ward Beecher:

> If one should give me a dish of sand, and tell me there were particles of iron in it, I might look for them with my eyes, and search for them with my clumsy fingers, and be unable to detect them; but let me take a magnet and sweep through it, and [it would] draw to itself the almost invisible particles, by the mere power of attraction! The unthankful heart, like my finger in the sand, discovers no mercies; but let the thankful heart sweep through the day, and as the magnet finds the iron, so it will find in every hour some heavenly blessings; only the iron in God's sand is gold. (*Life Thoughts Gathered from the Extemporaneous Discourses of Henry Ward Beecher*, ed. Edna Dean Proctor [Boston: Phillips, Sampson and Company, 1858], 116).

At that young age, the iron in the sand was plenty of reward for an afternoon of hard work. Now I am not so easily satisfied. The treasure I seek is the one Henry Ward Beecher has suggested—God's gold. My search is constant, the task both consuming and rewarding. I want to know the Savior.

Over two thousand years ago Jesus walked on this earth. Twelve men and a handful of women were given the opportunity to witness daily the miracle of His life. He told them, "Blessed are your eyes, for they see: and your ears, for they hear. For verily I say unto you, That many prophets and righteous men have desired to see those things which ye see, and have not seen them; and to hear those things which ye hear, and have not heard them" (Matt. 13:16–17). It must have been an amazing experience for those early Saints to see with their eyes and hear with their ears the moments and miracles that had been prophesied, the experiences that those of us who live today only read about. How disheartening and disappointing it must have been for the Savior to realize that "the world knew him not. He came unto his own, and his own received him not" (John 1:10–11). He was like iron in the sand; many were unable to discover His identity as the Savior of the world.

I often wonder how we can prevent ourselves from becoming like that. Can we discover, in every hour, something that will bring us closer to Christ? President Thomas S. Monson has said, "We need not visit the Holy Land to feel Him close to us. We need not walk by the shores of Galilee or among the Judean hills to walk where Jesus walked. In a very real sense, all can walk where Jesus walked when, with His words on our lips, His spirit in our hearts, and His teachings in our lives, we journey through mortality" ("The Paths Jesus Walked," *Ensign*, May 1974, 48).

On one of the Savior's many journeys, He traveled through Samaria and stopped at Jacob's well. I imagine that the day was warm and the city

"In a very real sense, all can walk where Jesus walked when, with his words on our lips, his spirit in our hearts, and his teachings in our lives, we journey through mortality."

—THOMAS S. MONSON

was loud with the comings and goings from such a central location. As Jesus sat by the well, a woman from Samaria approached, and He asked her for a drink. This surprised the woman because the Jews did not normally speak to the Samaritans. She had been taught that she was not good enough to speak to a Jew, and she wondered if this man had misunderstood who she was.

How many of us experience feelings such as hers? Sometimes when we consider having a relationship with the Savior, we may feel we are inadequate; we might question our worth and worthiness and wonder if the Savior recognizes us for who we really are. But herein lies an important lesson—even though Christ was a Jew, He considered this moment with the Samaritan woman of utmost importance because she was of great worth in His eyes. Before He began teaching her, He made her feel valuable. As they talked, Jesus revealed His insight into her life and the problems that she dealt with day-to-day, and she soon realized that He did in fact know who she was. He gently prodded until she finally allowed room for Him in her heart.

What began as an ordinary task suddenly became life changing. As she spoke to the Savior, the Samaritan woman developed a genuine longing for more insight. Who was this Jesus? The quest for knowledge had begun.

We quickly learn that this woman was not completely ignorant. She had been taught that Messiah would come, and she also knew his name would be Christ. Jesus took this knowledge and added to her faith, just as He does with each one of us. As the supreme teacher, He built upon her knowledge, line upon line, until He was able to finally testify that *He* was the promised Messiah. The same is true in our own lives. He will take what knowledge we have and add to it until we receive a fulness of knowledge. He knows us. Just as He knew every detail of this woman's life, He knows every detail of ours. And just as He taught her with the simple analogies that were a part of her daily work, He will teach us in ways that we can understand.

For the Samaritan woman, this powerful teaching moment came at a very unexpected time. "She had come—like so many of us, who find the pearl in the field which we occupy in the business of everyday life— on humble, ordinary duty and work" (AE, Vol. I, 408). And it was here that she was taught. Likewise, some of our greatest learning moments may come as we go about our ordinary daily tasks. We must learn to watch for these moments, for these "pearls in the field" of our everyday lives. Then we become true treasure seekers, daily discovering God's gold.

The Invitation . . . *Discover*

Read the account of the Samaritan woman in John 4:1–42.

The Journey

- Prepare to receive a simple learning moment, a "pearl in the field," as you go through your day. Let your search be constant. Try to discover, "in every hour," some heavenly blessing that will bring you closer to Christ. A treasure—God's gold.

When Hope Is Gone

And so, after he had patiently endured, he obtained the promise.

—HEBREWS 6:15

The bitterest times are black. When I look back at the hardest times in my life, the sensation I remember most is darkness. A sense that the world is closing in, the empty feeling of nothingness, the inability to see clearly enough to make simple decisions. That darkness has the ability to shroud the soul, preventing all light from penetrating. In the book of John we read of a man in this condition. This man was blind from birth. He spent every day in the dark. Although surrounded by people, he was completely forgotten and left alone with his trial. I wonder how many times he must have sat in the black world he lived in and pondered his existence. I wonder if at times he even doubted his ability to go forward. Were there days when he questioned everything he had been taught, the reality of God, the beliefs which had sustained him through life so far? I think so.

There is a moment of epiphany after the soul has doubted all it knows, when it begins to reach out for solid answers and firm ground. This moment is defined by one emotion that sustains and creates a desire for change. Before faith or knowledge is found, before joy or happiness is experienced, before the healing begins, one emotion starts to stir from deep within the depths of despair. It is hope. Hope is the light that will begin to lead through the darkest hour, which will enable us to move forward along the darkened path. It was this light that the blind man sought.

Sometimes this epiphany, this small portion of hope, will bring a change in thought. This change simply helps us to evaluate the situation from a different view than we have previously seen. We are given small portions of knowledge, line upon line, as we work through the abyss.

The blind man experienced this process. The Lord simply changed his point of view. Dust was turned into clay. Simple. And then he was told to go to a place of healing, Siloam, and wash—an ordinary experience that symbolized so much. Wash. Let go, rid yourself of what is holding you back, and heal. The man's eyes were opened. He could see (see John 9:1–41).

There are so many times I have prayed for the Lord to touch my eyes so I might see. In the darkness of the night I have wept and pled for sight, praying that the Lord will help me see the reason for the trial and what I am supposed to learn. I question how long it will be until the trial will finally be over. Sometimes the light is slow in coming, and I wonder if I have the strength to endure. When the reason for the pain is not forthcoming, I turn to the Savior and instead of pleading for answers, I beg for comfort. I remember that during one of the Savior's greatest struggles, Heavenly Father sent unto Him from heaven an angel to strengthen Him (see Luke 22:43). I have learned to trust that in my darkest hours, when I require strength to just exist, He will send an "angel" to help me through.

After spending five long days with Josh in the hospital after he was diagnosed with diabetes, we prepared to go home. We walked out of those hospital doors and into a whole new lifestyle. It was almost as if part of us had died, and with trepidation and uncertainty we faced an entirely new road ahead. Josh, who was three years old, couldn't figure out why he wasn't better since they had allowed us to leave the hospital. He had not anticipated bringing home the shots and needles that were necessary to keep him alive. I will never forget our first afternoon home. I set Josh up on the counter so I could poke his tiny finger to test his blood and then give him a shot in preparation for dinner. He began to cry, screaming and yelling, "I hate this, I hate you, you don't do this to any of the other kids in our family, why do you do it to me? Why did you ever think I wanted to do this?" I remember he grabbed my cheeks with his tiny hands, pinching as hard as he could. I didn't stop him. When the shot was over I sat down on the kitchen floor and burst into tears. How would we ever get through?

Sometimes a burden will exhaust our energy so much we can't even begin to remember what it feels like to have faith. Although we trust that Christ lives, we may have a hard time believing that we will ever get past the point where we are. There are so many occasions when I have prayed for the Lord to sustain me in a time of trial, to strengthen me, comfort me, and increase my faith and hope to the point that I can begin to heal. I have proved Him, and He has been there.

When the apostles asked Christ why the blind man was blind, He answered that it was for one reason, "that the works of God should be made manifest in him" (John 9:3). Never underestimate the purpose of the trial. The works of Christ will be made manifest in your life. It is through adversity that we experience the sweetest parts of the Atonement. Enduring our trials allows us to experience the healing power of Jesus Christ. This process strengthens our testimony of the reality of Christ and enables us to eventually help lift the hands of another.

President Heber J. Grant gave this sweet promise: "The Lord will be always near you. He will comfort you; you will feel His presence in the hour of your greatest tribulation" (First Presidency Message, in Conference Report, Apr. 1942, 96). In the hours of greatest tribulation we can feel the Lord's presence. He will bring us comfort and He will be our strength. Most important, He will give us the hope we need to move forward when hope is gone. Elder Jeffrey R. Holland once said, "On those days when we have special need of heaven's help, we would do well to remember one of the titles given to the Savior. . . . 'an high priest of good things to come'" ("An High Priest of Good Things to Come," *Ensign*, Nov. 1999, 36).

THE INVITATION . . . *Hope*

Read the story of the blind man found in John 9:1–38.

THE JOURNEY

• Attempt to analyze through different eyes a situation that has been troubling you. Pray that the Savior will *touch* your eyes so that you will see what you need to do differently.

- Now take some time to write down some of the *good things* that have come to you through Christ. How does recognizing these blessings bring you hope?

Search

Discover

Hope

A Promise without Parallel

Inasmuch as ye are humble and faithful and call upon
my name, behold, I will give you the victory.

—D&C 104:82

When I was twelve years old I took up running between two and four miles a day. I loved to run. During those years I ran a 10K (about 6 miles) race each September. I received my number and shirt and lined up on the starting line. My mom and dad would run with me. We would pace ourselves at the beginning of the race, reserving our energy for the end. I remember looking forward to reaching the tables offering water to the runners. I loved to pass one particular curve where I knew family members would be waiting to cheer us on. I hardly remember the fifth mile; every year I barely made it through, and often considered stopping, resting, giving up. At those times my dad would offer encouragement; we would count out the steady rhythm of our stride, and I would match my steps with his, not even looking up as I pushed myself to reach the final mile. When I knew the end was in sight, I would again begin to run my own rhythm, enjoying the feeling that comes when a victory is within reach.

Paul the Apostle has counseled us, "Let us run with patience the race that is set before us, looking unto Jesus the author and finisher of our faith" (Heb. 12:1–2). Each of us has been given the opportunity to run the race of life. We are given two guidelines as we run the race—to run with patience and to look to Christ. Running with patience suggests rhythm, pacing yourself, and being able to endure. Looking unto Jesus helps us understand we weren't sent to run the race alone. He is given two names as our race partner—the Author and the Finisher. The Author suggests one with authority, who helps us align our course, someone who knows every step of the race and who can encourage us through the journey. The Finisher suggests one who completes and perfects. If we choose to let Him, He will assure that we run the race correctly and that we will be able to reach the finish line. This name is one of comfort. He promises the victory. He will sustain us, even carry us if need be. He is the Finisher.

There will be times, however, when we will contemplate quitting the race because we can't see the end in sight. We may feel there are pros and cons to giving up early, and we spend the majority of each day weighing each decision. We forget to include our partner and try to find our own rhythm and pace, ending up exhausted and lacking the energy to continue. When this happens we experience pain. We cannot run the race alone. He knows we cannot make it without Him. We are told of things that have happened, the things that are, and the things that will come. He does not leave out any part of the course. But He does offer relief in the form of the strength to endure. He invites us to turn to our Father in Heaven with our needs as we continue the journey. He asks us to pray.

At the end of a general conference session several years ago, President Gordon B. Hinckley set aside his notes and said he would like to just speak with us. Immediately he had my attention. He said he would like to read us a scripture that was the summum bonum of it all. I could hardly wait. And then he read a scripture that I had heard so many times I scarcely listened to the message it contained. That scripture is found in Moroni 7:26:

> Whatsoever thing ye shall ask the Father in my name, which is good, in faith believing that ye shall receive, behold, it shall be done unto you.

That was it? The summum bonum of it all? I admit I was a little disappointed. During the following week, I read the scripture over and over again. I decided there must be something about it I had missed. I was entirely right.

In Moroni 7:26 we are taught five simple steps to improve our prayers:

1. He begins by saying, "Whatsoever thing ye shall ask the Father . . ." The first step is to *ask*. We must pause long enough to recognize what we are in need of and then ask. The Bible Dictionary explains, "The object of prayer is . . . to secure for ourselves and for others blessings that God is already willing to grant, but that are made conditional on our asking for them" (753).

2. The next step is to ask "in my name," that is, in the name of Christ. We do this because He is our Mediator. We ask the Father for things through Christ because Christ is our advocate; He pleads our case to the Father, giving us a greater chance at the victory (see D&C 45:3–5).

3. The third step is to determine "which is good." Sometimes it is

hard to know what to pray for. Our mind wanders as issues become unclear and complicated. We have to do a little research on our own. This step includes a lot of legwork. Many times we can determine what is good only after we have done all we can on our own. Then we can take everything we have learned and place it at the feet of the Lord and ask Him to help us make the decision.

4. The fourth step is to ask "in faith, believing that ye shall receive." It is much easier to have faith when we know the Savior and believe that we have done all we can on our own to receive an answer. There is a moment of silence that precedes this step—a time of reflection. That is when we listen for encouragement; we try to hear the steady rhythm the Spirit brings; and we match our steps with His, sometimes not even looking up as we wait for direction.

5. The last step is the best step of all: "Behold, it shall be done unto you." Elder Jeffrey R. Holland said, "Some blessings come soon, some come late, . . . but for those who embrace the gospel of Jesus Christ, *they come*" ("An High Priest of Good Things to Come," *Ensign*, Nov. 1999, 38; emphasis in original). The blessings will come. The answers will be forthcoming. We don't always know how, but we can learn to watch for and accept the answers that He will send our way. This watching requires the patience we talked about before. It also requires effort. Not many people can run six miles the first time they take up jogging. And so it is with answers. We learn to receive them, a step at a time, until we become familiar enough with the answers to prayer to appreciate them everywhere around us.

As we become more familiar with the way He answers us, we will learn to pray more often. We will come to expect the answers only He can bring, and we will seek for instruction from the Lord more frequently. "Blessed art thou for what thou hast done; for thou hast inquired of me, and behold, as often as thou hast inquired thou hast received instruction of my Spirit. If it had not been so, thou wouldst not have come to the place where thou art at this time" (D&C 6:14).

After suffering from cancer, my uncle faced a short round of chemotherapy. It was, in essence, an added insurance that the cancer would not return. But after his second treatment things went terribly wrong, quickly. My uncle suffered a severe reaction to the chemotherapy, which threatened his life. I remember the frantic phone call I received from my aunt. Things were looking bad, she said; call anyone you can think of, ask them to pray. She said that during the next twelve hours, things would go one way or the other—he would either pull through, or he wouldn't make it. The news was devastating. I began to pray. I prayed every fifteen minutes for the next twelve hours. Whoever happened to be in the room with me at that moment would kneel by my side. How do you teach your children to pray for a miracle and still trust God's will? Sometimes I prayed alone. I knelt by the couch, next to my bed, in the kitchen. I prayed in the car while driving. I continually poured out my heart to God. And finally, the answer came. Early that evening my aunt called with the news that he had rounded the corner, things were looking up, and he was going to make it. One more time that day my little family gathered together in the family room. We knelt in prayer again. We thanked God for the blessing of prolonging Uncle Dick's life.

Constantly and consistently praying will help us experience joy and the comfort that comes from knowing that the One who knows the path is helping us to finish the course.

THE INVITATION . . . *Pray*

Learn to recognize the steady rhythm of the One who accompanies you along the race by reading Moroni 7:26.

THE JOURNEY

• Ponder the five characteristics of prayer given in this verse. How will remembering these make your prayers more meaningful? Choose one step that you would like to focus on.

• As you kneel to pray tonight, thank your Heavenly Father for His Son, Jesus Christ. Share with Him the reasons why you are grateful for the Savior. Let Him know what your knowledge of Christ means to you.

Recognize His Voice

I am the good shepherd, and know my sheep, and am known of mine.

—JOHN 10:14

I come from a long line of shepherds. My father wanted us to under-stand this part of our heritage, so as we were growing up our family kept a small flock of sheep. One of the sheep I will never forget had the name of "Big Mama." She earned this title because she was the leader of the flock.

Each spring brought changes to the flock as new lambs were born and older lambs would be sold, but Big Mama remained a constant. She loved my dad. It did not matter where she was on the one-acre patch of ground where we kept the sheep, when she heard him call she would come run-ning. She had a very uncommon bleat, and my dad could mimic it exactly. And so he would call, and she would answer, and when she came, the rest of the flock would follow.

One morning my dad woke me up early and said that the sheep had gone missing. They had found a hole in the fence and had wandered off.

My dad had already driven through the surrounding streets but had not seen them anywhere. He had concluded that they must have wandered through the fields and joined a flock of more than one hundred other sheep about a mile away from our home. He wanted me to come with him to talk to the farmer and to see if we could retrieve our sheep.

The farmer was not pleased to see my father. Our sheep were not marked, and unfortunately, neither were his. To him all of the sheep looked exactly the same, with black faces and white wool, and he wanted to know how my dad thought he would be able to prove which were ours. My dad tried to explain that his sheep would come when he called, and the farmer just shook his head.

My dad climbed up on the tailgate of our old white truck and started to bleat. I wish you could have seen the look on that farmer's face. The first and second calls were followed by silence. I have to admit I was a little worried. Our sheep were probably happy to find so many new friends. I wondered how important my dad would be to Big Mama now. But my dad wasn't worried—he kept calling. And finally, from the back corner of the field there was the familiar reply. My dad repeated the call loudly and consistently as Big Mama made her way through the huge flock, followed by our other lambs. The farmer watched in amazement and then helped us load our sheep into the back of the truck so that we could take them home.

In John chapter 10, Christ gave the parable of the good shepherd. To fully understand this parable it is important for us to understand how a shepherd of that time period would care for his sheep. "In the East the flocks are at night driven into a large fold, and charge of them is given to an under-shepherd . . . when the shepherd comes in the morning, 'the doorkeeper' or 'guardian' opens to him. Having thus gained access to His flock . . . the Shepherd knows and calls them, each by his name, and leads them out. Then the Eastern shepherd places himself at the head of his flock, and goes before them, guiding them, making sure of their following simply by his voice, which they know" (AE, Vol. II, 189–90).

Jesus reminded His listeners that a good shepherd, "goeth before them, and the sheep follow him: for they know his voice" (John 10:4). The sheep learn to rely on this shepherd who earns their trust because of his watchcare. He leads them to green pastures and finds them still waters to drink from. He anoints their heads to keep insects away. He protects them from danger and offers healing when they are wounded or ill. He is their guardian, their defender, and their comforter. He makes sure they want for nothing.

Christ said of Himself, "I am the good shepherd: the good shepherd giveth his life for the sheep" (John 10:11). As the Good Shepherd, He has promised to lead us, protect us, heal us, defend us, and comfort us. He gave His life for us. In return He asks each of us to "come, follow me" (Luke 18:22). But to follow Him we must know His voice. In a world filled with confusion and commotion it can be hard to recognize the voice of the Shepherd. President Dallin H. Oaks has said, "From among the chorus of voices we hear in mortality, we must recognize the voice of the Good Shepherd, who calls us to follow him toward our heavenly home" ("Alternate Voices," *Ensign*, May 1989, 27).

The voice of the Shepherd can be heard

"I am the good shepherd: the good shepherd giveth his life for the sheep."

—JOHN 10:11

in many different ways. It may be the still small voice of the Holy Ghost that gently guides and prompts. Sometimes it is the clarion call from the prophet of the Lord, setting a clear standard by which we can direct our lives. Often it is the sure and steady witness of the scriptures that encourages us and increases our ability to recognize the voice of the Lord.

To know the voice of the Shepherd is a privilege and a blessing. Setting aside time to listen to the voice is our responsibility. We show our devotion to the Shepherd when we choose to listen to His voice and to come when we are called. His concerned and consistent call will beckon to us daily. It is up to us to quickly answer, "I'm coming!" For "if a man bringeth forth good works he hearkeneth unto the voice of the good shepherd, and he doth follow him" (Alma 5:41).

Sometimes we may find ourselves lost in a world of uncertainty. With so many concerns vying for our attention we may not hear the whisper of the still, small voice, we may not have time to seek out the clarion call, and the sure and steady instruction from the scriptures may be set aside. With time we may find that we are lost. In quiet moments we might feel a silent ache that is masked during the busy flurry of our lives. We might turn to loved ones or favorite pastimes for relief, but in the still moments a longing will remain.

In those tender moments we must remember that there is One who has set aside everything to seek us. He will not rest until He knows that we have heard His voice and we find ourselves nestled safely in His arms. "Is this not the very work of the 'Good Shepherd,' and may we not, each of us, thus draw from it precious comfort? It is not [difficult to imagine] how in folly and ignorance the sheep strayed further and further, and at last was lost in solitude and among stony places; how the shepherd followed and found it, weary and footsore; and then with tender care lifted it on His shoulder, and carried it home" (AE, Vol. II, 256).

The Good Shepherd knows our names and will lead us in the pathway we should go. He knows our deepest struggles and our greatest triumphs. But do we know Him? Do we seek out His presence, go to Him for counsel, and follow the pathway He has marked? How well do we know His voice? How often do we come when we are called?

Find a quiet moment to listen to His voice. How does it speak to you? Try to remember the times that you have found yourself under His watchcare. Reflect on moments when you have been safe folded, led, defended, stilled, restored, guarded, comforted, or provided for. Ponder the blessings that have come into your life because you have answered the call of the Good Shepherd. Looking back through such times in my life, I see blessings unmeasured. In fact, my cup runneth over.

THE INVITATION . . . *Listen*

Read the parable of the Good Shepherd in John 10:1–18.

THE JOURNEY

- Think about how you have learned to recognize the voice of the Shepherd. How has His "voice" come to you? Make a list of the moments when you have heard that voice and have heeded the call. Some ideas may include going to the temple, visiting someone in need, attending church, studying the scriptures, preparing a lesson, praying with a special purpose, or listening to the prophet.

- Find one way to "hear" His voice today.

Ancient Keys

*Surely the Lord God will do nothing, but he revealeth
his secret unto his servants the prophets.*

—Amos 3:7

A couple of years ago our extended family had the opportunity to
spend a vacation on a ranch located just outside of Zion National
Park. Since we would be staying a number of days, I packed plenty of
clothes, and we crammed ourselves into the minivan amongst coolers and
suitcases to make the four-and-a-half-hour trip. We had a wonderful vacation, but by the time Saturday rolled around, we were all ready to go
home. Caleb, my oldest son, woke up bright and early, begging us to leave
in time to make it home for his soccer game. My brother and his wife
were leaving early that morning, so we made the decision to send Caleb
home with them. The rest of our family would stay until the late afternoon when the others would be leaving.

I quickly helped Caleb gather up his things and then had a brilliant
idea: I would send all of our dirty clothes home in a suitcase with Caleb.

My brother had plenty of room in his car, and this would give us a little extra space for the ride home. In no time at all they were off, and we settled in for a final day of fishing, canoeing, and four-wheeling. Then we cleaned the cabin, packed the car, and by late afternoon we were ready to leave. Everyone loaded their belongings into the car, climbed into their seats, and settled down for the drive home. As my husband, Greg, was hauling out the last load of garbage, he yelled to me, "Make sure the keys are in the ignition." I checked, but they weren't there. Next he asked me to check under the seat. Again I checked, but they weren't there, either. As he came back around the cabin, he patted his pockets and then said, "Oh, I know where they are, they're in the pockets of the pants I was wearing yesterday."

My heart sank. That meant they were in the pile of clothes I had sent home with Caleb hours earlier. All of a sudden I wasn't as brilliant as I had originally thought. As remote as the area was, I figured we probably couldn't count on FedEx, and I found myself wishing you could email objects over the internet.

After the initial panic wore off, Greg called a very loyal friend who agreed to drive the keys back down to us. But as I sat there in the middle of nowhere and watched the rest of my extended family drive away, I couldn't help but feel abandoned.

I can't tell you how happy I was at midnight when our friend finally pulled up, pushing the electronic button on the keychain that made the headlights on our car flash on and off. I have never been so happy to see a set of keys!

When Christ was on the earth, He held the keys of the priesthood. He promised these keys to Peter, saying, "And I will give unto thee the keys of the kingdom of heaven: and whatsoever thou shalt bind on earth shall be bound in heaven: and whatsoever thou shalt loose on earth shall be loosed in heaven" (Matt. 16:19). These same keys were given to Joseph Smith by Peter, James, and John and have been conferred on every prophet who has served since that time. These keys allow our prophet to exercise "the same divine priesthood power and authority that was held anciently" (David B. Haight, "The Keys of the Kingdom," *Ensign*, Nov. 1980, 73).

If we want to know the Savior, we can look to the prophet who holds the keys and who will lead us closer to Christ. President James E. Faust has said, "Great temporal and spiritual strength flows from following those who have the keys of the kingdom of God in our time" ("The Keys That Never Rust," *Ensign*, Nov. 1994, 74). Throughout the ages the Lord has revealed sacred truths to his prophets. This knowledge has helped many weary travelers find their way back home.

"Great temporal and spiritual strength flows from following those who have the keys of the kingdom of God in our time."

—JAMES E. FAUST

In the Book of Mormon, Mosiah tells of a remarkable time when all of the people came together to listen to King Benjamin. They gathered as families, each pitching their tent to face the direction where the prophet of the Lord would be speaking. So vast was the multitude that they could not all hear him, and King Benjamin "caused that the words which he spake should be written and sent forth among those that were not under the sound of his voice, that they might also receive his words" (Mosiah 2:8). It was a Book of Mormon–style general conference. In his conference address, King Benjamin gave five items of counsel that will help us apply the words of the prophet in our life. These five items are found in chapters two through five of Mosiah.

The first is to "open your ears that ye may hear" (Mosiah 2:9). This is an invitation to take the time to listen to the prophet. We can hear the prophet speak at least twice a year at general conference. This event must become an occasion that we look forward to and plan for.

When I was growing up, our family looked forward to general conference the same way we anticipated an upcoming holiday. We knew it meant two days of relaxation with a lot of good food and no distractions. Throughout the sessions we gathered together to listen to the prophet and the apostles speak. In between sessions there were fun games, long walks, and an amazing omelette brunch to look forward to. I learned to love general conference because twice a year my parents created an experience we looked forward to. Just as the people of King Benjamin set up a tent facing the tower where he would speak, we need to make general conference a focal point in our life.

Second, King Benjamin reminds us to open "your hearts that ye may understand" (Mosiah 2:9). Sometimes we will hear counsel that we do not understand. We can pray that our hearts will be opened to receive new understanding. Then the Spirit can whisper a confirmation that what we have heard is true. It is important to receive our own witness. This is what set Nephi apart from Laman and Lemuel. Even though they all three listened to their father, the prophet, only Nephi prayed to receive a witness that the words his father spoke were true.

Third, we need to open our minds "that the mysteries of God may be unfolded to [our] view" (Mosiah 2:9). For me this includes study. We can look forward to the May and November issues of the *Ensign*, in which the conference talks are published. It is important to reread each of the talks, but particularly those that might have especially touched you. Study these talks and ponder how you can apply the principles in your life.

The fourth item is to remember the words we have been taught. This is not easy to do. After hearing so many words of counsel, it is sometimes hard to remember everything we have learned. I recommend trying to identify and apply one principle at a time. Write it down and stick it on your fridge or mirror until it is committed to memory. Then move on to another principle. Sometimes it might take the entire six months between conferences just to learn one principle. Other times you might be able to work on a different piece of counsel every month.

The fifth step is found in Mosiah 4:10: "And now, if you believe all these things see that ye do them." Once we have listened with our ears, come to understand in our hearts, studied it out in our minds, and learned to remember the counsel, we need to apply that direction in our life.

The result of doing these things will be to experience a mighty change, which will enable us to come to know Christ more fully. This mighty change will come as we learn to hear and know His voice. By following the counsel we receive from the prophet we can become more like the Savior.

At the close of one recent general conference, President Gordon B. Hinckley counseled us to gather our children and talk about some of the things we had heard. He suggested that we should write down some of these things, reflect on them, and put them into practice. Following that counsel can become part of our general conference traditions.

Our prophet is the watchman on the tower and the man who holds the keys that can lead us safely home. As I look back over the past several years I recall some of the counsel we have been given by President Gordon B. Hinckley: To stand a little taller and to reach out and help those who are in need. He has raised his voice in support of being self-reliant, getting out of debt, and practicing principles of thrift. He has testified of the blessings of paying an honest tithe and has taught the importance of attending the house of the Lord more frequently. Under his watchcare we have been taught to work harder to retain converts, pray more fervently, treat our children with greater kindness, and demonstrate more loyalty and respect for our eternal companions. He reminds us to be grateful, to be smart, to be clean, to be true, to be humble, and to be prayerful. By his very presence and by the things he has said, he has taught us to find peace in a world of uncertainty. He has also instructed us that "it is the opportunity, it is the responsibility of every man and woman in this Church to obtain . . . a conviction of the truth of this great latter-day work and of those who stand at its head, even the Living God and the Lord, Jesus Christ" ("Testimony," *Ensign*, May 1998, 70–71).

I am so grateful for a living prophet who exemplifies these teachings himself and has testified of these things. His conviction has strengthened my belief.

THE INVITATION . . . *Follow*

Read the account of King Benjamin's address in Mosiah 2 and focus on verses 5–6.

THE JOURNEY

- What counsel do you remember most from the last general conference? Glance through the *Ensign* or visit www.lds.org to help you recall some of your favorite talks.

- Write down the counsel given and place it somewhere that you will see it often. How can following that counsel strengthen your testimony of Jesus Christ?

- What is one way you can apply inspired counsel to your life today?

Pray

Listen

Follow

Stand

We are living in a part of the universe occupied by the rebel.
Enemy-occupied territory—that is what this world is.

—C. S. Lewis, *Mere Christianity*, 45–46

History is replete with wars and rumors of wars. In our day the news is overflowing with stories of combat and contention raging throughout the world. There is a price to pay for liberty, and in our country, all give something. But each of us knows a family who has lost a loved one in the fight for freedom. In that case we are reminded that some give everything.

The Fourth of July is one of my favorite holidays. It gives us an opportunity not only to celebrate the founding of our nation but also to remember those who have paid the price for our freedom. I remember going to a fireworks show the summer following the horrible events of September 11. Music played loudly in the outdoor amphitheater as we watched an amazing array of light dancing high above our heads. We were lying on our backs, with hundreds of families surrounding us, feeling the deep vibration each time a new shower of color burst above us. Toward the end of the show a familiar song came through the loudspeakers, "Oh say, can you see, by the dawn's early light, What so proudly we hailed at the twilight's last gleaming . . ." All around us people began to stand, as is the custom when the national anthem is played. You could hear parents urging their children, "Get up! Get up!" And soon the entire crowd was on its feet, gazing at the celebration in the sky, considering what it means to be free.

Along with the battles that rage throughout the world today, there is a spiritual war being fought in Zion. President Ezra Taft Benson explained, "There has never been more expected of the faithful in such a short period of time than there is of us. Never before on the face of this earth have the forces of evil and the forces of good been so well organized. Now is the great day of the devil's power. But now is also the great day of the Lord's power. . . . Each day the forces of evil and the forces of good enlist new recruits. Each day we personally make many decisions showing the cause we support. The final outcome is certain—the forces of righteousness will win. But what remains to be seen is *where* each of us personally, now and in the future, will stand in this battle—and *how tall* we will stand. . . . We will never have a better opportunity to be valiant in a more crucial cause than in the battle we face today. . . . Christ . . . is the most successful warrior that ever walked the earth, and He wants to help us win every battle" ("In His Steps," *Ensign*, Sept. 1988, 2).

Those who serve in our nation's military regularly meet with a captain who gives needed direction. The soldiers show their respect to this officer by standing "at attention" while he speaks to them. It is common when the commander is finished talking for him to tell his men to stand "at ease." There is an interesting parallel to this common practice that can be found in our scriptures. As our Captain in this battle, Christ asks us to stand "at attention" in many different ways. We have been instructed to:

Stand by faith (Rom. 11:20)

Stand fast in the faith (1 Cor. 16:13)

Stand and testify (Alma 5:44)

Stand spotless (3 Ne. 27:20)

Stand in the place of our stewardship (D&C 42:53)

Stand in holy places (D&C 45:32)

Stand as witnesses (Mosiah 18:9)

Take upon us the Lord's whole armor, that we may be able to stand (D&C 27:15)

Having done all, to stand for truth, righteousness, peace, and faith (Eph. 6:13)

The Lord also gives us a caution, saying, "Woe to them that are *at ease* in Zion" (Amos 6:1; emphasis added). In this fight, we do not have the luxury of "standing down," for as John the Beloved warned: "And the [adversary] was wroth with the woman, and went to make war with the remnant of her seed, which keep the commandments of God, and have the testimony of Jesus Christ" (Rev. 12:17).

One of our greatest strengths comes from *knowing* our Captain. Our relationship must never become stagnant; our communications must never become delayed. "We must know Christ better than we know him; we must remember him more often than we remember him; we must serve him more valiantly than we serve him" (Howard W. Hunter, "What Manner of Man Ought Ye to Be?" *Ensign*, May 1994, 64). In doing so we will become fully converted and able to fight for what we believe.

President Ezra Taft Benson has said that people who are "captained by Christ will be consumed in Christ. . . . Not only would they die for the Lord, but more important they want to live for Him. Enter their homes, and the pictures on their walls, the books on their shelves, the music in the air, their words and acts reveal them as Christians" ("Born of God," *Ensign*, Nov. 1985, 6–7).

Full conversion means that we have complete reliance on our Savior. Toward the end of Christ's earthly ministry, He cautioned Peter, "Simon, Simon, behold, Satan hath desired to have you, that he may sift you as wheat." But then He quickly encouraged, "I have prayed for thee, that thy faith fail not: and when thou art converted, strengthen thy brethren" (Luke 22:31–32).

As our Captain, the Lord will do the same for us. I believe that He prays for each of us, that our faith will not fail, that we will remain strong in the fight. He will watch over us and strengthen us so that we, too, may become fully converted. Then, as our part in the battle that is raging every day, we are to strengthen those around us.

In ev'ry condition—in sickness, in health,
    In poverty's vale or abounding in wealth,
At home or abroad, on the land or the sea—
    As thy days may demand . . . so thy succor shall be.

Fear not, I am with thee; oh, be not dismayed,
    For I am thy God and will still give thee aid.
I'll strengthen thee, help thee, *and cause thee to stand,*
    Upheld by my righteous . . . omnipotent hand.

—*Hymns*, no. 85; emphasis added

THE INVITATION . . . *Stand*

Read Luke 22:31–32.

THE JOURNEY

- When you see the battle raging, where do you see yourself in the fight? Consider your church calling, your role as a parent, or your role as a friend. Do you give some, or do you give all?

- Find one way that you can strengthen someone today.

Calm the Storm

Seek the Lord . . . [for] he be not far from every one of us.

—Acts 17:27

Late one evening the disciples found themselves aboard a ship in the midst of the sea. The wind was contrary, and as they approached the darkest hours of the night they were tossed with waves. Surrounded by the stormy water and howling wind, turbulent enough that none were able to sleep, they were filled with fear. While suffering these afflictions, they looked up and saw Christ walking on the sea. He quickly assured them, "Be of good cheer; it is I; be not afraid." And Peter answered Him and said, "Lord, if it be thou, bid me come unto thee on the water." "Christ's answer was as it always is every time: 'Come'" (see Matt. 14:27–28), said Elder Jeffrey R. Holland.

Instantly, as was his nature, Peter sprang over the vessel's side. In this defining moment we are shown the character of Peter and the magnitude of his faith. In his desire to come unto Christ he willingly left the safety of the ship and stepped out onto the churning water. "While his eyes were fixed upon the Lord, the wind could toss his hair and the spray could drench his robes, but all was well—he was coming to Christ." But Peter was quickly distracted. He realized the force of the elements around him; he felt the boisterous wind and saw the turbulent waters; and he became afraid and began to sink. "It was only when his faith wavered and fear took control, only when he removed his glance from the Master to look at the furious waves and the ominous black gulf beneath, only then did he begin to sink into the sea. In . . . terror he cried out, 'Lord, save me'" (Jeffrey R. Holland, "Broken Things to Mend," *Ensign*, May 2006, 71).

The important part of this story is that when Peter cried unto the Lord, Christ was there immediately. Jesus stretched forth His hand and caught him.

Many times we find ourselves in a similar situation. We become overwhelmed with the magnitude of the path before us. Questioning our ability to move forward, we begin doubting our ability to go on. And so the storm begins to churn within. We find ourselves faltering, sinking, losing the ability to believe. We wonder if the Lord will carry us through our own raging waters, if He will stretch forth His hand and catch us. Peter's mistake was taking his eyes off the Savior and letting the raging of the world around him become his focus. So often in the process of learning we take *our* eyes off the Savior. We lose sight of the goal and find ourselves focusing instead on the turmoil that surrounds us, losing faith that He is able to calm the storm.

Distractions come quickly in the busy world we live in. Sometimes the pressure comes from discouragement or depression that can somehow turn our lives upside down. Often we find ourselves caught in a whirlwind of demands and time constraints that do not allow us to focus on the Lord. Finding time to pray and have daily scripture study always sounds so simple when suggested in a Sunday School lesson. But how do we fit it into our real-life situations? Sometimes the simplest tasks are the ones that become forgotten first.

An important step in coming closer to Christ is finding time to focus on the Lord daily. One of my favorite scriptures is found in 2 Nephi, chapter 25. In this chapter Nephi gives specific advice on how we can remain focused on the Savior. In verse 26 he says, "We talk of Christ, we rejoice in Christ, we preach of Christ . . . that our children may know *to what source they may look*" (2 Ne. 25:26;

"We talk of Christ, we rejoice in Christ, we preach of Christ . . . that our children may know to what source they may look."

—2 NEPHI 25:26

emphasis added). When I am analyzing my relationship with Christ, I turn to this verse. It helps me to sharpen my focus. Not only do I want my children to know to what source they should look, I also want to remember to focus on Christ. Nephi gives us three distinct ways we can look to Christ in our homes.

First, Nephi encourages us to *talk* of Christ.
- Do our conversations with our spouse, our children, even our friends reflect personal experiences we are having daily with the Savior?
- Do we share our testimonies regularly with the people we love the most?

Second, he encourages us to *rejoice* in Christ.

- How often do we take the time to literally rejoice when we receive an answer to a prayer or a tender mercy from the Lord?
- Do we take time from what we are doing to slow down and offer up a prayer of thanksgiving in the very moment when we recognize the merciful hand of the Lord in our lives?

Third, he suggests that we *preach* of Christ.

- How faithful are we in regularly holding family home evenings?
- Do we take the time on Sunday to reflect with our families on what we have heard or felt at church?
- Do we find frequent opportunities to teach about the Savior in our homes?

Individually these practices may seem simple, but combined they can have a profound effect on our lives and the lives of the members of our families. Living this counsel can redefine our focus. Then Christ will become more than just a painting hanging in our homes or a porcelain figure displayed on our bookshelves—He will become a friend. When we focus on Him, Christ will become the center of our lives—someone we long to talk to and someone we long to be with.

In the last chapter of John we find some of the disciples again riding in a boat without the Savior. This time they are fishing. Many things had transpired since the day Peter walked on water. Their faith had been tested and tried. They had experienced miracles and disappointment. Christ had been crucified and then raised from the dead.

Imagine the learning that had taken place, imagine the powerful gift of knowledge these men carried with them—the knowledge that the

Savior truly does visit His people in the daily course of their lives. They were true witnesses of Jesus Christ.

They had fished through the night, and when morning came, a man they did not immediately recognize stood on the shore watching. Then "that disciple whom Jesus loved" said to Peter, "It is the Lord," and the disciples began rowing toward the shore to meet the Lord.

But not Peter. In his exuberance, his excitement to be with Christ, he jumped right into the sea and began to swim. His focus was on the Lord. He longed to be near Him. He could not wait (see John 21:1–19).

THE INVITATION . . . *Focus*

Read the accounts of Peter's focus on Christ in Matthew 14:22–33 and John 21:1–19.

THE JOURNEY

• Today remember to focus on Christ. Allow Him to become part of your conversations, your celebrations, your teaching moments, and your thoughts. Long to be near Him.

The Gift

Go home to thy friends, and tell them how great
things the Lord hath done for thee.

—Mark 5:19

One Thanksgiving I will never forget was when I visited the Youth Detention Center in Salt Lake City. This facility is a temporary home for boys and girls ranging in age from eight to seventeen. Most are there because they have committed a crime. Some have been affiliated with gangs. Their days consist of school classes and meals; their nights are spent in a cell. Many of their memories are filled with violence and drugs.

I was asked to speak to them about gratitude on the night before Thanksgiving. It was one of the hardest talks I have ever prepared. When it was time for the meeting to begin, I watched them silently file into the room; each group followed a counselor to make sure they behaved. The young people were not allowed to talk or to make any signals with their hands. As I looked into their faces, I noticed that each seemed set in stone, as if they were determined not to show any emotion. I wondered what kind of lives had led them to this place—how many of them had come from homes that were empty of love or affection? How many of them had been born addicted to a drug they had received from their pregnant mothers? What chance for success could they possibly have?

I had prepared a talk that focused on gifts that we could all be grateful for, such as joy, wisdom, and strength, but as I watched them walk into the room I realized I had prepared the wrong lesson. Under the circumstances I expected my heart to fail from fear, but instead I felt the Spirit wash over me as I suddenly realized that the Lord had prepared His own message. I felt prompted to open my scriptures to Luke 17, the story of the ten lepers. I keep a small print of a painting of the ten lepers in this chapter of my scriptures. I took it out and held it up so that all of the kids could see it.

The picture portrays the healed lepers, running with pure exuberance at their good fortune. Inexpressible joy is written on their faces as, in unbridled celebration, they rush to be declared clean by the priests and to show family and friends the miracle that has changed their life. In the painting, the artist has depicted one man, a Samaritan, standing at the back of the group. He is clearly in awe of what has occurred, obviously reflecting on the fact that he has miraculously been made whole, and he is looking to where the Savior must be standing. The scriptures tell us that rather than running off, this man turned back "and fell down on his face at [Jesus'] feet, giving him thanks" (Luke 17:16). In his commentary on this miracle, Alfred Edersheim speculates on how Christ may have viewed this event. He talks of how the Savior must have watched them turn to go: "he may have followed them with His eyes, as, but a few steps on their road of faith, health overtook them." Then he talks of the grateful

Samaritan, who, "with voice of loud thanksgiving, hastened back to his healer . . . and in humblest reverence fell on his face at the feet of Him to Whom he gave thanks. This Samaritan had received more than new bodily life and health: he had found spiritual healing." Edersheim goes on to explain that it was one thing to apply to Jesus for healing, "but it was far different to turn back and to fall down at His feet in lowly worship and thanksgiving. That made a man a disciple" (AE, Vol. II, 329–30).

If we turn to the Savior and seek His counsel, we too can be healed and given the chance to live again.

Walking up and down among the incarcerated youth, I shared the story of the ten lepers with them and watched their faces soften as they considered the story. Just like the lepers who lived outside the village, completely isolated from society, each of these young people had been brought to this place alone, without friends, family, or anything familiar. Each of their lives was different now. Perhaps this was a story they could relate to.

Then I spoke to them of the unexpected opportunity the lepers had been given to change. For a leper, becoming clean was an impossible dream, and there was only One who could make it happen, and that was Jesus Christ. We talked about those times in life when we find ourselves in a situation we might not know how to get out of. Unable to solve the problem on our own, we become isolated. Distancing ourselves from what is familiar, we wonder if we can ever return. During times of reflection we need to remember that there is always a way back.

We are given the opportunity, any time we choose, to make a life change. That opportunity comes from Christ through the Atonement. If we turn to the Savior and seek His counsel, we too can be healed and given the chance to live again. This healing requires giving our whole heart to follow the counsel of the Lord.

As I talked with the kids at the detention center, I watched them ponder that thought as they carefully studied the picture. I wondered if they could really give up the things that held them bound. Their challenges seemed so massive; could they make the change? How many would have the strength it takes to choose Christ? I couldn't refrain from asking them as they intently searched the picture, "Look at these ten lepers. Of all of them, which one do you think loved Jesus the most?" Out of the silence one boy raised his eyes to meet mine. He pointed to the one who stood still, and whispered confidently, "That one."

One boy had realized the full magnitude of the moment.

It was more than celebrating the gift—it was recognizing the Giver.

THE INVITATION . . . *Change*

Read the account of the lepers in Luke 17:11–19.

THE JOURNEY

- Identify a change that you would like to make in your own life. It could be something amiss in your family, your work, your relationships, or an individual weakness. Write down a plan that will enable you to make that change. Approach the Lord in prayer and ask for His help.

Out of Darkness

Let us walk in the light of the Lord.

—Isaiah 2:5

A youngster walking through a dense London fog was carrying a lighted lantern.

"'Guide me back to my hotel,' said a voice from out of the fog, 'and I'll give you a shilling.'

"'Yes, sir.'

"And so the boy, holding his lantern high, started walking in the fog and soon reached the hotel. As he paused, not one man but four stepped forward with a shilling. The other three had seen the light and followed without question. It is so with any who lead the way to truth and light" (See N. Eldon Tanner, "The Power of Example," *Ensign*, Dec. 1981, 4).

It is amazing what darkness can do. It has an unsettling effect, altering our perception and creating a sense of unease. In a recent general conference, I noticed how many apostles alluded to the fact that we live in perilous times. Uncertainty surrounds us and often the dangers that are lurking around us are hidden from our view. The best way to move forward through these perilous times is to focus on the teachings of Christ. Through the scriptures and the living prophet we will be guided in the direction of safety. But is this all it will take for His light to shine through the darkest hours and inspire us to make good decisions?

Isaiah asks, "Who is among you that feareth the Lord, that obeyeth the voice of his servant, that walketh in darkness, and hath no light? let him trust in the name of the Lord, and stay upon his God. Behold, all ye that kindle a fire, that compass yourselves about with sparks: walk in the light of your fire, and in the sparks that ye have kindled. This shall ye have of mine hand; ye shall lie down in sorrow" (Isa. 50:10–11).

This scripture teaches a very important lesson, but it has to be learned line upon line. None of us wants to lie down in sorrow. To avoid that we have to understand what this scripture tells us to do. The first line describes a person who has learned about Christ and follows the commandments from the prophet, but who walks in darkness because he has no light. It seems that Isaiah gave us a contradiction. How could this happen? If we skip down a line, Isaiah makes it clear by painting a very interesting description. He describes a light that is man-made with sparks that the individual has kindled. This is a person who has obtained knowledge, but instead of relying on the light of Christ, has chosen to rely on his own light and strength.

One of the greatest struggles Christians through all time have faced is apathy. Going through the motions won't prevent us from distancing ourselves from the Lord. It is important that we remain focused as to where our commitment and devotion lie. President M. Russell Ballard said, "As I read and ponder the scriptures and carefully consider the Lord's counsel to His followers in every dispensation of time, it appears to me that the most important thing *every* one of us can do is examine our own commitment and devotion to the Lord Jesus Christ. We must carefully guard against spiritual apathy and work to maintain the full measure of our loving loyalty to the Lord" ("How Is It with Us?" *Ensign,* May 2000, 31; emphasis in original).

> "The people that walked in darkness have seen a great light."
>
> —ISAIAH 9:2

To avoid walking in darkness, Isaiah encourages us to trust in the name of the Lord and stay upon our God. It takes a lot of faith to realize that we can't do everything on our own and then to learn to trust in and be supported by the Lord. It is by doing this that we come to know His will for us. That knowledge will define our actions. When we trust Him enough to accept His will and learn to lean on Him for our support, then we will be filled with His light.

As we walk through one of the darkest times in history we would be wise to look to the Light. Then it will be said of us as it was of the people in Isaiah 9:2, "The people that walked in darkness have seen a great light." That "great light" is Christ. He is the sure and steady beam that will lead us safely home.

THE INVITATION . . . *Reflect*

Read Isaiah 50:10–11.

THE JOURNEY

- Write down some ways that you have been able to turn to the Lord for direction and support.

- Write down some of the ways you have learned to trust Him.

- Today find one way to share your testimony of these two principles with someone who is struggling.

The Better Part

One thing is needful.

—LUKE 10:42

We were on vacation one beautiful November morning, and I found myself wandering through a straw market in the middle of an island in the Bahamas. Although the tent held hundreds of little booths, by the time we walked down the third aisle we were aware that all of the vendors were peddling the same goods. Every booth offered one of five different items—straw purses, lava lava skirts, tiny glass trinkets, rattles, or $5 T-shirts. Squished together, on either side of a very small aisle, the island people who owned the shops would call out, "You want a purse, ma'am, your pretty daughter would like a purse?" And sure enough, four-year-old Grace did want a purse, a purse with a matching wallet to boot! And so we searched up and down every aisle. I wasn't sure what we were looking for—it seemed all of the purses were of identical design, each one boasting a face of one of many different popular cartoon characters, but to Grace, none was right, and so the search continued.

We passed by woman after woman, hand-sewing the identical faces onto the purses. Some even offered to sew Grace's name onto the purse, but still she could not be persuaded.

Finally, after what seemed like a very long time, Grace stopped. She had found what she was looking for: a tiny purse with little pink rosebuds sewn on top and a bonnet and matching slippers to go with it. This was it! We could finally make the purchase.

I knew exactly what to do—this wasn't my first trip to a straw market—I began to barter. The woman had offered her price, ten dollars for the purse, eight dollars for the slippers, and ten dollars for the hat. Because I was buying three items, I knew I had room to maneuver. I offered twenty dollars for the lot. She wouldn't budge! I played along and began to walk away, fully intending that she would call me back, but she never yelled out a larger dollar amount. Finally, I turned around. "I'm not going to buy that purse for ten dollars when I can buy every other purse in this market for six dollars," I told her.

"Go buy the other purses," she said, "You won't find another purse like this anywhere here. I do quality work." The old woman sat patiently in her chair with her wrinkled hands folded in her lap. She was right. I looked down at the purse. It was beautiful and unique. One could see the care she had taken in placing each pink rosebud. And it matched the slippers and the bonnet perfectly. She even agreed to sew on Grace's name. We ended up buying the set for twenty-eight dollars.

The old woman smiled as Grace put on the bonnet and the slippers. As Grace pulled the purse over her little shoulder, the vendor giggled and clapped her hands with delight. I didn't feel one ounce of remorse that I had lost. I was most grateful I had met that woman; she taught me a valuable lesson on self-worth: she knew who she was; she believed in the quality of her work.

How often in our lives do we choose to give the better part? I think of that island woman: every day she wakes up and walks to a hot, over-crowded tent filled with dozens of competitors and sells items crafted by her own hands to a group of travelers who barter to pay a meager sum. And yet, she has found joy and accomplishment in the quality of her work. Every day she gives the better part.

It reminds me of the story of Mary and Martha found in Luke 10. Most often when we hear this story, we are reminded that Mary chose the good part, which shall not be taken away from her. But what about Martha? While Mary sat listening to the words of the Savior, "Martha was cumbered about much serving." It sounds as though she also felt a little sorry for herself, for she questioned the Master, "Lord, dost thou not care that my sister hath left me to serve alone?" (v. 40).

How often do we feel that what we do goes unnoticed or is unap-preciated? Sometimes we might even feel taken for granted by those we serve. But we need not wonder if the Lord cares. He cares deeply about each of us. And He loves those who selflessly serve just as much as He loves those who pause to listen to His teachings. In John 11:5 we read, "Now Jesus loved Martha, and her sister."

As we read on through the New Testament and into the last week of the Savior's life, we again find ourselves in the home of Mary and Martha. In John 12:2 it says, "There they made him a supper; and Martha served." I don't think it is happenstance that in two different scriptural accounts we read about Martha serving. I believe that was her talent. I believe it brought her great joy. I believe it was what she did best. In her life perhaps doing the dishes and sweeping the floor, mending the tattered and the torn, feeding the weary and the worn, and simply giving her heart was the better part of all that she had to offer.

Each day we have the opportunity to give the better part. We too may feel cumbered and troubled about many things, but we can take the opportunity to lift and brighten the lives of others by simply doing that which we do best. President Gordon B. Hinckley has said, "I have been quoted as saying, 'Do the best you can.' But I want to emphasize that it be the very best. We are too prone to be satisfied with mediocre performance. We are capable of doing so much better. Brethren and sisters, we must get on our knees and plead with the Lord for help and direction. We must then stand on our feet and move forward" ("Standing Strong and Immovable," *Worldwide Leadership Training Meeting,* 10 Jan. 2004, 21).

Our Heavenly Father will give us the direction we need as we try to determine what qualities make us unique. Each of us has been blessed with gifts and abilities that are individual to us. With use, these abilities will make a difference in our lives and in the lives of the people we come in contact with. Discovering what we do best will bring a happiness and contentment that cannot be found any other way.

Spend some time in conversation with Heavenly Father. Ask Him to help you recognize the gifts you have been given. Take time to listen for a response. Pondering the following questions might also help you become more aware of what makes you unique.

What motivates you spiritually?
What is one gospel subject that you enjoy studying?
What meaningful activities bring you the most joy?
Which of those activities help you feel closer to Christ?
What qualities do you have that can help others feel closer to Christ?

We do not all have the same gifts or talents. Mary and Martha were very different from each other. We need to learn to celebrate the gifts we have been given and then learn how to be the very best we can in those areas. At different times in our lives we might be given different gifts or qualities that will benefit us or those we serve. Learning to utilize those gifts to the best of our ability is what constitutes giving the better part.

When we know who we are and have identified the qualities and gifts we have been given, the service we offer will be our very best. In a message to the women of the Church, President Hinckley said, "Thank you for being the kind of people you are and doing the things you do. May the blessings of heaven rest upon you. May your prayers be answered and your hopes and dreams become realities. . . . You are doing the best you can, and that best results in good to yourself and to others. Do not nag yourself with a sense of failure. Get on your knees and ask for the blessings of the Lord; then stand on your feet and do what you are asked to do. Then leave the matter in the hands of the Lord. You will discover that you have accomplished something beyond price. . . . You may never know how much good you accomplish. Someone's life will be blessed by your effort" ("To the Women of the Church," *Ensign*, Nov. 2003, 113–15).

THE INVITATION . . . *Do Your Best*

Read the story of Martha found in Luke 10:38–42.

THE JOURNEY

- Remember who you are. What are you best at? What gift can you offer? How can that gift bring more joy to the people around you?

- Choose to give the better part today. Find one way that you can use your gift to serve someone else's need.

Stand

❖

Focus

❖

Change

❖

Reflect

❖

Do Your Best

The Sycomore Tree

The Lord be with us till the night
Enfold our day of rest,
And be in ev'ry heart the light,
In ev'ry home the guest.

—*Hymns*, no. 161

Luke, chapter 19, tells the story of a man named Zacchaeus who hoped to see Jesus when He passed through Jericho. The scriptures tell us that this man held a high position and was quite rich. Zacchaeus was also "little of stature" and "could not for the press" see the Savior. But he was not about to let the circumstances prevent him from seeing "who [Jesus] was" (v. 3). He ran ahead and climbed up into a sycomore tree for a better view.

There he waited and watched for the Lord to come near. "And when Jesus came to the place, he looked up, and saw him, and said unto him, Zacchaeus, make haste, and come down; for to day I must abide at thy house. And he made haste, and came down, and received him joyfully" (Luke 19:5–6).

How many of us frequently find ourselves in a similar situation? We live in a world that moves at a very fast pace. With email, cell phones, and FedEx, our lives are never still. We work longer hours with shorter deadlines. Success today has become more than holding an important position or acquiring wealth; we want the most for our children, our families, and ourselves. Often this means filling our schedules and every spare moment with more and more of what we hope will bring us joy. Somewhere in the press of all of these demands, we try to make room for the Savior. But are we wise enough to take the time and remove ourselves to a place where we can sit apart from the daily grind and allow Him a place in our lives? Walking away for even a moment can help us receive needed counsel from the Lord.

To catch an unimpeded view of the Savior, Zacchaeus had to climb into a sycamore tree. Where is your sycamore tree? Think of a place where you can go, which will allow you unimpeded access to the Lord. Spend a moment there and take the time to prioritize what is most important in your life. In doing so, consider the direction that the Savior gave Zacchaeus: "To day I *must* abide at thy house" (Luke 19:5; emphasis added). That guidance is just as important for each one of us. The Savior's Spirit *must* abide in our homes every day, but it is up to us to decide how, or even if, we will invite Him in.

The Savior did not suggest that Zacchaeus should stay in that place where he had discovered the Lord. He told Zacchaeus to come down, to come back into the press, and then follow the direction He had given. Likewise, we cannot ignore the responsibilities and pressures that surround us. Being wise enough to remove ourselves for a short time to focus on the Savior will give us the opportunity to move forward with determination in the direction that we need to go. Then we need to come back to our everyday life with a resolution to follow the guidance we have been given. Zacchaeus was told to "make haste" (v. 5) as he prepared for the Lord, and he did. Once he had *come down* there was

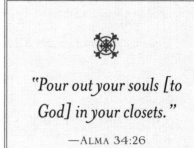

"Pour out your souls [to God] in your closets."

—ALMA 34:26

an urgency, a higher level of priority given to this task than to any other task he might have had. Because of his preparation he was able to receive the Savior joyfully.

Joseph Smith once said, "Seek to know God in your closets" (*History of the Church*, 5:31). Next to the fireplace in the master bedroom of Joseph and Emma's home in Nauvoo there is a small closet. Inside the closet there is ladder that leads up to a tiny alcove. The secret haven at the top of the ladder is just large enough for one person to sit comfortably, and we are told it was a private place where Joseph could go and ponder. I wonder how many conversations between Joseph and the Lord took place there. It seems that the Prophet knew the importance of having a special place where he could escape to find a quiet moment with the Lord.

Today you might not have the opportunity to sit in a tree or climb a ladder into a hidden alcove, but set aside some time to find your own secret haven. Spend a moment there to ponder. Sometimes reaching higher can fill the longing deep within our hearts.

Let that secret haven become your sycamore tree. Go there to seek the Lord, then make haste to prepare and receive Him joyfully.

THE INVITATION . . . *Be Still*

Read the story of Zacchaeus found in Luke 19:1–6.

THE JOURNEY

- First, find your sycomore tree, or the quiet place you can go to focus on the Lord.
- Second, make haste and invite the Lord into your home. How will you prepare to receive Him?

Help Thou Mine Unbelief

Without ceasing I make mention of you always in my prayers; . . .
for I long to see you, that I may impart unto you some spiritual gift,
to the end ye may be established; that is, that I may be comforted
together with you by the mutual faith both of you and me.

—ROMANS 1:9–12

A simple request. All I wanted was life. I never knew that we'd have to pray him here. But for those nine months I cried to the Lord for His blessing, day after day. And I'd say, *"As his mother, this burden is too hard to bear—what will it take?"*

He answered simply . . . faith.

I was fourteen weeks into my second pregnancy when I threatened to miscarry. After two trips to the emergency room and several more to the doctor, I was put on complete bed rest to try to save the baby's life.

Three days prior to my receiving this mandate, the bishop had come to our house to extend a calling for me to serve as the Relief Society president of our ward. Now, a week later, he was back, wondering how the

Lord's inspiration fit in with this medical condition. As he sat on a chair next to my bed, he told me about the many trips he had taken to the temple that week, seeking direction from the Lord on proceeding with the call, and described the peaceful assurance he had felt that we should move forward. So I suggested to him the names of the sisters I wanted as my counselors, though I was unable even to show up for the sacrament meeting in which we would be sustained.

Later that week, I was set apart. The experience was one of the most powerful moments of my life. In the blessing, I was told that the baby would be born healthy, *if* I had enough faith and followed the direction of my doctor with exactness. I knew that I could follow the direction of my doctor, but the responsibility of having enough faith completely overwhelmed me. As soon as Greg and I were alone, I burst into tears. I couldn't do it. So much doubt crept into my mind daily that I knew I was not spiritually strong enough to have the faith to make the pregnancy succeed. I went to bed discouraged. Stuck in bed, I felt that I was unable to accomplish anything. I was failing as a wife, as a mother, and now as a Relief Society president. And to make matters worse, if the pregnancy failed, I would forever know that it was because of my lack of faith.

The day after I was set apart, I called a friend to ask for advice. As she had done on many previous occasions, she sent me to the scriptures to find my answer. I found myself in the ninth chapter of Mark, standing in the same shoes as the man who had

"If thou canst believe, all things are possible to him that believeth."

—MARK 9:23

come to the Savior, begging Jesus to heal his son, who was possessed of a "dumb spirit" (v. 17). The man explained that he had previously asked Jesus' disciples to heal his boy and they had been unable to do so. "But," he said, "if thou canst do any thing, have compassion on us, and help us" (v. 22).

Jesus had compassion on the man and his afflicted son and said: "If thou canst believe, all things are possible to him that believeth" (v. 23).

When I read those words, I immediately echoed the pleading of the father in my own heart. I felt quietly prompted that this man was not actually asking "*if* thou canst do any thing." He knew the Savior could, or he would not have come to Him. In my mind I heard instead the distraught father saying, "*Because you can do anything, have mercy on us.*" And then I could hear the Savior say to me, not "*if* thou canst believe," because He knew that I was capable of believing in miracles—I had before, and if it were not so, I would not have come to the place where I was at that time (see D&C 6:14). Instead, I heard this reply, *Because you can believe, all things are possible.*

Seeking the miracle, "the father of the child cried out, and said with tears, Lord, I believe; help thou mine unbelief" (Mark 9:24). Reading this, I instantly felt relief. The man was not perfect in his faith. He felt doubt, just as I had since moments after the priesthood blessing. But there was a difference. Willing to admit that his faith was not perfect, he offered everything he had and asked the Lord to make up what he lacked.

Here was the answer I needed. I was to plead not only for the healing to take place but also for the added faith I would need to *allow* the healing to take place.

And so it is in our everyday life. As we attend to difficulties, we can turn to the Savior. When we feel we are lacking as a mother, a wife, or a friend, we can rely on Him for answers. When we are not enough in our callings at church or in the many other areas in which we serve, we can look to Christ. And any time the task at hand seems more than we can bear, we can plead for His assistance. Then, "although our faith were only . . . the smallest, and the result to be achieved the greatest . . . nothing shall be impossible unto us. For all things are ours, if Christ is ours" (AE, Vol. II, 109).

Part of the promise of the Atonement is the blessing that comes after all we can do. When we are not enough, Christ can make up the difference. But we have to ask Heavenly Father, in the name of Christ, for the added strength. For drawing closer to Christ is not an event but a process. As we walk along that trail, we will find not only that Christ is aware of our limitations but that, after all we can do, He will compensate for them. The sense of falling short or falling down is a natural part of each of our lives. But we need to believe that after all we can do, Christ can fill that which is empty, straighten our bent parts, and make strong that which is weak. Never forget that the Lord is on our side (see Bruce C. Hafen, "Beauty for Ashes," *Ensign*, Apr. 1990, 85).

He can make us enough.

THE INVITATION . . . *Develop Faith*

Read the account of the pleading father in Mark 9:17–27.

THE JOURNEY

- Take time to identify and write down an area in which you feel you are not enough. This could include challenges that are physical, temporal, spiritual, or emotional.

- Take it to the Lord. Plead your case in prayer. Don't be afraid to acknowledge your weakness and ask for greater faith. Then be still and listen to the promptings that will come.

What Lack I Yet?

Till thou hast paid the very last mite.

—LUKE 12:59

His suit was well worn and out of place with the crisp, sharp suits the other missionaries wore. But the boy did have one thing in common with the other elders; they had each arrived at the mission home for the first time. As the missionaries prepared to leave for their assigned areas, the mission president pulled the humble boy from South America aside and asked him where he had gotten his suit. He explained that his father had taken it off after church the Sunday before he left on his mission and had placed it in the small suitcase. Looking down, the mission president asked where the elder's weathered shoes had come from. The missionary replied that his father had taken them off his feet when they arrived at the airport and had given them to him just as he was ready to leave.

The boy's humble family had given all they had so this young man could serve the Lord.

Contrast this with the young man we read about in Mark 10. I imagine this boy was about the same age as the missionary. As Jesus was going forth, this rich young man came to speak to Him. We read that he came running and knelt at the Savior's feet. With seeming pure intent, he explained to the Lord that he had kept the commandments since he was a boy and now wanted to know what he needed to do additionally to inherit eternal life. He questioned the Lord, "What lack I yet?" (Matt. 19:20).

We can assume the question was sincere, for Mark tells us, "Jesus beholding him loved him" (Mark 10:21). The Lord then gave the boy specific counsel; but what He asked was not easy: "One thing thou lackest: go thy way, sell whatsoever thou hast, and give to the poor . . . and come, take up the cross, and follow me" (v. 21).

For the young man, the requirement was too great. Surrendering all he had was too much to ask, and rather than committing his all to the Savior, he "went away grieved" (v. 22).

The same might be true for many of us. Each must determine if he or she is willing to give up something of lesser value to obtain something of infinite value—whether to pay the price to "inherit eternal life" (v. 17).

How might we liken this story to our own lives? Do we willingly give all that we have to serve the Lord? It means more than just giving the visiting teaching message; it's being the friend. It means adding the final touches every time we serve in our callings. It means paying just a little more in our fast offerings, knowing that our small effort will make a significant difference to someone in need. It means getting out of our comfort zone to talk to someone new at church. It means remembering that "in the quiet heart is hidden sorrow that the eye can't see"

(*Hymns*, no. 220) and learning to be less critical and more understanding. Sometimes it means giving up our seat, and other times it means giving up our entire afternoon. It means I'll be there, you can count on me, and I'm on your side. It means that we are always on the Lord's errand. It means that we are a true follower of Christ. Although it is hard to imagine at the time of our sacrifice, we receive, in the giving, something of far greater worth in its place.

There is a story found two chapters later in the same book of Mark that depicts this true devotion to the Lord. Interestingly, it seems that the woman in this story, who gave everything she had to the Lord, never met the Savior during His ministry on earth. Her reward was not immediate, but still, her devotion was sure.

I imagine Jesus sitting out of the way, watching the activity in the temple around Him. As He sat, "His gaze was riveted by a solitary figure. We can see her coming alone, as if ashamed to mingle with the crowd of rich givers. . . . She held in her hand only the smallest of coins, but it was all her living" (AE, Vol. II, 388). As Jesus watched, the woman threw in her two mites, giving every earthly thing she possessed to the Lord, without thought of recognition or reward, but in humble, quiet sacrifice. With great respect, Christ spoke of her to His disciples, saying, "This poor widow hath cast more in, than all they which have cast into the treasury: for all they did cast in of their abundance; but she *of her want* did cast in all that she had, even all her living" (Mark 12:43–44; emphasis added).

The scriptures do not define this woman's want. She may have wanted for food, shelter, or clothing. Perhaps she was following the commandment to pay her tithing and prove the Lord therewith, desiring the promised blessings she knew would follow. We do not know for certain, but we do know this: *of her want* she gave all she had.

I want to be like that.

THE INVITATION . . . Give All

Read the account of the rich young man in Mark 10:17–22 and the widow's mite in Mark 12:41–44.

THE JOURNEY

- Think of someone you know who has given all in service to the Lord. What lesson can you learn from that person? How can you be more like him or her?

- Commit today to give *all you have* in your service to the Lord. Choose one area where you feel you could give more. What changes will this require in your daily routines?

DAY EIGHTEEN

After All

And there will I meet thee, and I will go before thee. . . .
And there will I bless thee. . . . And thus I will do unto thee
because this long time ye have cried unto me.

—ETHER 1:42–43

It must have been frightening to be alive at the time when the Lord confounded the language of the people at the great tower. Imagine the confusion and panic as people were suddenly unable to speak or communicate with each other. Two brothers, worried for the welfare of their families, came up with a solution. Jared told his brother to cry unto the Lord that their language and the language of their families would not be confounded. The Lord heard their prayer and had compassion on them. He told the brother of Jared to gather his friends and families and all of their flocks and prepare to go to a land that was "choice above all the lands of the earth" (Ether 1:42).

The brother of Jared was commanded to build barges that would help the family reach their destination. The barges were built according to the

94

instruction of the Lord. Because the brother of Jared was obedient at each step, he was able to receive the next level of knowledge. After the brother of Jared finished building the barges he reached a moment of indecision, questioning his next step. Knowing that he and his people would be spending a large amount of time traveling closed up inside the barges, he worried about two very significant problems: how would they breathe and what would they do about light?

Consider these two problems: one is an inconvenience, and one is a life-threatening situation. The brother of Jared took these problems to the Lord. A lesson can be learned from the way the Lord answered. The Lord did not want this group of people to perish. In answer to the humble pleading of a faithful servant to a question of immediate need the Lord answered directly. He gave a solution to the request for air, suggesting that the brother of Jared should make a hole in the top and in the bottom of the barges. When the people traveling in the barge needed air they were to unstop the hole and receive air, and when water began to come into the barge they were to stop up the hole again. A simple solution, and the brother of Jared did as the Lord had commanded.

Then he cried again unto the Lord, worried that there was no light in the barges, wondering if they were to cross the sea in darkness. The reply came quickly, just as it had with the first question, but the answer was entirely different. The Lord asked the brother of Jared, "What will ye that I should do that ye may have light in your vessels?" (Ether 2:23–25).

The brother of Jared did not sit and wait for a solution. He immediately went to work. He climbed up a mountain, and not just any mountain but a mountain of exceeding height, to find some stones. And he didn't take just any old stones, but rather he did "molten out of a rock sixteen small stones; and they were white and clear, even as transparent glass" (Ether 3:1) He did all the work he could do on his own, and *then* he cried unto the Lord.

The scriptures teach us, "Ye receive no witness until after the trial of your faith" (Ether 12:6). The brother of Jared faced a trial of faith, and his witness was twofold. The blessing came, the stones were touched and they received light. But more important than that is what happened in the process. As the Lord touched the stones, the mortal man saw the finger of the Lord. "And the brother of Jared fell down before the Lord, for he was struck with fear" (Ether 3:6). And the Lord said unto him, "Never has man come before me with such exceeding faith as thou hast" (Ether 3:9). Because of that exceeding faith, the Lord showed Himself to the brother of Jared, revealing, "Behold, I am he who was prepared from the foundation of the world to redeem my people. Behold, I am Jesus Christ. . . . Behold, this body, which ye now behold, is the body of my spirit; and man have I created after the body of my spirit; and even as I appear unto thee to be in the spirit will I appear unto my people in the flesh" (Ether 3:14, 16).

"Ye receive no witness until after the trial of your faith."

—ETHER 12:6

In verse 19 we are told that the brother of Jared had "faith no longer, for he knew, nothing doubting." He had received a witness; he had come to *know* the Lord.

After the Jaredites had prepared everything they needed for the voyage—their food, their flocks and herds, and everything they should carry with them—"they got aboard of their vessels or barges, and set forth into the sea, *commending themselves unto the Lord their God*. And it came to pass that the Lord God caused that there should be a furious wind blow upon the face of the waters, towards the promised land; and thus they were tossed upon the waves of the sea before the wind" (Ether 6:4–5; emphasis added).

I am always amazed at the faith of the Jaredites. How many of us would climb into a barge that we could not steer or direct in any way, to go to a destination we knew nothing about, and be willing to travel without even knowing how long the journey would take? And then, not only did they commend themselves to the Lord, the journey was not a calm one. Instead, furious winds blew them toward the promised land.

I love that even though the wind did never cease to blow, and the people were constantly driven, they sang praises unto the Lord. In the very midst of their adversity, they "did thank and praise the Lord all the day long; and when the night came, they did not cease to praise the Lord" (Ether 6:9). What a lesson of gratitude, of joy in the journey, of enduring to the end. When the Jaredites finally reached the promised land the first thing they did was bow themselves down upon the earth and "did shed tears of joy before the Lord, because of the multitude of his tender mercies over them" (Ether 6:12).

Have you received a blessing after all you could do?

Through the process did you come to know the Lord?

I was seventeen weeks into the pregnancy of our fourth child when I went into labor. Discouragement does not come close to describing the despair that encompassed me as I checked myself in to the women's center. After three hard pregnancies, I knew the odds were not good that we would keep this child. Any hope I might have had was dashed when the nurse who had been assigned to watch over me informed me that until twenty weeks of gestation this wouldn't be considered a viable pregnancy. There was nothing they would do to stop the contractions.

I had been extremely nauseous with this pregnancy, I had felt the baby growing inside me, and for the past week I had become aware of the initial kicking inside. I didn't know how anyone could fathom that this was not a viable pregnancy. After monitoring the baby and the contractions for two hours, the nurse confirmed my fears. I was contracting regularly. I begged her to call my doctor who knew my history to see if there was anything we could do. And then I began to pray. I prayed he would make the right decision—that we would try to save the tiny life that I had become fiercely attached to. And hope came. He put me on a medication to calm the contractions, and I was to stay down on complete bed rest. I went home and continued to pray.

My life consisted of constant bed rest, frequent baths to calm the contractions, weekly trips to the doctor, and a succession of priesthood blessings as we tried to cope with the magnitude of what we were facing. Finally, after four ultrasounds within three weeks, the doctor suggested there was one procedure we could try that could save the baby's life. This would do one of two things: it would either force me into hard labor, and I would deliver immediately, or it would slow down the damage being caused by the constant contractions. At twenty-one weeks it would be risky, but it was our only choice. To make matters worse, I would need to fast for twelve hours before the operation. This meant I could not take the medication I had been taking every two hours to calm the contractions. I was a nervous wreck. I remember lying on the operating table just before the surgery was to begin. I was completely exhausted. I had not slept soundly for weeks. It seemed that I had been using every muscle in my body to keep the baby inside. I hurt all over. I had done all I had been asked. I had given my best effort. We had fasted and prayed. We had called upon the Lord through the power of priesthood blessings. There was nothing more I could do. It was in the hands of my doctor. It was in the hands of the Lord. As I began to receive the anesthesia, I said the shortest prayer I had offered in the last four weeks, "Lord, thy will be done." I could do nothing more. It was out of my hands.

The first time I woke up in the recovery room I saw the anesthesiologist sitting next to me. Groggy and only halfway alert I asked the question pounding in my heart: "Did it work? Is the baby still alive? Am I still pregnant?" His answer was a simple yes. As I drifted back off to sleep I vividly heard a voice whisper in my head, "Thanks be unto God for his unspeakable gift." Later that day, I returned home to my familiar routine of complete bed rest. I was concerned that the contractions were not calming, but I was also intrigued by the whisper I had heard. I began to search the scriptures for the source of the simple message. The words had offered the first glimpse of hope I could cling to. The Spirit had spoken to my soul. I found the reference to my simple message in 2 Corinthians 9:15. For the first night in many weeks I slept in peace.

I spent almost six months in bed. Even up to the final week, the outcome was uncertain. As we walked into the delivery room the nurse asked if there was anything she could do to make our visit better. I told her, "Just deliver us a healthy baby, alive." She couldn't possibly understand the weight of that request. But Grace was born on September 21, healthy and full-term. My doctor couldn't believe it. As he pulled her out and laid her on my stomach, we admired every healthy bit of her from her tiny toes up to the curly white hair that covered her wrinkled head. "This is an angel baby," he told the nurses. "Look at this baby, and you'll see a miracle—you don't know what it took to get this one here."

My father told me to write it all down. He didn't want any of us to forget the miracle we had witnessed. We had also "seen the finger of the Lord" as He had brought Gracie to the earth. Just like the brother of Jared, my witness was also twofold. God had given me an unspeakable gift in my perfect baby daughter, but through the trial I also had come to know the Lord. The days that had turned into weeks and months of doubt, discouragement, and despair had led me to call on the Lord for intercession, for help, and for comfort. I had come to know my Savior. I recognized His voice. I had felt His Spirit and His constant companionship as I struggled to go on. He had become real to me. I knew, nothing doubting.

In Ether 6:3 we read: "And thus the Lord caused stones to shine in darkness, to give light unto men, women, and children, that they might not cross the great waters in darkness." The Lord has promised each of us—men, women, and children—that He will not leave us to suffer in darkness or despair, He will send light to every one of us. As it says in Ether 2:25: "And behold, I prepare you against these things; for ye cannot cross this great deep save I prepare you against the waves of the sea, and the winds which have gone forth, and the floods which shall come." Isn't it interesting that the Lord told them they would not be able to face the task at hand unless He prepared a way for them? There comes a point in the midst of every trial when we submit to the will of the Lord. We give our best effort, and after all we can do, we lay the burden at His feet. We believe, we trust, and we allow Him to prepare a path for us toward the promised blessing.

Often we don't realize that the trial is what enables us to reach the destination the Lord has in mind for us. He will not let it destroy us, but He will let it move us in the direction we need to go. Just like the Jaredites, when we are encompassed about and in the depths of the trial, if we cry unto Him, He will bring us forth again.

After the greatest trial comes the greatest gratitude. I no longer question why we see so many pictures and read so many accounts depicting followers of Jesus who fall down at His feet in reverence when they meet Him. I imagine the weight of gratitude is so significant they cannot bear to stand in His presence; the gift He offers is unspeakable.

Faith is an unspeakable gift. It is the indescribable promise. It sustains the soul through moments that otherwise would destroy us. It is a gift that can be constantly replenished if we are willing. And the reward that awaits the true seeker is a treasure beyond compare.

If you are searching for your promised land, "seek this Jesus" (Ether 12:41), the One who encourages us to build, to perform great works, to prove ourselves worthy and obedient. Who offers solutions, who encourages us to search for ourselves and find the answers we long for. Seek this Jesus, who will not let you cross the water in darkness, who will prepare the way before you, who knows what you have been through, who knows

After the greatest trial comes the greatest gratitude.

what is still to come. The One who allows the trials because He knows the blessings that will follow. The One who will show you the greater things, who will bring the unspeakable gifts. The One who leads us to the promise. "Seek this Jesus . . . that the grace of God the Father, and also the Lord Jesus Christ, and the Holy Ghost, which beareth record of them, may be and abide in you forever" (Ether 12:41).

THE INVITATION . . . *Understand Grace*

Read Ether 12 and look for the blessings.

THE JOURNEY

• Remember, grace comes after all you can do. Take time today to analyze a trying situation in your life. After you have done all that you can do, place it at the feet of the Lord. Keep a written record of the *greater things* and the *unspeakable gifts* that will come as He leads you to the promise.

Be Still

❖

Develop Faith

❖

Give All

❖

Understand
Grace

Seek for More

Weeping may endure for a night, but joy cometh in the morning.

—PSALM 30:5

The world around us is filled with discouragement. Adversity abounds, and in almost every home one can find a burden being shouldered. Like Lazarus, who lay dead in the enclosed tomb, we sometimes find ourselves surrounded by darkness. How often in the midst of our sorrow do we hear the voice of the Savior as He calls out with a loud voice, "Come forth" (John 11:43). Come forth from the darkness, despair, and discouragement that surround you, come forth from the sorrow and be healed.

In the midst of tribulation every soul takes a moment to ask why. Why me? Why now? What is the purpose for the anguish and the pain that I am experiencing? The mind searches for explanation; the heart questions its ability to withstand such intense emotion. In the search for a definite answer hope becomes dim and the struggle to simply exist takes over. It is hard to understand why bad things happen to good people. In these moments of despair we turn to God for answers. We become like the people of Alma: "And it came to pass that so great were their afflictions that they began to cry mightily to God" (Mosiah 24:10). We beg to understand the reason for the suffering.

We do not experience trials just to see if we will make it through. Each of us experiences the refiner's fire for one reason—to come to know the Refiner. We are not just tried; we are proven. Priceless lessons can be learned from the Master during times of adversity. It is in these moments of heartache that we come to know the Savior and more fully appreciate His atoning sacrifice. Lessons thus learned will prepare us to better endure what may follow and will sustain us through the darkest days of our lives.

Christ is always there. In the darkest hours of the night and the longest hours of the day, He is there. He is accessible and available at a moment's notice. His hope for us is taught in Hosea 5:15, where He says, "In their affliction they will seek me early." He knows that those who believe in Him will, in fact, prove Him. This process takes time, but in the end "a brother is born for adversity" (Prov. 17:17).

In the hours of suffering perhaps the greatest comfort comes in the realization that we are not alone. Christ has said, "Ye may know of a surety that I, the Lord God, do visit my people in their afflictions" (Mosiah 24:14). He will come to each of us. In our times of greatest trial He will visit, He will stand by us, and He will wait for us to acknowledge His presence and allow Him to intercede. Through the gift of the Atonement we will experience His healing power, if we but take the time to ask.

Mary Magdalene is a favored woman in the scriptures. She had the privilege of coming to know and love the Savior. Perhaps she was a dear friend, even a close confidant. We do not know much about Mary, but we do know that she was the first person to see the risen Lord. I have often wondered why.

Was her faith the most sufficient?

Was she the most prepared to receive the Savior?

Did Christ know she would recognize Him when He called her name because she had before?

For whatever reason she was thus favored, she went to the tomb early one morning after Christ had died, and here an important lesson was learned. She went seeking the Savior. In her hour of greatest need, in deep despair and longing for answers, she did what she had learned to do—she turned to Christ.

Arriving at the sepulchre and discovering the Lord's body was missing, she stood weeping outside the tomb. When she looked again into the empty crypt, she saw two angels in white, "And they say unto her, Woman, why weepest thou?" She replied, "Because they have taken away my Lord, and I know not where they have laid him." It was then "she turned herself back, and saw Jesus standing, [but] knew not that it was Jesus" (John 20:13–14). He also asked her, "Woman, why weepest thou? Whom seekest thou?" (v. 15). She supposed the man to be the gardener, and it was only when He spoke her name that she recognized the resurrected Lord.

Mary was a woman who had a great level of knowledge of the teachings of Christ. She lived on the earth and really knew the Savior during His ministry. Yet still, she did not at first recognize Him.

On that Easter morning Mary's level of understanding was that Christ was dead. Weeping in frustration and sorrow, she sought to find

Him. She did not recognize His voice at first because in her mind it was not possible. But then—it was! Mary's testimony of Christ increased. She had reached a new level of understanding.

How often do we come to a point in our lives when we are comfortable and confident in our relationship with Christ? We may go forward for a time serving and learning. Inevitably a trial will come that will test our knowledge. We may question our trust in the reality of the Lord. At these times we realize that our testimony is never stagnant. Trials provide an opportunity for us to seek the Savior. As we prove Him, we gain more understanding and knowledge.

Mary did not recognize the Savior until He called her name. Then, suddenly, light and understanding came. A new level of knowledge: Christ was risen; He lives; there is life after death. He had triumphed and was victorious. The Savior stood by her in her moment of learning. He waited patiently until she was ready, and then He taught.

Do we recognize the voice of the Lord? We can prepare to hear His voice by reading our scriptures, remembering to pray, keeping the commandments, and attending the temple. But even when we are regularly doing these things there will be times when our faith is tried. We will plead for greater understanding. And perhaps as Mary did, we will weep. It is at such times, when we are downtrodden enough to find ourselves humbly pleading, as Mary was, that we will recognize the voice of the Savior. Our understanding will be increased, and we will be led out of darkness into light. Then we will celebrate with great joy in praise of the Lord. He will know when we are ready for the lesson because He knows our hearts.

Through every trial our faith is tested. Sometimes faith precedes the miracle. Other times we must have faith to trust in God's will. At both of these times our spirit seems to be stretched to the limit as we learn, line upon line, how faith works. When we find ourselves asking, *Where is the promise, where is the reason for this pain, and where do I turn now?* I hope we will follow the example of Mary and go to Christ, for He is the greatest Healer, the Healer of all wounds.

THE INVITATION . . . *Seek*

Read the account of Mary Magdalene in John 20:1–18.

THE JOURNEY

- Examine your life. What is your greatest need?
- Sometime today find a way to seek the Lord. Find in Christ the answers you long for. Dare to reach a new level of understanding.

Art Thou Only a Stranger?

And it came to pass that I . . . having great desires to know . . .
did cry unto the Lord; and behold he did visit me.

—1 Nephi 2:16

Three days before our wedding, my soon-to-be husband, Greg, went to an Instacare medical clinic because he had a sore throat and the beginnings of a head cold. During the examination the doctor informed us that he could feel a tumor on Greg's thyroid. Worried that it might be cancerous, he suggested Greg have an additional examination as soon as we arrived home from our honeymoon. We did so. Greg saw a specialist at the University of Utah Medical Center, and the findings were not good. The biopsy revealed that there was a ninety-seven percent chance of the tumor being malignant, and we were terrified. Within six weeks, Greg was scheduled for surgery.

Change is never easy, and facing something of this magnitude so early in our marriage scared us both. Following the surgery, I sat alone next to Greg's bed in the hospital room. My parents lived out of town, and

Greg's parents had gone home for the night. Greg was heavily sedated, and I found myself sitting in that dark room in the middle of the night completely alone with my thoughts. Sometimes loneliness is frightening. I tried to hold on to all that was familiar, to all of the dreams that we had planned. And in the depths of my heart I wished that there could have been someone who would sustain me and stay the night with me.

Never before in my life had I been faced with a trial that depleted all of my reserves as this one had. Over time, I would come to know that God would hold me in the palm of His hand. But that understanding didn't come immediately. I was beginning to realize that sometimes it has to hurt to make you strong, and in the days that followed, I took comfort in the words of familiar verses of scripture: "Draw near unto me and I will draw near unto you" (D&C 88:63); "My peace I give unto you" (John 14:27); "Be still and know that I am God" (D&C 101:16). These whispered messages from the Lord became my greatest comfort. Although it would take months for Greg to return to full health, which he did, I had begun the most important journey of my life—my own road to Emmaus, where I would come to know and recognize the Savior.

"Be still and know that I am God."

—D&C 101:16

Imagine being with the two unnamed disciples who left the city in the early afternoon of one spring day. We would walk for almost an hour, passing country houses along the way. Beyond a dreary, rocky region, we would climb a path with streams running alongside. We would pass orchards of orange and lemon trees, olive groves, and shady nooks. In all, our walk would encompass almost six or seven miles, and every mile of it would be filled with talk of Jesus Christ, the disciples each sharing memories, tinged with sadness because of His recent passing and the mystery of the empty tomb (see AE, Vol. II, 639).

Somewhere in our journey, a stranger would join us on the road, but caught up in conversation we would not at first recognize Him. After inquiring about the source of our sorrow, the stranger would then begin to expound to us the scriptures that pertained to the coming of the Messiah. By now it would almost be evening, the day far spent, and reaching our destination, the disciples would invite us and the stranger to tarry with them. And while partaking of a simple meal, the eyes of our understanding would be opened, and we would recognize the resurrected Lord before He suddenly vanishes from our sight.

Imagine our wonder, expressed by one of those disciples: "Did not our heart burn within us, while he talked with us by the way, and while he opened to us the scriptures?" (Luke 24:32; see vv. 13–32).

Often we walk our own road to Emmaus, so consumed by life's demands that it is hard for us to open our eyes to the miracles that surround us. If we are able to recognize our spiritual longing, we might be moved to plead: "O Savior, stay this night with me; Behold, 'tis eventide" (*Hymns,* no. 165).

And He *will* abide with us. We can draw nearer to Christ by reading the scriptures. If we do not take the opportunity to read the words of the Lord daily, we may fail to recognize the Master who accompanies us along the journey. How sad it would be to arrive at the end of the journey and realize we never came to know the Visitor with whom we have traveled.

For we do not travel alone. We have been given the same promise that was given the disciples: "In the silence of our hearts, if only we crave for it, and if we walk with Him, He sometimes so opens from the Scriptures . . . the things concerning Himself" (AE, Vol. I, 642).

There have been many evenings, as the shadows have fallen around me, when I have turned to the scriptures for comfort. In those quiet moments, just like the unnamed disciples, I have found verses that have caused *my* heart to burn within *me*. Often, those whispered assurances from the Lord have been just what I have needed to sustain and lift me and carry me through. Great blessings will come if we learn to acknowledge the presence of the Savior along this journey of life. As we turn to the scriptures and begin to recognize the voice of the Lord, there will be moments when our hearts will burn within us. These moments will teach us to look to Him more often. "When other helpers fail and comforts flee" we will instinctively cry out: "Help of the helpless, oh, abide with me!" (*Hymns*, no. 166).

> *"In the silence of our hearts, if only we crave for it, and if we walk with Him, He sometimes so opens from the Scriptures . . . the things concerning Himself."*
>
> —ALFRED EDERSHEIM

THE INVITATION . . . *Abide*

Read the account of the disciples walking on the road to Emmaus, found in Luke 24:13–32.

THE JOURNEY

- Learn to use the scriptures to receive personal revelation from the Lord.

- Take some time today to find a scripture that speaks to you.

- Let His Spirit abide in your heart by reflecting on that scripture throughout the day.

What Mean These Stones?

Take you hence . . . twelve stones.

—Joshua 4:3

One early March I traveled with a group of about sixty fifth-grade boys to Clear Creek Camp located up Spanish Fork Canyon. Shortly after we arrived, the principal of the school informed us that we would be taking a two-mile hike through nearly three feet of fresh snow. When we left the valley there had been no snow on the ground, and many of the boys did not think to bring boots. However, we were all required to make the trek, so we were told to dress as warmly as we could.

The hike proved to be exciting, as excursions usually are with eleven-year-old boys. Within the first hour we stopped to discuss wildlife and the difference between deciduous and coniferous trees and paused to climb a twenty-foot, handmade wall.

As we were beginning the last half of the hike, I noticed the boy in front of me was missing a shoe. We searched all around but could not find it anywhere. The scary thing was his foot was so numb with cold that he hadn't even realized he had lost the shoe, and he had no idea how long it had been missing.

As a mother, I was worried, and we decided that the boy should put on both of my boots, because his feet were so wet and frozen. I resorted to the next best thing. Each of the boys had been asked to bring a large plastic garbage bag on the hike, so I put two bags on over my socks and then pulled his wet socks over the top of the bags to keep them in place. Once we had made the switch we began to hike again through the snow.

History proves the love the Lord has for His people and His willingness and ability to lead them to a promised land.

The principal had passed us in the process of switching boots and was fully aware of the situation, so it really surprised me when he directed us to continue up the mountain instead of returning home. Since we had been hiking for more than an hour, I didn't want to turn back alone, and so I followed. I made it for about five minutes before the cold started to sink in. With the use of a pair of snowshoes I was able to keep from sinking, but my feet still came in direct contact with the snow with every step. I was freezing, and still we were making our way *up* the hill.

I tried thinking of the pioneers to convince myself that this sacrifice was minimal compared to what they must have walked through, but that lasted only about fifteen minutes, and then I was fighting back tears and frustration. I wondered what the principal was thinking. By the time we finally stopped our climb, I realized we were more than an hour from our cars by the way we had come, and I knew I wasn't going to make it back; I was pretty sure they would have to send in a helicopter to rescue me. I looked with some irritation at the principal, who was now explaining to the boys why some of the trees on the mountain had grown in the valleys and why some areas had no trees at all. We were standing almost at the crest, with the mountain falling below us at a steep angle, and far below us, I could see our three cabins nestled in the trees. By now I was standing on my heels to keep the rest of my feet out of the snow, and I wondered how I would ever get back. I figured the principal had forgotten about me. Surely he must have, or he would have raced us all home the way we had come.

Then, just when I thought I couldn't take it any longer, the principal did the strangest thing. He lay down flat on his back on one of the large plastic bags and began sliding down the hill, full speed toward the cabins. The rest of us were shocked! And then it dawned on us what he was doing. This was the purpose of the plastic bags. We were to sit on them and slide home.

I have never been so grateful for a plastic garbage bag in my life! I sat down and started sliding and found myself back at the cabins within ten minutes. I had made it! And I realized that all along the principal had known what he was doing. He knew I would be fine, because he knew the plan, and he had prepared the quickest way to get me out of a tough situation.

"History proves the love the Lord has for His people and His willingness and ability to lead them to a promised land."

In a small way, this experience reminds me of how many scripture stories testify to the fact that the Savior truly does deliver His people.

Think of Moses and the Red Sea, Noah and the flood, or the people of Alma who were in bondage for so many years. History proves the love the Lord has for His people and His willingness and ability to lead them to a promised land. The power of God is amazing. The scriptures provide countless examples of times when the Lord stretched forth His hand to offer relief for His children who were struggling. In every dispensation He has provided miracles for His children as they have wandered through the wilderness toward a better life. They have proved the Lord, and He has been there.

A favorite poem reads:

> *When you come to the Red Sea place in your life*
> *In spite of all you can do*
> *There is no way back, there is no way round*
> *There is no way but through*
> *Then know God with a soul serene*
> *And the dark and the storm are gone*
> *God stills the wind*
> *God stills the waves*
> *God says to your soul "Go on"*
>
> —BAIRD T. SPALDING

Many years after Moses and his people experienced the miracle of crossing the Red Sea on dry ground, Joshua found himself in much the same situation, required to lead the Lord's people across a great river to the other side. As the people gathered to ford the river Jordan, Joshua promised them in the name of the Lord that the Lord would gather all the water into a "heap" and told them that they would be able to cross on dry ground. Joshua assured the people that the Lord, *without fail*, would provide their need (see Josh. 3:10–13).

As that miracle occurred, the Lord instructed Joshua to have twelve men each haul "upon his shoulder" a stone from the riverbed, to be used to erect a monument to the event on the other side of Jordan (see Josh. 4:5–7).

I imagine that making the crossing was quite a task. These twelve men probably had families, young children, cattle, and personal belongings they were required to move across this great riverbed. Now, as if they were not shouldering enough, they were asked to add more weight to their load. As they experienced this added burden, some may have questioned the Lord: *Could we not set up a monument with stones from the far side of the river and still remember the journey?* What was the purpose of the extra burden?

Once they reached the other side of the river, Joshua had the twelve stones placed together as a memorial. "And he spake unto the children of Israel, saying, When your children shall ask their fathers in time to come, saying, What mean these stones? Then ye shall let your children know, saying, Israel came over this Jordan on dry land. . . . That all the people of the earth might know the hand of the Lord, that it is mighty" (Josh. 4:21–24). These twelve men left a legacy to their families for generations to come of their testimony of the Lord and the great power He has to bless His people.

We also can leave a legacy for our families. One of the ways we can do this is to have visual reminders in our homes that testify of Jesus Christ. These might include statues, paintings, or framed scriptures. We once had a stake president who suggested that each of our children hang a picture of the Savior in his or her bedroom. Then he added a second, very important piece of counsel: this picture should represent the way they view the Savior. We spent an entire month helping our children find paintings that were just right. Each chose something different—the paintings each reflecting their personal testimony of what the Savior means to them.

Another way we can leave a legacy is through bearing our testimonies of the ways the Lord has touched our lives. These written or spoken declarations can serve to encourage those who are dear to us to recognize the hand of the Lord in their own lives. Share your testimony of Christ today with someone who is dear to you. There are many ways that you can do that; it might be through a letter or in a conversation. Find a way that is meaningful to you.

Experience has taught me that throughout the journey, the faithful traveler holds close to his heart the hope of reaching a promised land. In this case, the "promised land" we are searching for is a greater awareness and a stronger testimony of Christ. By drawing closer to Him we will be able to reach that destination. If our heart is willing He will *without fail* lead us to where we want to be.

"He knows the way because He *is* the way" (Jeffrey R. Holland, "Broken Things to Mend," *Ensign,* May 2006, 71; emphasis in original).

THE INVITATION . . . *Remember*

Read the story of Joshua and the crossing of the river Jordan in Joshua 3 and 4.

THE JOURNEY

- Either figuratively or literally, gather twelve stones. Assign each stone to represent a blessing that you have recognized in your journey toward Christ.

- Share these blessings with your family. Testify how you are coming to know the Healer, the Master, the Son of God, even Jesus Christ. What are the stories you can tell about how He has strengthened, enlightened, comforted, or otherwise blessed you?

Seek

Abide

Remember

The Celebration

Hang on the walls of your mind the memory of your successes.
Take counsel of your strength, not your weakness. Think of the good
jobs you have done. Think of the times when you rose above your
average level of performance and carried out an idea or a dream for
which you had deeply longed. Hang these pictures on the walls of
your mind and look at them as you travel the roadway of life.

—ATTRIBUTED TO WHISTLER BY
STERLING W. SILL, "GREAT EXPERIENCES," *ENSIGN,* JUNE 1971, 43.

I love celebrations that include each guest receiving a favor. Often this favor comes wrapped in a clear cellophane bag containing small treasures that have something to do with the theme of the party. As you go home you carry with you a tangible memory. Each time you look at one of those small treasures you are reminded of the celebration.

Think of this chapter as your own favor—a way for you to carry with you a memory of your journey. The best way to capture lessons learned is to write them down. Then, when we have moments when we need strength, guidance, or direction, we can look back to times in our lives when we have been blessed with those gifts.

Find a quiet time to reflect on the past twenty-one days. Read your journal entries. As you do, note the treasures you have found and the discoveries you have made. Have any of those experiences helped you to see more clearly the hand of the Lord in your life? Pause to reflect on the lessons you have learned. Have you felt joy, peace, strength, or understanding? What are the moments when you have felt closer to Christ?

Recalling the treasures and celebrations experienced along this journey closer to Christ will provide you with a lasting reminder to turn to Him in times of future need.

I have never enjoyed goodbyes, or any type of endings for that matter, so I am thrilled that this is not the end of our journey. These twenty-one days have only been the beginning of a journey closer to Christ that can last forever. A Chinese proverb wisely counsels, "The journey is the reward." I hope you have found that to be true. In the days to come may your on-going search be constant. Consider the rising of the sun every morning as a personal invitation to make the most of each new day—an invitation to know and recognize the hand of the Lord in your life—an invitation to *come and see*, to continue the personal journey that will bring you closer to Christ. Respond, if you please.

*"How great reason have we to rejoice;
for could we have supposed when
we started . . . that God would have
granted unto us such great blessings?
And now, I ask, what great blessings has
he bestowed upon us? Can ye tell?"*

—ALMA 26:1–2

Becoming His

A DAILY JOURNEY

TOWARD DISCIPLESHIP

*The first step on the path of discipleship begins,
luckily enough, in the exact place where we stand!*

—ELDER DIETER F. UCHTDORF

Just a Little Book

As I begin to write this manuscript, I have just finished reading an antique book titled *Flower of the Dusk,* by Myrtle Reed. The book begins with a conversation between two friends who are discussing their hopes. One asks the other, "What would you do, if you could choose?"

"I'd write a book," the friend replies, and then she describes the most wonderful book I can imagine. "Just a little book," she says. "The sort that people who love each other would choose for a gift. Something that would be given to one who was going on a long or difficult journey. The book a woman would take with her when she was tired and went away to rest. A book with laughter and tears in it and so much fine courage that it would be given to those who are in deep trouble. I'd soften the hard hearts, rest the weary ones, and give the despairing ones new strength to go on. Just a little book, but so brave and true and sweet and tender that it would bring the sun to every shady place."

In the inmost part of my heart, that is the book I wish this one would be. So I place that heartfelt desire into the hands of the Lord and simply pray that I might be the writing instrument that will allow His words to fill these pages.

If you are in the middle moments of a long or difficult journey,
if you are tired and in need of a rest,
if you just want to laugh a little and cry a little,
if you are yearning for something more,
if you are in deep trouble and you are looking for courage,
or if your heart is weary or despairing and you are looking for strength to go on,
then hopefully this book is just what you need.

Before you begin, let me make one thing clear—as much as I wish they could, in and of themselves the simple words that fill these pages cannot offer you the hope, courage, or strength you seek.

But the Savior can. Of this, I am certain.

I pray this book will lead your heart to His.

The Beginning

We do not really grasp who we are until we know whose we are.

—Truman G. Madsen

Becoming is an interesting process. It is what takes us from where we are to where we want to be. Oh, there are so many things I want to become—more intelligent, more filled with discernment, more kind. But there is one desire that fills my heart with longing over and above any other. I want to become a disciple of Christ, and in the course of my life's journey I hope to become His.

It is a process I have been studying for years, and although I haven't discovered all of the answers, I have found an interesting pattern that could perhaps be applied to each of our lives. I recognize this pattern as a journey toward discipleship. My studies have encompassed the lives of Paul, Nephi, Caleb, and Joshua, along with many other ancient and modern prophets. I have studied the progression of the early Church in Jerusalem and the journey of the modern-day pioneers. My research has filled notebooks, covered paper napkins, and been penned within the margins of my scriptures.

Inspiration leads me to share this journey with you, but I am confident that the writing upon these pages will be only a simple roadmap along your own journey to discipleship. I believe that He who authors the course will carefully guide your steps, just as He guides mine. The path to discipleship is a very individual process, a deeper journey than simply coming closer to the Lord. As we follow this pattern, we will come to understand that becoming a disciple of Jesus Christ is a lifelong process that will ultimately define who we are.

For the purpose of this book, this pattern of discipleship has been broken into twelve parts. Each part highlights one piece of the pattern.

Within every part you will discover four common themes—to consider, to act, to ponder, and, finally, to become. Considering, acting upon, and pondering each principle within the pattern gives us an opportunity to walk the path of discipleship. Each step leads us closer to becoming His.

Elder Robert D. Hales encourages us to **consider.** "The first step to finding faith in the Lord Jesus Christ is to let His word . . . touch your heart. But it is not enough merely to let those words wash over you, as if they alone could transform you. We must do our part. . . . It means taking seriously what is taught, *considering it carefully,* studying it out in our minds." Elder David A. Bednar encourages us to **act.** He counsels on the "necessity to not only express but to do, the dual obligation to both plead and to perform, the requirement to communicate *and to act.* . . . True faith is focused in and on the Lord Jesus Christ and *always leads to righteous action.* . . . Thus, faith in Christ leads to righteous action, which increases our spiritual capacity and power." President Gordon B. Hinckley suggested we should **ponder.** "Let us study the ways of the Lord, reading His life and teachings in the sacred scripture He has given us. Let us *take a little time to meditate,* to think of what we can do to improve our lives and to become better." President Dallin H. Oaks encourages us to **become.** "Now is the time for each of us to work toward our personal conversion, *toward becoming what our Heavenly Father desires us to become.*"

At the end of each of the twelve parts you will find a section entitled **Solo Time.** Here you will be invited to open your scriptures. One of the best ways we can draw closer to the Lord is by turning to the scriptures. This is your individual time with the Lord—this is the process that will make your experience personal. As you open your scriptures, focus on the promptings that you receive that are specific to your needs and your situation at this time in your life.

The rate at which you progress through this book is completely up to you. The book is designed to follow a yearly format, with one of the twelve parts for each month. Within each monthly section you will find the four themes. Perhaps you could consider focusing on one theme each week during that month. However, you might move at a faster pace, covering a chapter a day, or a slower pace, taking time to focus on each section until it becomes part of who you are. Once you have settled the lessons from one section into your heart, move on to the next. Remember to carry each lesson with you throughout your journey—letting each part of the pattern build upon the one before. These pages are meant to create an experience. Each section will act as a guidepost along your journey. Each chapter will include an invitation for growth.

This path will include moments for learning, growing, and stretching. There will be times of stillness, and situations that require great courage and strength. This trail is vertical—leading upward, lifting your heart, requiring reaching. In the still moments, promptings will come. Perhaps you will be reminded of the quiet invitation the Lord continually extends, ". . . and whosoever will come, him will I receive; and *blessed* are those who come unto me" (3 Nephi 9:14; emphasis added). Accepting the invitation to come unto Christ leads us through a transformation. In reality, the process is one not just of coming but really of *be*coming. As we come unto Christ, we *be*come something more. Something better. We *become* His.

Become More

Down in the wild garden, when she brushed aside the snow,
Rose found a blushing hepatica in full bloom.
"How indiscreet," she thought, and then added, to herself,
"but what sublime courage it must take to blossom now!"

—MYRTLE REED

Consider . . .
You're Worth It

Many years ago I had an experience I will never forget. I was serving as a visiting teacher. My assignment was to a woman who was struggling with a trial that had the potential to destroy her life. I had been visiting this woman for four years. She was one of my dearest friends.

On this particular night, things were not going well, and at nine thirty in the evening we ended up at the bishop's office over at the church building. We counseled together with the bishop for a time, and then, in an attempt to try to find some solutions, we called a private counselor this woman had been working with to see if he could help us. He happened to be driving home from a party with his wife and agreed to come to the church.

When he arrived, he left his wife in the car with a book and spent an hour and a half counseling with this woman, the bishop, and me. At eleven o'clock that evening we finally came up with a solution. The course we settled upon would include changes that had the potential to affect the rest of my friend's life for good. It would require courage. It would require strength. It would require great sacrifice. She had chosen to make the decision that we had all been praying about for weeks. I was so proud of her, and I found myself humbled by the magnitude of the journey that lay ahead of her and grateful for the encouragement of a good bishop and a kind counselor who had helped her reach that decision. As we prepared to go home, my friend walked over to the counselor, took him by the hand, and said, "Thank you for coming."

I thought of the sacrifice he had made to be there that night. It wasn't regular office hours. He had dropped everything to come. His wife had been sitting in the car in a dark parking lot in the middle of winter for an hour and a half. In the quiet recesses of my heart I echoed her gratitude, *Yes, thank you for coming.*

I will never forget his reply.

Most people would have said, "You're welcome." But that wasn't his response. When my friend said, "Thank you for coming," the counselor replied, "You're worth it."

He taught a powerful sermon in three simple words. He knew the potential she had. He knew she was meant for more. In his eyes, she was worth the sacrifice.

As I drove home from that experience, I found myself wondering if I knew someone who would sacrifice like that for me if I were in a time of need—someone who would come to help me under any circumstance because I was worth it, because he saw the potential for more within me. Immediately my mind was filled with one of my favorite paintings of the Savior, one in which He is dressed in white and His arms are outstretched. As clearly as if the painting were right in front of me, I could see the prints of the nails in His hands. Instantly I remembered the words found in Isaiah 49:15–16, "Yet will I not forget thee. Behold, I have graven thee upon the palms of my hands."

For a moment my mind was filled with the thoughts of what it would be like to have a personal, one-on-one experience with the Lord, an experience like the one had by the people we read about in Third Nephi: "Arise and come forth unto me, that ye may thrust your hands into my side, and also that ye may feel the prints of the nails in my hands and in my feet, that ye may know . . . and this they did do, going forth *one by one* until they had all gone forth, and did *see* with their eyes and did *feel* with their hands, and did *know* of a surety . . ." (3 Nephi 11:14–15; emphasis added).

Every time I read this account, I wonder, What would I have said if that opportunity had been mine? What would I have thought? What would I have felt? As I ponder upon what it will be like to meet the Savior, I feel certain that my thoughts will be flooded with memories of the times on my own earthly journey when I have felt Him near me— when I recognized an answer to prayer, when I saw miracles in the ordinary moments, the tender-mercy experiences of my life.

Recently I have decided that perhaps that one-on-one experience with the Lord need not be a future event. Could it be possible that I might have that Third Nephi experience every time I turn to the Lord with longing to draw closer to Him? Looking back on the most personal experiences of my life—the moments when I have turned to the Atonement as a healing balm, as a source of strength, or as a means of change—I realize I *have* had the sweet opportunity to know the Lord in a very personal way. In my darkest hours, I *have* felt the prints; when my way has been obscured, I *have* seen with my eyes; and in the moments when I have been given strength beyond my own, courage to do what I otherwise could not, and peace within a heart that could not be comforted, I *have* come to know the Lord. I have seen, I have felt, and I have known of a surety.

This Third Nephi experience was not meant for just twenty-five hundred people. The Lord's invitation is extended to each of us, "Ye see that I have commanded that none of you should go away, but rather have commanded that ye should come unto me, that ye might *feel* and *see*" (3 Nephi 18:25; emphasis added).

The Lord invites each of us to have our own one-on-one experience with Him, to feel Him with us, to see Him along the way, and, in doing so, to become more. Deciding to accept that invitation is the very first step on this journey. We must remember that He has graven us on the palms of His hands. He will not forget us because we are worth it to Him. Perhaps as we learn to recognize Him along this journey we will find our hearts overflowing with gratitude, and in moments of quiet prayer we will say, just as my friend did, "Thank you for coming."

I can already hear His gentle reply, "You're worth it."

CONSIDER THIS . . .
Read 3 Nephi 11

"With this commitment to who we can become, the spiritual doors swing open. There is a new freedom to feel and to know, a freedom to become" (Elder Neil L. Andersen).

Today is the first day of this journey toward discipleship. Consider how you might set aside some time during this journey to create one-on-one experiences with the Lord. Open your scriptures. Listen to your favorite hymns. Spend some time meditating after prayer. The moments that we spend privately with the Lord can be life changing if we let them. Through Him we begin to recognize our true worth. He can help us become more.

Open your eyes that you might *see* these moments. Open your heart that you might *feel* them.

Act . . .

A Waters of Mormon Experience

The first step on the pathway to discipleship requires us to make a choice. Either we can remain in the place where we are, or we can become something more. Sometimes the choice is made in quiet moments. At other times the choice requires great courage. I am reminded of Alma, who experienced a change of heart after listening to the testimony of Abinadi. After pleading with the king to save Abinadi, Alma fled for his life. In that instant everything changed. He had come to know the Lord, and through that personal experience he came to understand that he was meant for more. That knowledge led to a journey that changed the course of his life.

From Alma we learn that the first step toward discipleship is to make a conscious choice to know the Lord, believing that through Him we can become more.

After Alma left the king, he began to teach privately among the people. "And as many as would hear his word he did teach" (Mosiah 18:3). Those who believed his words followed the same path he had—they too came to know the Lord. Their journey to discipleship included a covenant that ultimately changed their hearts. The scriptures teach us that "all this was done in Mormon, yea, by the waters of Mormon, in the forest that was near the waters of Mormon; yea, the place of Mormon, the waters of Mormon, the forest of Mormon, how beautiful are they to the eyes of them who there came to the knowledge of their Redeemer"

(Mosiah 18:30). It seems that this place called Mormon within the forest of Mormon near the waters of Mormon must have been a breathtaking place. But it wasn't the scenery that made it so beautiful to the people; it was the fact that in that place they had come to know the Lord, their Redeemer.

As I have studied the lives of many disciples of Christ, I have found that this experience is not unique. Each disciple had a Waters of Mormon experience—an experience during which he came to know the Lord. In that moment, each disciple allowed the Lord to change his heart, to make him more. A man on the road to Damascus, a young boy in the Sacred Grove, a silent listener in Noah's court, a lame man at the pool of Bethesda, three witnesses surrounded by fire, the list goes on and on.

This lesson leads me to wonder, What are the Waters of Mormon experiences in my own life? Where are the beautiful places where I have come to know my Redeemer—where I have let Him take me by the hand and allowed Him to make me more than I could have ever become on my own? Glimpses come to mind: sitting in a hospital room at the University of Utah, kneeling beside my bed in the darkest hours of the night, walking down a tulip-lined sidewalk in March. These are moments I will never forget because they are mile markers on my own journey toward discipleship. They are sacred to me because they are the places where I have come to know my Redeemer. These are some of the defining moments when He helped me to become more.

If you choose, this journey to discipleship has the potential to include many Waters of Mormon experiences—experiences where you can come to know the Redeemer in a very individual and personal way. The scriptures teach that, "If any man love God, the same is *known* of him"

(1 Corinthians 8:3; emphasis added). He knows each one of us on an individual basis; He hears the prayers of the boy kneeling in a grove of trees and those of a woman kneeling at the hospital bed of her husband in the middle of the night.

And just as He spoke to Moses, His words to us will be "given in *our* own language" (Moses 6:46; emphasis added). When we seek to recognize the Lord, He will change our hearts. He will make us more. Through the process He will teach us in personalized ways that we can understand and hold on to. Our experiences will be given in our *own* language because we are *known* of Him.

Sometimes we have to make a conscious choice to watch for these Waters of Mormon experiences. As it did for Alma, the silent listener in King Noah's court, often that choice includes sacrifice. For some it might be time. For others it might be pride. Perhaps we are too afraid to hope. Maybe our priorities will have to be adjusted. One thing I am confident of: When our desire to know the Lord becomes the priority of our life, the most important things will not pass us by. Often the greatest sacrifice leads to the greatest understanding. Interestingly the sacrifices made along this road seem to pave the pathway toward obtaining more, not less—more opportunities to know the Lord, more opportunities to experience His love, and more opportunities to become His disciple.

Might I share another thing of which I am certain? There is no adventure greater than a journey toward discipleship, and there is no reward more satisfying than to find that somewhere along the way you have lost yourself and become His.

As you begin this journey, ask Him to be your guide. Turn your life over to Him one month at a time, for this one year, and prepare your heart to recognize your own Waters of Mormon experiences. Great miracles await you.

This I know.

Act upon this . . .
Read Mosiah 18

What are the Waters of Mormon experiences in your life?

Try to think of an experience through which you came to know the Lord. It could be an experience where you allowed the Lord to change your heart, to make you more. If you have one in mind, reflect on its importance in your life. If you are unsure, find ways to invite the Lord into your life. Let your desire to know the Lord become the priority of your life.

Ponder . . .
He Is Set . . . Come to Him

The chapter containing one of the Lord's most famous sermons begins with two important lines: "And seeing the multitudes, he went up into a mountain: and when he was set, *his disciples came unto him*" (Matthew 5:1; emphasis added). Close your eyes and picture this. The Lord climbed the mount, and *once He was set,* His disciples *came unto Him.* He left behind the multitudes and the crowds of people and walked up the mountain to wait.

This sermon was meant only for those who were willing to ascend to it.

It was the choice of each individual. A journey. One had to come unto Christ to receive the lesson needed for the journey toward discipleship, the outline for who he or she might become. The first lesson of the Sermon on the Mount is the realization that a true disciple must go to the Lord to receive the message. Leave behind the multitude and go to Him. This will not be the choice of the masses, but it is the choice of a disciple. The pattern within the story of the Sermon on the Mount is clear—the Lord's disciples ascended the mount to Him, and *then* He taught.

"To comprehend the works of Christ, one must know Him as the son of God. . . . [One must] come to Him, to see and hear, to feel and know. . . . The response must be an individual one" (Elder James E. Talmage).

Once we have come unto Him, the way of the Lord is to teach us individually, one by one—to help us become more.

Open the scriptures to any book. Search the chapters, and read through the verses. The stories of Jesus are filled with these one-on-one teaching moments. In my mind's eye I can see them.

A Samaritan woman approaches a man sitting at a well. *She comes to Him.* The moment is spent in conversation that leads to conversion, prompting her to leave behind her water pot to bring others back to Him.

Sixteen clear stones molten out of rock and carried in work-worn hands to the top of the mount. He climbed to where the Lord was, one with great faith asking the Lord to touch the stones, to prepare them to shine forth in the dark. And "the Lord stretched forth his hand and touched the stones *one by one* with his finger" (Ether 3:6; emphasis added). First there was faith, and then pure knowledge. Touched. One by one.

Twelve men in an upper room. Dusty, thirsty, tired. It was His last supper, and they came to Him. Humble, the Servant rose from supper, took a towel, and began to wash the disciples' feet. Tenderly. One by one.

A man who was blind, a daughter who lay dying, the centurion's servant. It was always about the individual. To love the one.

And again, in the midst of the great multitude who, when they beheld Him, ran to Him. And *"one of the multitude"* brought unto Him his son. One of the multitude. *One.* "I have brought unto thee my son" (Mark 9:17; emphasis added).

In the darkest hours they would seek Him. Remember Nicodemus, ruler of the Jews? "The same *came to Jesus* by night" saying "Rabbi, we know that thou art a teacher come from God: for no man can do these miracles that thou doest, except God be with him. . . . How can these things be?" (John 3:2, 9; emphasis added). The same *came to Jesus.*

"And, behold, *one came* and said unto him, Good Master, what good thing shall I do . . . what lack I yet?" *One came,* and He answered privately, Savior and friend. "Come *and* follow me" (Matthew 19:16, 20, 21; emphasis added).

No matter where we are in our journey, one thing is certain—there will be hours where we need strength beyond our own, miracles within the ordinary moments, blessings that only He can give.

To know Him as the Son of God.

To see and hear. To feel and know.

The response must be an individual one.

He is set—come to Him.

PONDER THIS . . .
Read Matthew 5

The journey to discipleship, this journey to become His, will be life changing only to the extent that we allow it to be. It might require us to ascend to a higher level. We may need to leave behind the multitude and the crowd to come to Him. Often it is only under those conditions that we can truly hear His message. We must find the time for these private excursions.

"And thus they all received the light of the countenance of their lord, every man in his hour, *and in his time,* and in his season" (Doctrine and Covenants 88:58; emphasis added).

What is it that you need from the Lord? Remember, the Lord is willing to give us however much time we need, whether it is an hour out of our day, or perhaps an entire season of our life. No matter the hour, the time, or the season, His invitation is constantly extended.

He is set . . . come to Him.

Become . . .
Meant for More

Louise Yates Robison, a former Relief Society general president, once said, "Welcome the task that takes you beyond yourself."

The journey to discipleship is a journey that has the potential to take you beyond yourself. The pattern is clear and the destination is certain. No matter where we are on our journey, this process will require letting go of who we are to become who the Lord knows we can be. President Ezra Taft Benson encouraged, "Men and women who turn their lives over to God will discover that He can make a lot more out of their lives than they can. He can deepen their joys, expand their vision, quicken their minds, strengthen their muscles, lift their spirits, multiply their blessings, increase their opportunities, comfort their souls, raise up friends, and pour out peace." It is not necessarily that the Lord wants us to be something different; in essence He is inviting us to become something more.

Several years ago my friends took me out to lunch for my birthday. The afternoon was filled with good conversation and laughter. In a moment of pause, one of my friends asked me to sum up what I had learned over the past year. It is amazing how quickly memories can flash through the mind, and I was surprised at how vivid they still were.

I thought through the lessons I had learned and realized that many of them were lessons I would not have chosen to learn had I been given the option at the beginning of the year. However, in that moment I realized I was grateful for each one of them. Lessons like the courage and serenity that only God can bring. The importance of stopping right now to say, "I love you," "I'm proud of you," and "I'm so glad you're mine." Moments when a heart was completely overwhelmed with gratitude that words could not express. I remembered a time of quiet desperation when a prayer for strength led to the realization that angels are always standing near. A day when hope won out after others believed that the time for miracles had gone. A mother's true sacrifice—letting life pass by so she could cherish that tiny one. Understanding that the gift of discernment allows you to *see* the good. Knowing that giving everything can lead to exhaustion but also to miracles, and that tears of joy can fall at the same time as tears of pain.

How do you explain all of that to a group of friends at a ladies' luncheon? To sum it all up, I looked at my friends and replied, "This was a year of *more*." I saw the puzzled look on their faces and then tried to explain, "Looking back, it seems that I have never learned more in one short year. It feels like I have never cried more. I can't remember if I've ever laughed more, or loved more, and it's been a long time since I've grieved more. Honestly, I'm not sure if I've ever given more. It just has been one of *those* years."

Suddenly I realized that there were moments in that year when I remember feeling like I was not enough, and in those moments I found myself turning to the Savior. I don't know how it happened, but every time I was in need, He gave me more—more hope, more faith, and more strength. Somehow it seemed there was more peace and more understanding. He sent more miracles. And, in some way, through it all, I had felt more love. Through Him I had become more.

Looking back on your own life, have you felt those same stirrings? At times the desire for more pulls at us like a kite tugging impatiently, drawing us forward one step at a time, leading us toward Him. But at other times it seems as though the wind has completely quieted and there is no longer an uplift to beckon us ahead. In those moments perhaps we are too cynical, our own knowledge preventing room for belief. Maybe we have been hurt, and the place in our heart that needs to be healed can't be, because we are too afraid to trust. We might be keeping score with God, feeling that we will never measure up to His expectations. We may long for the desire to know more but just don't know where to begin.

As we become willing to let Him take whatever we have to offer and make it more, we will begin to experience a transformation. Sometimes these transforming experiences are unexpected and painful. At other times we seek them out because deep within our heart we know we are ready for something more. Each experience will lead to flashes of insight and moments of growth. Through deeply personal moments of inspiration we will begin writing His name on our heart, filling our mind with one-on-one moments we want to remember, and weaving His tender mercies throughout our life. It is a process that requires letting go and trusting. It is a journey that could become the adventure of our life, if we choose to let it.

Let this journey take you beyond yourself. What the Lord has in mind for you will exceed all of your expectations.

He knows you were meant for more.

BECOME . . .
Read the conference talk "More Holiness Give Me," H. David Burton, October 2004; Read the words of the hymn "More Holiness Give Me" (Hymns, no. 131).

"The virtues expressed in 'More Holiness Give Me' fall into several groups. Some are personal goals, like more holiness give me; more strivings within; more faith, gratitude, and purity; more fit for the kingdom; more purpose in prayer; and more trust in the Lord. Others center on adversity. They include patience in suffering, meekness in trial, praise for relief, strength to overcome, freedom from earth stains and longing for home. The rest firmly anchor us to our Savior: more sense of His care; more pride in His glory; more hope in His word; more joy in His service; more tears for His sorrows; more pain at His grief; more blessed and holy; and more, Savior, like Thee" (Bishop H. David Burton).

Consider your life. Are you missing something? Do you struggle with being enough? Have you ever longed for more? This week, could you allow the Lord to make up the difference? Then write down the experiences when you feel yourself becoming more.

Become

Willing to feel and see one-on-one moments with the Lord

Mindful of the Waters of Mormon experiences in your life

Not just interested in the Sermon, but willing to ascend to it

Ever mindful of Him along the way

Accepting of the journey that takes you beyond yourself

Meant for more

Solo Time
Become More

"I beseech you therefore, brethren, by the mercies of God, that ye present your bodies a living sacrifice, holy, acceptable unto God, *which is* your reasonable service.

"And be not conformed to this world: *but be ye transformed*" (Romans 12:1–2; emphasis added).

The process of becoming more is unique to each of us. It can't be shortened, and no one can do it for us. Think of a butterfly. Part of the transformation is a building process, which requires hard work and dedication from the caterpillar—first gathering strength and sustenance, then spinning and weaving. But that process in and of itself is not enough. The other part of the process requires a season of stillness, of patience, of waiting. It is the combination of the two that allows the caterpillar to be transformed from what it once was into what God intended it to be—to become more.

Just as a butterfly will die if the human hand assists the process, our transformation will not be complete without total effort on our part. It is the personal nature of our experiences that enables the transformation to take place. Because of this, there is no process more insightful than becoming. It is the act of leaving behind something you already are in the hope of what you might become.

A true disciple learns to balance the moments of hard work and dedication with the moments of stillness. Both the working and the waiting require sacrifice. Both require a change of heart. The sacrifice becomes worth it once we come to believe that we are truly meant for more. "They rose to that height which makes sacrifice the soul's dearest offering, as the chrysalis, brown and unbeautiful, gives the radiant creature within to the light" (Myrtle Reed).

Through personal daily experiences that prompt us to work and dedicate our lives to Him, combined with moments of deep reflection in which we patiently wait for His guidance and direction, the transformation begins to take place. In the process we become tougher and yet more tender as well—not in an instant, but in the Lord's time. "For he knoweth all things, and there is not anything save he knows it" (2 Nephi 9:20). He will balance the moments of work and the moments of waiting, and through Him we will become more than we could have ever become through our own effort.

"For since the beginning of the world have not men heard nor perceived by the ear, neither hath any eye seen, O God, besides thee, how great things thou hast prepared for him that waiteth for thee" (Doctrine and Covenants 133:45).

It has always been so.

Become Willing

A cathedral without windows, a face without eyes, a field without flowers, an alphabet without vowels, a continent without rivers, a night without stars, a sky without a sun— these would not be so sad as a . . . soul without Christ.

—James L. Gordon

Consider...
The Name Written Always in Your Heart

I am prepared to like you very much."

The other night my daughters and I watched *Miss Potter,* the story of Beatrix Potter. If you have seen it, you will remember the unforgettable scene that shows the very first meeting between Beatrix Potter and Millie Warne, who are destined to become the best of friends. Just after Miss Potter enters through the door, barely moments after their first introduction, Millie whispers to her, "I must warn you, I am prepared to like you very much."

It's such a simple phrase, but you just can't help but smile when you hear it. Millie had prepared a place in her heart for Beatrix, and that relationship became a source of strength to both of them throughout their lives.

The simple quote gives pause for thought. This journey of Becoming His invites each of us to strengthen our relationship with Christ. Are you serious about developing that kind of relationship—one that will become a source of strength for the rest of your life? Do you have a heart prepared to like Him very much? To love Him? To trust Him? If so, what are you prepared to do?

The second principle of discipleship I'd like to suggest is to become willing to prepare a place in our lives for a relationship with the Lord. The first principle encouraged us to make a choice, with the understanding that within that process we could become more. This principle includes becoming willing to live according to that choice. It includes becoming willing to write His name upon our hearts, becoming willing to ponder continually upon the things of the Lord, becoming willing to reach out to Him, and becoming willing to consider our ways. Within this section we will talk about all four of these aspects of becoming willing.

Last fall I was preparing to go on vacation. I asked my daughter Megan if I could borrow her iPod. I left on Friday and returned home on Sunday. I was so busy I never got a chance to listen to Meg's iPod. On Monday, as I started unpacking, I realized I couldn't find the iPod anywhere. I sadly realized that it must have fallen out of my bag on the plane. Immediately I called the airline, only to get an automated recording that proved less than helpful: "Hundreds of passengers leave items on our planes every day. We have no way to categorize or sort these items. Thank you." That was it! They didn't even ask for my name. (I don't know why, but leaving my name would have made me feel a little bit better.)

Obviously I was going to have to buy Meg a new iPod. So I got online and began the ordering process. Megan and I checked the tracking number daily (because when you are fourteen, you can't exist without an iPod). We determined that the delivery date would be a Wednesday, and I wasn't going to be home. So I told Meg, "They don't leave stuff like this on the porch, so you need to be here, and when you hear the doorbell, you need to answer." She sat at home all afternoon, and finally the anticipated moment arrived.

When Megan answered the door, the UPS man handed her the small cardboard box, and then he handed her an automated handheld machine. Megan wasn't sure what she was supposed to do with the machine. She looked at it for a minute and finally thought, *Oh, he must want to know what is in my box.* So, on the small screen, with the pen he had provided, she very carefully drew a picture of an iPod with earphones coming out of it. (Yep, she really did that!) Then she handed it back to the UPS man. He stared at the box for a minute and then said, "Well, what's your last name?"

Megan replied, "Freeman," and shut the door.

I am sure that man went home and told his wife, "You are not going to believe what happened to me today."

When I came home, Megan was mortified. "Mom!" she said, "you didn't tell me I was supposed to sign my name!" She told me the whole experience and then asked, "Why did the man want my name?" I explained to her that a signature shows you are taking responsibility for something. A signature can show ownership, or it can show that an item is being placed into your care. Then I told her, "It's okay, Meg. It's funny."

"I know, Mom," she said. "I just wish I knew about the name."

Several weeks after that happened, I was reading in the book of Mosiah, "I would that ye should take upon you the name of Christ. . . . I say unto you, I would that ye should remember to retain the name, written always in your hearts . . . that ye hear and know the voice by which ye shall be called, and also, the name by which he shall call you" (Mosiah 5:8, 12). I stopped at that verse and heard the echo of Megan's voice, *I just wish I knew about the name.*

How important is it for us to remember the name written always in our hearts? I recently attended a women's conference. At one point all of the women were gathered into groups of about twenty. The purpose was to get to know each other better. We were asked to introduce ourselves and then tell the group why we were there and what we hoped to gain from the experience. As I listened to each woman share, I felt my heartstrings being tugged. One woman had lost her husband to cancer four months earlier. Her daughter was really struggling, making decisions that had the potential to ruin her life. Another woman spoke of bringing her sister to the conference so that she would be surrounded by women who would be kind to her, because that would not be the case when she returned home. Another asked, "Do you know what it feels like when you are swimming and swimming trying to reach the surface so you can finally take a breath? That is my life. At least I am still swimming. I just wish I could breathe." I looked around at those women and again heard my daughter's voice—*I just wish I knew about the name.*

Have you ever had a moment like that? In those moments I try to remember the name written always in my heart. There I find courage; there I find peace; there I find strength beyond my own.

From King Benjamin we learn the importance of being willing to write the name of the Lord on our hearts. He teaches that writing the name of the Lord on our hearts is not something that can be done in one afternoon. The process often requires preparation and dedication. He explains that it is a covenant we should be willing to keep all the remainder of our days. It will lead to a change of heart. It will require obedience. Most important, it is our choice. We take His name if we are willing. *We* choose to make the covenant; *we* choose to allow our hearts to change.

In Samuel we are told to "prepare [our] hearts unto the Lord" (1 Samuel 7:3). Hearts are interesting things. They are both a source of life and a source for emotion. We know they can be broken and mended— both physically and spiritually. And although the human heart weighs less than a pound and is the size of a fist, somehow it has the capacity to grow, enlarge, and swell—making room for kindness, love, and other important feelings. Just as a physician is concerned with the health of our heart, the scriptures tell us that the Lord is concerned with the condition of our heart. Part of the process of keeping our spiritual heart healthy is to prepare it to receive the Lord. This is the process by which we begin to imprint His name there. But our heart must be willing.

The second step on this journey toward discipleship is crucial because His signature written on our heart signifies our willingness to be placed into His care. "Yea, blessed is this people who are *willing* to bear my name; for in my name shall they be called; *and they are mine*" (Mosiah 26:18; emphasis added).

CONSIDER THIS . . .
Read Mosiah 5

"It is significant that when we partake of the sacrament we do not witness that we take upon us the name of Jesus Christ. We witness that we are willing to do so (see Doctrine and Covenants 20:77). The fact that we only witness to our willingness suggests that something else must happen before we actually take that sacred name upon us in the most important sense. . . . Our willingness to take upon us the name of Jesus Christ affirms our commitment to do all that we can to be counted among those whom he will choose to stand at his right hand . . . at the last day" (President Dallin H. Oaks).

There are three important things that we do in the name of Christ: we pray in His name, we repent in His name, and we serve in His name. With those in mind, consider one way you might show that you are willing to take the name of the Lord this week.

"And they came, every one whose heart stirred him up, and every one whom his spirit made willing" (Exodus 35:21).

Act . . .
Upon These I Write the Things of My Soul

In a corner of my bathtub there is a cylinder glass vase filled one-fourth full with soft beach sand and the rest of the way full of seashells. I did not buy the seashells; they have been gathered over a lifetime. One of our family's favorite places to visit is San Diego, and one of our favorite pastimes is to stroll down the beach searching for seashells. The hobby can occupy much of an afternoon.

My children learn to become expert shell seekers at a young age. We do not walk along the shoreline where the beach meets the surf; we walk within the breaking waters at low tide, our eyes carefully scanning the calm waters between the rolling waves. At just the right moment, after the first wave leaves and just before the second one hits, there is a moment of stillness, of settling, when the surface becomes calm and a clear view of the ocean floor spans below. In that split second, the most priceless seashells can be found—perfect sand dollars not yet destroyed by the constant pounding of the surf. We gather them as each day ends. The shells accompany us on our journey home.

Over the years these seashells have been carefully placed into the vase in my bathroom. I love to look at the vase. Sometimes, on particularly discouraging days, I carry the vase around with me from room to room so that it is continually in my view. It reminds me of some of my happiest days, of memories made with my family, of some of our most precious moments together. The simple vase has a powerful way of reminding my heart to ponder on good things.

In the Book of Mormon we read of a prophet who teaches a great lesson about pondering. Not many days after the death of their father, Nephi got in an argument with his brothers. I am sure his heart was heavy from the passing of his father; I think his emotions were probably close to the surface. It must have been a particularly discouraging day. Nephi does not go into detail about the argument. Instead, he sits down to write on the plates, and what follows is a heartfelt journal entry often referred to as the Psalm of Nephi.

Nephi begins the entry by saying, "Upon these I write the things of my soul" (2 Nephi 4:15). Think for a minute about the emotion that must have filled Nephi's soul—heartache from just losing his father, discouragement after having argued with his brothers. The verses of this psalm contain tender impressions from the raw emotion of a prophet. Within his writings on this discouraging day we can find great counsel for our own discouraging days. One of my favorite verses reads, "Behold, *my soul delighteth* in the things of the Lord; and *my heart pondereth continually* upon the things which I have seen and heard" (2 Nephi 4:16; emphasis added).

This is the second lesson for this section—becoming willing to ponder continually upon the things of the Lord. Nephi did not carry around a vase of seashells on his particularly hard days. Instead he carried with

Him the things of the Lord, and his heart pondered continually upon them. His willingness to remember the memories of his experiences with the Lord had the power to lift his heart.

The same can be true of our lives. We must be willing to experience personal moments with the Lord—first, to write His name on our hearts, and second, to ponder continually upon the things of the Lord. Just like our family when hunting shells in San Diego, we need to set aside moments to spend with the Lord. Sometimes these moments come from reading our scriptures; other times they come during humble, heartfelt prayer. The Lord's Spirit can be felt in the tearstained hours of trial and in the most tender moments of service. His Spirit can sustain us through the deepest heartache and strengthen us to face our unmasked fears. The undeniable warmth that settles within our heart signifies His answer, accompanies His peace, and confirms His witness. These are the things of the Lord; these are the moments we must remember.

It is crucial to find a way to preserve the memories so that we will be able to look back on them on our most discouraging days. This will require some preparation on our part. The memories can be saved within the pages of a journal. We might hang a particular painting of the Lord on the walls of our home to remind us of our testimony. Perhaps there is a favorite hymn or song that reminds us of our feelings of the Lord. Becoming willing to experience these moments will help us to walk the path of discipleship. Filling our life with these remembrances will allow our hearts to ponder continually on the things of the Lord, and within those pondering moments our hearts will be lifted.

Read 2 Nephi 4

"Maintain your personal journals. Those who keep a book of remembrance are more likely to keep the Lord in remembrance in their daily lives" (President Spencer W. Kimball).

This week, become willing to continually ponder upon the things of the Lord. Perhaps you might consider finding a journal or notebook where you can keep track of *the things of your soul* during this process. Become willing to write down your personal reflections as He begins to mold you into the person He knows you can become.

Ponder . . .

Reaching

I was seventeen, my heart freshly cut open because I had moved from what was familiar to what was not and I faced the future with uncertainty and raw emotions. My mother sat next to me. We were on two orange plastic chairs, and we sat in the high school hallway, and we waited for someone to call my name. When it was my turn, we stared down at subjects that were familiar—English, history, algebra—and names of teachers that were not. We talked about what would be best, and how I would start my senior year in a new high school, friendless. We decided that if I could find just one thing to look forward to, one class that would be fascinating enough to make a lonely heart happy, I could get out of bed in the morning and my mother could spend the school day at home peaceful.

Finally we stumbled upon the answer to the longing. While my friends back home in Utah studied biology in a classroom from a book, I would study marine biology from sandy California beaches and sometimes from a boat, and an instructor would provide the text. He would call me Utah because I was the only one who came from there.

One morning in the spring we took a field trip. We didn't go by bus, like all of my friends back home did, we went by boat, and we traveled across the waves to an island where we would explore. I sat at the back of the boat, the calm blue water stirred up into white foam. The text of the lesson included a blue whale surfacing on the right side of the boat, later a shark hovering in the shadows, and, as we neared the destination, dolphins playing in front of the bow. Droplets of water splashed into the sky, glinting of yellow, and just off the side of the boat, fish flew.

I had studied science on white pages with black type and four-color photographs specifically chosen to complement the text. I had memorized, and visualized, and categorized, and yet I had not learned. Now my knowledge was stretched, and I heard text from the instructor, and I saw the biology swimming, and I was learning.

Against the pounding rhythm of boat meeting ocean, I pondered. I had left behind security and stability—a zone of comfort in which I excelled and my grades and my relationships and my accomplishments suggested that I was proficient and that my schooling was nearly complete. Then change, unexpected and unanticipated, had sent me reeling into a situation of unaccomplishments with no familiar relationships and text that was unconventional. Sometimes life walking straight ends up at corners turning, and the previous learning becomes insufficient, the current text unfamiliar. In those moments, our hearts, grasping for what once was certain, are forced to reach for possibilities undefined.

As the boat reached the island, I realized what would have been immediately and apparently clear if my eyes had been focused on what lay ahead rather than what filled the moment and undefined the past. The island was compassed about on every side by steep cliffs. There were no warm beaches sandy with white water lapping, no sturdy dock for the boat that would surely drift.

Then, once again, the instructor guiding, text spoken, knowledge forthcoming. In that moment when the heart is willing to learn, again the teacher appears.

If we looked carefully, we would see a ladder bolted to the sheer face of the cliff. The boat would hover next to the face. The water would not still. In between the ebbing and the flowing, the rising and the dropping, the constant rolling of the sea majestic beneath us, our instructor would navigate the boat to the spot on the cliff just below the ladder. Then, in that instant when the sea heaved and the boat rose, we would reach our hands as high as we could—reach to grasp the ladder rung. Immediately the boat would pull away from the cliff, so that in case we fell into the ocean we would not be crushed between the boat and the formidable cliff face.

It was daunting. This was not in my comfort zone, my list of accomplishments, my level of learning sufficient. This was not walking down black steps off a bus onto asphalt pavement. This was a course uncharted. Perhaps I was not equal to the task.

I watched the others climb, one by one, boat inching close to the ladder, the heaving, the reaching, the boat pulling away from the cliff face, the climber ascending. I wished my heart brave.

The instructor suggested that if I wasn't up to the climb I might wait in the boat anchored to the safety of the sea floor. Perhaps there was safety within, but I remembered the shark without. My heart considered the exploration of the unknown ahead and filled with butterfly wings, and the lift gave me courage to reach.

And so the heaving. And the reaching. And the safety falling away. My heart dropping into my toes. Butterfly wings beating. And then the climb.

Interestingly, I don't remember what my eyes saw when I reached the top of the ladder. I don't remember the exploring. I don't even remember any of my fellow students who accompanied me there.

I remember only the kind instructor and the moment of reaching.

Even now, decades later, it is the same.

In that moment when my heart, grasping for what once was certain, is forced to reach for possibilities undefined, in that moment when I find myself turning corners with knowledge insufficient, when I feel safety falling away . . .

Like the woman, twelve years ill, who spent all she had and, instead of growing better, grew worse. Like Peter, surrounded by furious waves, fear growing, drowning imminent . . .

I reach. Willing.

Isn't that just what they did? Two separate stories. Two separate chapters. But my fingers touch gilded pages, my eyes skim holy words, and therein I find the similarity.

The willingness to reach.

For strength. For healing. For something more.

But the similarity does not end there. Two words clear as promise define the Master's response: *straightway* and *immediately*. As clear in the one text as it is in the other. One waited twelve years, the other perhaps twelve seconds, but the response is consistent for both. A prayer for strength never goes unanswered.

And so, in the moments when I have moved from what is familiar to what is not and I face the future with uncertainty and raw emotions, He is who I reach for.

The answer comes privately.

He reaches my reaching.

I am strengthened straightway and immediately.

The third lesson on becoming willing is daring to reach. It is within those reaching moments that we come to know the Lord.

PONDER THIS . . .
Read Luke 8:41–48 and Matthew 14:22–33

"Let us therefore *come boldly* unto the throne of grace, that we may obtain mercy, and find grace to help in time of need" (Hebrews 4:16; emphasis added).

Have you ever found yourself in a time of need—a reaching moment that required strength beyond your own? How could you become more willing to reach out to the Lord in those moments? Determine to set aside whatever holds you back. Then, come boldly.

Become . . .
Willing to Consider Your Ways

Sometimes becoming willing requires a self-inventory of sorts, an analysis of where we are compared to where we want to be. This process of defining our priorities often requires consideration.

The last lesson in this section is to become willing to consider our ways. Haggai was a prophet who taught this lesson in a profound way. His people had become sidetracked on their journey to discipleship. They were meant to be building the temple but had lost focus somewhere along the way. The Lord said to the people, "*Consider your ways.* Ye have sown much, and bring in little; ye eat, but ye have not enough; ye drink, but ye are not filled with drink; ye clothe you, but there is none warm; and he that earneth wages earneth wages to put it into a bag with holes. Thus saith the Lord of hosts; *Consider your ways*" (Haggai 1:5–7; emphasis added).

This description sounds a lot like our day. Our world is filled with people who work hard but bring in little, who are unsatisfied and lack a feeling of fulfillment. Unfortunately, the illustration of money slipping away is an idea that many of us can relate to. Perhaps we too should consider our ways.

The Lord explains the problem, "Ye looked for much, and, lo, it came to little . . . the heaven over you is stayed from dew, and the earth is stayed from her fruit" (Haggai 1:9, 10). Somehow these people had lost focus. What counted in their eyes as much was in reality little. They had laid aside the most important thing. Their building the temple would have allowed the Lord to remain at the forefront in their lives. Why was that so important? Without Him the dew from heaven and the fruit of the earth were stayed.

Dew is often used figuratively to represent inspiration from heaven. When the Lord and His house became of lesser importance to the people of Haggai, inspiration from heaven also decreased. Without inspiration from the Lord, the people were left to their own means, their own strength. Their lives lacked the blessing that comes through being guided by the Lord. The Bible Dictionary explains that the worldly behavior of the people had brought about "a curse on all their labor and increase." As unfortunate as that is, it makes sense, and we are led to wonder if the same is true in our day.

But the Lord did not forget His people. He stirred up their spirits in remembrance, and He was forgiving. As soon as they laid the foundation for the temple, the Lord became their focus, and their lives began to change for the better. "Consider now from this day and upward . . . even from the day that the foundation of the Lord's temple was laid, consider it. Is the seed yet in the barn? yea, as yet the vine, and the fig tree, and the pomegranate, and the olive tree, . . . from this day will I bless you" (Haggai 2:18–19).

Their willingness to turn to the Lord, to make Him a first priority, allowed Him to send great blessings they otherwise might not have obtained. Because their thoughts were focused on Him, they were able to receive inspiration for their lives, direction from Him that would otherwise have gone unheeded.

Is it possible that this counsel would work in our lives? What if we were to ask ourselves that same question? *Consider your ways.*

Do your ways lead you to seek inspiration on a daily basis?

Is the Lord a first priority?

Are you asking Him for input concerning your home, your profession, and your way of life?

Do you take the time to consider the blessings in your life and recognize that they come from the Lord?

This week, become willing to be the type of person who can answer yes to each of those questions. Then consider now from this day and upward. Consider it.

From this day He will bless you.

BECOME . . .
Read Haggai

Become

Willing to prepare your heart, open your heart, and soften your heart

Willing to take His name

Willing to ponder continually

Willing to write the things of your soul

Willing to reach

Willing to consider your ways

Willing to place your will on God's altar

Willing

"The submission of one's will is really the only uniquely personal thing we have to place on God's altar. . . . When you and I finally submit ourselves, by letting our individual wills be swallowed up in God's will, then we are really giving something to Him! It is the only *possession which is truly ours to give*" (Elder Neal A. Maxwell).

Often, considering our ways prompts us to set aside what we want to make way for what the Lord wants. Just like the people of Haggai, our willingness to turn to the Lord, to make Him a first priority, will allow Him to send great blessings we otherwise might not be able to obtain. When our thoughts are focused on the Lord, we become able to receive and recognize inspiration for our lives.

Become willing to consider your ways this week. What might need to change so that you can receive more inspiration from the Lord?

Solo Time
Become Willing

I love this definition of willingness:

"Those who humble themselves before God, . . . and come forth with broken hearts and contrite spirits, . . . and are willing to take upon them the name of Jesus Christ, having a determination to serve him to the end" (Doctrine and Covenants 20:37).

When I think of people who are willing to write the name of the Lord on their hearts, to ponder continually upon the things of the Lord, to reach for the Lord in their darkest hours, to consider their ways, I am reminded of the pioneers—a group of Saints who set aside their entire lives, sacrificing everything for God's will.

President Joseph F. Smith spoke particularly of the pioneer women, saying, "Could you turn one of these women away from their convictions

in the Church of Jesus Christ of Latter-day Saints? . . . Could you blind
them with reference to the divine mission of Jesus Christ, the Son of
God? No, never in the world could you do it. Why? Because they knew
it. God revealed it to them, and they understood it, and no power on
earth could turn them from what they knew to be that truth. Death was
nothing to them. Hardship was nothing. . . . All they felt and knew and
desired was the triumph of the kingdom of God and the truth that the
Lord had given to them."

And then, with all of the sincerity of a prophet of God, he pled, "My
soul, where are these women now?"

I believe the conviction of these women came from what they knew
deep inside. Their strength came from their willingness to live up to those
convictions.

I believe they were women who were willing to write the name of the
Lord on their hearts.

I believe they were women who were willing to ponder upon the
things of the Lord continually.

I believe they were women who were willing to reach for the Lord in
every hardship.

I believe they were women who were willing to consider their ways,
and then to align their ways with the ways of the Lord.

What would it take for you to develop the conviction the pioneers
had? What are you willing to sacrifice to know the Lord?

Become a Builder

*That which I have I can easily give you, but that
which I am you must obtain for yourself.*

— PRESIDENT DALLIN H. OAKS

Consider . . .

How Is It That He Cannot Instruct Me That I Should Build?

Recently I walked into Sharing Time and noticed there was a visitor in my five-year-old Primary class. I sat down, and immediately he changed seats so he could sit right next to me. As the opening song began, he introduced himself, and then he said, "What do you want to be when you grow up?" I haven't been asked that question in years, and I couldn't help but smile.

"Maybe a writer," I said. "What do you want to be?"

"I don't know," he replied with a twinkle in his eye. "Maybe a doctor; maybe a Walmarter." I couldn't help but picture him as a Walmarter.

"Maybe you could be a teacher, like your dad," I suggested.

"No," came his quick reply, "you have to get a shot to be a teacher." He thought for a moment and then asked, "Do you have to get a shot to be a dad?"

"No," I answered.

"Okay," he replied, "then I think I will just be a dad."

One thing I love about five-year-olds is that the whole world is open to them. They believe that they are good at everything and that they can become anything they want to be. We were all like that many years ago. When our kindergarten teacher asked who could paint, we all raised our hands. Who could dance? Again, every hand. Who is good at soccer? Unanimous.

Then we grew up. We put boundaries and definitions upon our

dreams. Reality set in. We said to ourselves, *I can't be a doctor; I don't have a degree. I can't fly the airplane; I am not a pilot. I can't paint; I don't have any talent.* Sometimes I wish we could be in kindergarten again, to have that kind of faith in ourselves.

Nephi had faith like that.

The Lord spoke to Nephi and said, "Arise, and get thee into the mountain" (1 Nephi 17:7). Nephi didn't ask any questions—he just went. When he got to the mountain, the Lord told him, "Thou shalt construct a ship" (1 Nephi 17:8).

Was Nephi a shipbuilder?

I searched through the first seventeen chapters of the Book of Mormon and couldn't find any record of that information. No schooling. No previous experience as a shipbuilder. But for some reason, the Lord thought he was.

I love the lesson we learn from Nephi's answer to the Lord. He didn't say, "I can't build a ship, I don't have a degree in shipbuilding." Instead his answer was, "Whither shall I go that I might make tools?"

This answer is even more incomprehensible to me. Not only was Nephi not a shipbuilder—he didn't even own the tools for the trade. Before Nephi could begin building the ship, he had to make the tools.

Through Nephi's example we learn the third principle of discipleship—we must become builders. Just like Nephi, we will find that sometimes the greatest building experiences of our life will require having faith and being willing to go to work, even if we have to begin by constructing the tools.

As Nephi got to work building the tools, his brothers began to murmur, saying, "Our brother is a fool. . . . We knew that ye were lacking in judgment. . . . *Thou canst not accomplish so great a work*" (1 Nephi 17:17–19; emphasis added).

But Nephi didn't give up; instead he remembered Moses and said to his brothers, "Ye know that Moses was commanded *to do that great work*" (1 Nephi 17:26; emphasis added). Then he spoke to them of the parting of the Red Sea, the manna in the wilderness, the water in the rock, and the Promised Land. Finally he told them, "And now, if the Lord has such great power, and has wrought so many miracles among the children of men, *how is it that he cannot instruct me, that I should build a ship?*" (1 Nephi 17:51; emphasis added).

Nephi wasn't afraid of the task at hand because he believed in a God who was capable of helping His servants accomplish great things. In the next chapter, we read, "And I, Nephi, did go into the mount oft, and I did pray oft unto the Lord; *wherefore the Lord showed unto me great things*" (1 Nephi 18:3; emphasis added).

What great things does the Lord have in mind for you? What tools could you use to help you achieve those great things?

Think for a minute of the tools Nephi used to build the ship. Obviously he used tools made from "the ore which [he] did molten out of the rock" (1 Nephi 17:6). But there were other tools. I think of his trips to the mountain, and I am reminded of the temple. I consider his memories of Moses, and I am reminded of the scriptures. I know that he spoke consistently to the Lord, and I am reminded of prayer. You might not think of these as tools, but could they be? A favorite quote from the movie *Mr. Magorium's Wonder Emporium* reminds me, "Unlikely adventures require unlikely tools."

The Lord sent Nephi on an unlikely adventure. Through the use of what some might call unlikely tools, the Lord was able to help Nephi recognize his ability to accomplish great things during that adventure.

One more lesson we learn from Nephi, the builder, is the importance of an instructor. Nephi couldn't teach himself to build the boat. He needed to go somewhere for instruction. If we really want to obtain instruction from the Lord, we must go to the places where He is—the temple, scriptures, and prayer.

I have come to believe that what Nephi said is true, "If the Lord has such great power, . . . how can he not instruct me?" (1 Nephi 17:51). The Lord can instruct us in personal and individual ways if we let Him. Through temple visits, prayer, and scripture study, this instruction becomes clear. It is through these individual and personal experiences that our testimonies are built. Then we become just who the Lord would have us become—a builder, a disciple who is capable of accomplishing great things.

CONSIDER THIS . . .
Read 1 Nephi 17

The third step on the pathway toward discipleship is to become a builder, knowing that the Lord has a great work in store for you. Consider what your great work might be. Where could you go to obtain instruction? What tools will you use in your building process? What are some steps you might take as you begin your great work?

President Dallin H. Oaks told a story of a great man instructing his son: "All that I have I desire to give you—not only my wealth, but also my position and standing among men. That which *I have* I can easily give you, but that which *I am* you must obtain for yourself. You will qualify for your inheritance by learning what I have learned and by living as I have lived. I will give you the laws and principles by which I have acquired my wisdom and stature. Follow my example, mastering as I have mastered, and you will become as I am, and all that I have will be yours."

Act . . .
Location, Location, Location

If you were to decide to build a home today, and you spent the afternoon with a realtor looking at pieces of land, I am fairly certain that realtor would give you three words of advice, "location, location, location." Now, I know you are thinking that is just one word, and you are right. But every realtor I have ever heard say that word always says it three times, and there is a reason why.

Location is crucial.

It is crucial now, and it was just as crucial thousands of years ago. When Abraham and Lot left Egypt, they were looking for a place to settle. Between them they had so many belongings that they realized they could not live together. So, when they arrived in the place where they were going to stay, they stood shoulder to shoulder and looked out over the land. Abraham told Lot, "If thou wilt take the left hand, I will go to the right; or if thou depart to the right hand, then I will go to the left" (Genesis 13:9).

CLOSER TO CHRIST

I wonder if Lot thought to himself in that moment, "Location, location, location." If not, he probably should have. "And Lot lifted up his eyes and beheld all the plain of Jordan, that it was well watered every where, . . . and Lot dwelled in the cities of the plain, and pitched his tent *toward Sodom*" (Genesis 13:10, 12; emphasis added). It seems Lot made his choice by choosing what was easiest, underestimating the importance of inquiring after the character of his neighbors. Perhaps there was a curiosity, even a desire to be entertained by the wickedness while keeping it at arm's length. In our day, some might say he chose to "live on the edge."

Rather than choosing quickly, Abraham left his choice of location up to the Lord. He walked the length and breadth of the remaining land. The scriptures tell us that he chose his land by faith and pitched his tent in Hebron.

It wasn't long before war rose up within the cities surrounding Lot's location. Sodom and Gomorrah were plundered, "and they took Lot, . . . who dwelt in Sodom, and his goods, and departed" (Genesis 14:12). Lot may have faced his tent toward Sodom hoping to stay at arm's length from the wickedness, but this scripture leads us to wonder if eventually Lot and his family were consumed by the wickedness and taken right up into Sodom. Their choice led to their captivity.

Abraham came to the rescue. He armed 318 of his own servants and left to rescue Lot—318 men to rescue one man from a situation that resulted from the direction in which he had placed his tent.

How important is location?

I find several interesting lessons within Lot's experience. First, he chose the course that was easiest without first consulting with the Lord. Second, he faced his tent toward Sodom, the most worldly city on Earth. Lastly, somehow the way of Sodom became so much a part of his life that he was carried away captive with those he associated with. The rescue from this predicament was so dangerous that Abraham could not attempt it alone. It required 318 men to rescue Lot from the choice he had made.

Could the same be true in our day? If we face our tent to the ways of the world, could those ways become so much a part of our life that we risk becoming held captive by them? Rather than putting ourselves in a situation that might necessitate our being rescued by an army, perhaps we could just face our tent in a different direction.

In the days of King Benjamin in the Book of Mormon, a proclamation was sent throughout all the land. The people were invited to gather to hear the voice of the king. A great many people came. In fact, there were so many that they could not be numbered. "And it came to pass that when they came to the temple, they pitched their tents round about, every man according to his family, consisting of his wife, and his sons, and his daughters, and their sons, and their daughters, from the eldest down to the youngest, every family being separate one from another. And they pitched their tents round about the temple, *every man having his tent with the door thereof towards the temple*" (Mosiah 2:5–6; emphasis added).

Consider the difference between these two choices:

"And Lot dwelled in the cities of the plain of Jordan, *and pitched his tent towards Sodom*" (Genesis 13:12; emphasis added).

"And they pitched their tents round about the temple, *every man having his tent with the door thereof towards the temple*" (Mosiah 2:6; emphasis added).

How important was the direction of the tent? One led to captivity; the other led to a mighty change of heart. In chapter five of Mosiah we read a great list of blessings that came to these families as a result of facing their doors toward the temple:

They were led to believe, to understand truth.

They experienced a mighty change in their hearts.

They wanted to do good continually.

They were able to have great views of that which was to come.

Through faith, they acquired a great knowledge, which caused them to rejoice with exceedingly great joy (see Mosiah 5:2–4).

The world we live in today does not allow us to be casual with the direction in which we face our tent. As disciples who are builders, we must consider location. Great blessings will come if we leave the ways of Sodom behind and choose instead to face our tent with the door toward the temple.

ACT UPON THIS . . .
Read Genesis 13 and Mosiah 5

Facing your tent toward the temple is a symbolic illustration. What are some ways you could literally apply this direction in your own life? Would you be willing to find a way to act on that direction this week?

Ponder . . .
And Still, the Builders Build

I will never forget one October afternoon when my children decided to build sand castles on the beach. Taking a few steps from the line of towels we had occupied all day, they knelt in the sand, and the building began. Minutes stretched into hours. The sun began to set, the tide changed, and still they worked, molded, created, formed, and shaped the sand.

Each asked for assistance. The younger ones wanted help getting the right texture of sand, filling the mold, setting it into place without cracks. The older ones came looking for inspiration, design ideas, encouragement. The process took hours; once they were focused, they could not be dissuaded. The other beach families packed up and left for home, the seagulls left shortly after, the lifeguards closed up shop, and still the builders built. Finally they were finished. Exhausted from their efforts, and after a fairly extensive show and tell, they left the beach with their dad to unwind in the swimming pool.

I couldn't resist the serenity of the moment, and, promising to follow momentarily, I listened to their happy voices floating toward the hotel and took one last look at the horizon. The beach was silent except for the tide rolling in. Almost at the horizon, the small speck of a huge aircraft carrier made its way across the blue ocean. The waves, now empty of surfboards and surfers, rolled into the shore, one after the other, over and over again, their white foam lapping at what had become the castles of my children's dreams. I wandered from one to the next, thinking how my children had somehow captured themselves within the sand.

The two boys had built their castles, one next to the other, as close to the surf as they dared. They were mighty fortresses, with huge moats spanning the entire length of each, fortified by mounds of sand packed to withstand the constant pounding of the surf. The mounds blended into each other, as if, by combining the two, one might gain from the strength of the other. Grace's castle was a little higher up the beach, a simple square with a roof of carefully placed turrets. Each turret boasted a treasure from the beach—a seashell, a piece of seaweed, and other simple joys. Megan's castle had been built clear up on the sand, almost next to our towels. Safe from the surf, the now dried sand sparkled in the setting sun. The curves were soft and simple, the landscape smooth, the tower designed to resemble a beautiful seashell.

I retrieved my camera and sat on the edge of my towel. Lifting it to my eyes, I was thrilled to find that I could capture all four castles with one shot. The picture became the background of my computer screen. I love to look at it. It reminds me of the memory but also, more important, of what my children are becoming. I see them building even now. The boys withstanding the constant pushing of the world we live in—seeking inspiration, fortifying, gaining strength from each other. Grace loving every moment life has to offer. Megan, dependable—a constant source of safety, calmness, and serenity.

Each building. Each becoming.

As you undertake this building process yourself, allow the minutes to stretch into hours. Let the sun rise and set and the seasons change around you as you lose yourself to molding, creating, forming, and shaping your beliefs. Pray for inspiration. Surround yourself with people who will encourage you. Allow the process to take time, and once you are focused, do not let yourself be dissuaded.

Others may pack up, close up, and become distracted.

But still the builders build.

PONDER THIS . . .
Read Ezra 4:4–5

"Then the people of the land weakened the hands of the people of Judah, and troubled them in building,

"And hired counsellors against them, to frustrate their purpose" (Ezra 4:4–5).

Think about your efforts to build right now. It might be with your family, your own testimony, or an area in which you serve. Does it ever feel like someone is trying to frustrate your purpose?

I love the Lord's response in the above situation, "Moreover I make a decree what ye shall do . . . [that] expenses be given unto these men, that they be not hindered. And that which they have need of, . . . let it be given them day by day without fail" (Ezra 6:8–9).

Remember the promise of the Lord. He will send us what we are in need of, day by day without fail, so our efforts to build will not be hindered. Pray that He will send you the answers you need. Watch for those answers as you read your scriptures. The Spirit will guide you. Remember to write the promptings down.

Become . . .

A Wise Masterbuilder . . . Bring Your Finest

THE BRIDGE BUILDER
By Will Allen Dromgoole

An old man, going a lone highway,
Came at the evening, cold and gray,
To a chasm, vast and deep and wide,
Through which was flowing a sullen tide.
The old man crossed in the twilight dim;
The sullen stream had no fears for him;
But he turned when safe on the other side
And built a bridge to span the tide.

"Old man," said a fellow pilgrim near,
"You are wasting strength with building here;
Your journey will end with the ending day;
You never again must pass this way;
You have crossed the chasm, deep and wide—
Why build you the bridge at the eventide?"

The builder lifted his old gray head:
"Good friend, in the path I have come," he said,
"There followeth after me today
A youth whose feet must pass this way.

184

This chasm that has been naught to me
To that fair-haired youth may a pitfall be.
He, too, must cross in the twilight dim;
Good friend, I am building the bridge for him."

When I ponder this process of building, I am reminded of Paul, who gave himself the title of a wise masterbuilder and said, "According to the grace of God which is given unto me, as a wise masterbuilder, I have laid the foundation, and another buildeth thereupon" (1 Corinthians 3:10).

Paul, at eventide, laid the foundation. Before his journey's end, just like the bridge builder, he left a foundation upon which each of us can continue to build if we so choose.

In the book of First Corinthians, Paul gives us great counsel for the building process:

"But let every man take heed how he buildeth thereupon.

"For other foundation can no man lay than that is laid, which is Jesus Christ.

"Now if any man build upon this foundation gold, silver, precious stones, wood, hay, stubble;

"Every man's work shall be made manifest: for the day shall declare it, because it shall be revealed by fire; and the fire shall try every man's work of what sort it is. If any man's work abide which he hath built thereupon, he shall receive a reward" (1 Corinthians 3:10–14).

If we want to be a wise masterbuilder, we must consider Paul's advice. How we build upon the foundation of Jesus Christ is completely up to us. Knowing our works will be tried by fire might help us to better analyze what we will use to build. Wood, hay, and stubble will fail us—they cannot abide the heat. Instead we must choose gold, silver, and precious stones.

Where do we find these precious materials? The scriptures teach, "The *words of the Lord* are pure words: as silver tried in a furnace of earth" (Psalm 12:6; emphasis added). "I counsel thee to buy of me gold *tried in the fire*" (Revelation 3:18; emphasis added). Some ideas that immediately come to mind from these scripture hints are prayer, the scriptures, God's prophets, and lessons learned from adversity. Quiet time spent pondering will lead us to discover many more places where these materials can be found.

The Lord gives His Saints advice on how to build. In counsel given as the Saints prepared to build the Nauvoo Temple, He said, "Come ye, with all your gold, and your silver, and your precious stones, and with all your antiquities; . . . [all] that will come, may come, . . . and build a house to my name, for the Most High to dwell therein" (Doctrine and Covenants 124:26–27). All were invited to come, bringing their gold, their silver, and their precious stones. In essence, He asked them to bring their finest.

Ours is the work of building the kingdom. Every day we build, starting first with our own testimonies and then reaching out to those who will follow behind us. Think about your own building process for a moment. How is the work coming along?

Sometimes I wonder how different that building process might look if each of us were bringing our finest. When we search the scriptures, when we serve in our callings, when we teach within our homes, do we bring our finest? Our very best? Gold tried in the fire. Silver tried in a furnace. Are the stones that come from the refinement of our experiences the most precious parts of our testimony?

In the New Testament, Peter says, "Unto you therefore which believe he is precious" (1 Peter 2:7). Is he speaking to you? Are you someone who believes Christ is precious? One of the most important steps of this building process will come about as our testimony of the Savior becomes more precious to us than anything else. If He is precious to us, if our testimony of Him is valuable, it will determine not only how we will build but also what materials we will choose to build with. It will also help to shield us from the moments of intense heat or pressure that will certainly be part of the journey.

We must learn to trust that "the foundation of God standeth sure, having this seal, The Lord knoweth them that are his" (2 Timothy 2:19).

Let Him become precious to you.

Then, bring your finest.

Become

Willing to use unlikely tools

Focused on accomplishing great things

Serious about your location

Lost in the process

Determined to mold, shape, create, and form your belief in Christ

A gold refiner, and a purifier of silver

Someone who thinks Christ is precious

Willing to bring your finest

A builder

Become . . .
Read 1 Corinthians 3:11–14

"And they shall be mine, saith the Lord of Hosts, in that day when I make up my jewels" (3 Nephi 24:17). We are precious to the Lord. What are some ways we can allow Him to become more precious to us? As we serve Him, how might we remember to bring our finest? Study these three scriptures: Isaiah 48:10; Zechariah 13:9; Job 23:10. What can you learn from them about bringing your finest?

Solo Time
Become a Builder

I love the story of Nehemiah. He was the prophet when the walls of Jerusalem had been broken down and all of the gates had been burned by fire. Worried about what should be done, Nehemiah prayed day and night for direction. Finally, the Lord told Nehemiah to rebuild the wall. He gathered all of the people together and said, "See the distress that we are in . . . come, and let us build up the wall of Jerusalem" (Nehemiah 2:17).

The people gathered together and prepared to work. Meanwhile, the enemies of Jerusalem also gathered together. They pointed fingers at the people and despised them, and as they laughed they said, "What is this thing that ye do?" (Nehemiah 2:19). And Nehemiah answered, "The God of heaven, he will prosper us; therefore we his servants will arise and build" (Nehemiah 2:20).

When we get to this part of the story, we have reached chapter three of Nehemiah. I love this chapter. It lists all of the people who said they would help build the wall. The list includes the men of Jericho, the goldsmiths, the merchants, and the priests. We read about the son of Urijah, the son of Koz, and many other sons who had come to help build. And then, in verse 12, we read about Shallum the son of Halohesh, the ruler of the half part of Jerusalem, and his daughters.

I love considering this group of people because it includes people from every walk of life—the rulers, the merchants, and the families, including the sons *and* the daughters. This building process was important to all of them. They wanted to protect what was most precious to them, and they were each willing to help. I love the thought that fathers gathered their children, both sons and daughters, to join them as they built.

As they worked, the enemy wondered about the people who were building and asked his men, "Will they fortify themselves? will they sacrifice?" (Nehemiah 4:2). The wicked men conspired against the people who were building, day and night. So Nehemiah gathered the people together. He armed them with swords and spears and bows, and he told them, "Be not ye afraid of them: remember the Lord" (Nehemiah 4:14). And so they returned to the wall, "every one unto his work" (Nehemiah 4:15).

I love how Elder Dieter F. Uchtdorf finishes this story:

"But as the walls of the city began to rise, opposition intensified. Nehemiah's enemies threatened, conspired, and ridiculed. Their threats were very real, and they grew so intimidating that Nehemiah confessed, 'They all made us afraid.' In spite of the danger and the ever-present threat of invasion, the work progressed. It was a time of stress, for every builder 'had his sword girded by his side, and so builded.'

"As the work continued, Nehemiah's enemies became more desperate. Four times they entreated him to leave the safety of the city and meet with them under the pretense of resolving the conflict, but Nehemiah knew that their intent was to do him harm. Each time they approached him, he responded with the same answer: 'I am doing a great work, so that I cannot come down.'

"What a remarkable response! With that clear and unchanging purpose of heart and mind, with that great resolve, the walls of Jerusalem rose until they were rebuilt in an astonishing 52 days.

"Nehemiah refused to allow distractions to prevent him from doing what the Lord wanted him to do."

Turning back to the scriptural account, we read, "So the wall was finished. . . . And it came to pass, that when all our enemies heard thereof . . . they perceived that this work was wrought of our God" (Nehemiah 6:15–16). Their work had become their testimony.

One of my favorite parts of this story is when the enemy asks, "Will they fortify themselves? Will they sacrifice?" As one who is a builder in the Lord's kingdom, how are you fortifying and strengthening your belief in Christ? What are you willing to sacrifice to know Him better?

Become Who You Might Have Been

It's never too late to be who you might have been.

—ATTRIBUTED TO GEORGE ELIOT

Consider . . .
Go Forward and Not Backward

It has been my opportunity to have my eyes opened to a world that I always knew existed, but for which the intricate details have not been mine to experience. Memories made and lessons learned over the course of four years remain sacred in my heart. I have gained a great appreciation for volunteers who serve faithfully to support, and a profound admiration for those who have courageously determined to recover. The most priceless memories have come in the moments when I walk on hallowed ground where those who battle to change their lives are finding strength through Christ.

The fourth principle on the path of discipleship is rooted in this battle for change. It is the principle of becoming who you were meant to be. Have you ever stopped to consider how many of the Lord's truest disciples experienced a less-than-perfect past? Has your study ever led you to understand that ours is a God of second chances? This chapter could be filled with the stories of men such as Enos, Paul, or Alma the Younger. These were valiant disciples whose battle for change enabled them to stand as powerful witnesses for the Lord. But one of my very favorite scripture stories on change, on becoming who you are meant to be, is the story of the man from the tombs of Gadarene.

Jesus and His apostles had crossed over the sea into the country of the Gadarenes. Immediately after the Lord left the ship, a man who was plagued with devils came to Him. The man lived within the tombs, "and no man could bind him . . . neither could any man tame him. And always, night and day, he was in the mountains, and in the tombs, crying" (Mark 5:3–5). The description of this man speaks not just of his unhappiness but, more important, of his daily struggle against a problem or habit that consumed his entire life.

Given these details, perhaps it is surprising that upon seeing the Lord the man ran to Him and worshipped Him, saying, "What have I to do with thee, Jesus, thou Son of the most high God?" And Jesus asked him, "What is thy name?" (Mark 5:7, 9). This tender moment is one of my favorite parts of this story. In my mind I picture the man wondering if he is someone the Lord has time for, if he is past saving, if, perhaps, he is wasting the Lord's time. I love that the Lord looked past the outward appearance, past the very visual condition that seemed beyond repair, and asked, "What is your name?" The appearance was of lesser importance; the individual was of greatest consequence. Even then, the man's true identity was hidden by his struggle, for he answered, "My name is Legion: for we are many" (Mark 5:9). Alfred Edersheim explains that a legion conveys the idea of *six thousand* armed and strong warriors of evil. Imagine being tempted daily by a legion. No wonder no man could bind him or tame him. But the Lord saw past the broken man, knowing it wasn't too late for him to become the person the Lord knew He could be.

The man was fearful of the change that was about to take place, but still the Lord commanded the unclean spirits to leave him. The devils entered into a herd of swine, ran violently down a steep place, and drowned in the Sea of Galilee.

Most often when we hear this scriptural account, this is where the story ends. However, my very favorite part of the story takes place in the next few verses. The men who cared for the pigs went into the city and told the people what had happened, and the people came to see what was done. When they came to the place where Jesus was, they "found the man . . . *sitting at the feet of Jesus,* clothed, and in his right mind" (Luke 8:35; emphasis added).

There is an important lesson here. The first step in making a change is to recognize the Lord, to understand our worth in His eyes, and to turn our life over to Him. The second step requires sitting at the Lord's feet, learning from Him, and understanding His words. There is strength to be found at the feet of the Lord, sufficient strength to give courage. But this in itself is not enough.

The man begged the Lord that he might stay with Him always, but this was not what the Lord had in mind. Instead He replied, "Go home to thy friends, and tell them how great things the Lord hath done for thee, and hath had compassion on thee" (Mark 5:19). After a life-changing experience like that, leaving the feet of the Lord would be hard counsel to follow.

Sometimes it is easier to make a decision to change for good when we are sitting at the feet of the Lord: when we feel the Spirit through a message at church, when our eyes are opened as we read the scriptures, or when we hear the whisperings of an answer to prayer. But then life goes on. When we are not caught up in the moment, sometimes we forget what prompted the change. The Lord has an answer for this: "Return to thine own house, and shew how great things God hath done unto thee" (Luke 8:39). The answer for making the change and then for keeping it is to testify of the Lord's hand concerning the change all the rest of our days.

This man took the Lord's counsel to heart. Not only did he share his testimony at home and with his friends, but the scriptures tell us that he published it throughout the whole city. "Such was to become his life work," says Alfred Edersheim. "In this there would be safety and happiness."

Great healing comes when we recognize the hand of the Lord in our lives and come to understand our worth. Even greater healing comes as we sit at His feet and learn His word. But the greatest healing comes when we bear testimony of His hand in our lives to all we know.

Within every great healing moment there is change. Sometimes the change is painful. Sometimes it requires great strength and courage. Sometimes it requires compassion. Always it requires recognizing the hand of the Lord, bending our will to His, and then testifying of what we have experienced. Sometimes the greatest healing comes through the bearing of this testimony and the compassion we are able to extend to others who walk the path we trod.

It is interesting that when the multitude saw what had happened to the man from the tombs, they besought the Lord to depart from them, "for they were taken with great fear: and he went up into the ship, and returned back again" (Luke 8:37). But the man and his story remained. In a time afterward when Jesus returned to that place, "the people *gladly* received him: for they were all waiting for him" (Luke 8:40; emphasis added). The healed man had prepared the way for the Lord. His change had enabled many to follow his example, and through him and the testimony of his experience their hearts had been prepared to receive the Lord.

Do you feel a prompting of something you would like to change in your life? Begin by finding a way to understand your worth in the sight of the Lord. Then sit at His feet. Find courage. Gather strength. Once you are ready, move forward. Share your testimony with those who need your compassion and encouragement. Go to your friends and tell them what great things the Lord has done for you. Perhaps your story will prepare someone else to know the Lord.

When our journey includes the Lord and we recognize our worth in His eyes, we begin to realize that it is never too late to become the person the Lord wants us to be. Often becoming that person requires great change on our part. It will require moving in the direction He prompts us to go. I am reminded of a favorite scripture, "Shall we not go on in so great a cause? *Go forward and not backward.* Courage, . . . and on, on to the victory! Let your hearts rejoice, and be exceedingly glad" (Doctrine and Covenants 128:22; emphasis added).

Go forward and not backward. Take courage, on to the victory.

CONSIDER THIS . . .
Read Mark 5

"I bear testimony that you cannot sink farther than the light and sweeping intelligence of Jesus Christ can reach. I bear testimony that as long as there is one spark of the will to repent and to reach, he is there. He did not just descend to your condition; he descended below it" (Truman G. Madsen).

The scripture story we have just been considering emphasizes the importance of every individual in the eyes of the Lord. He invites every one of us to sit at His feet. He enables us to change. He offers a second chance.

Just for a moment, consider your worth to Him.

Did you know there is an entire section in the Topical Guide dedicated to understanding the worth of souls? Perhaps you might begin your process of change by studying those verses.

Act . . .
There Are Good Things Found in Thee

Perhaps this far into the journey is a good time to address expectations. What does the Lord expect from us? If our path is uncertain, if our heart is unsure, if our intentions are unclear, are we still known and loved of the Lord?

What if our life is broken?

What if we have made choices that prevent us from allowing room for Him in our life?

In those moments we must remember one important aspect of the Atonement, as taught by President Boyd K. Packer: "Restoring what you cannot restore, healing the wound you cannot heal, fixing that which you broke and you cannot fix is the very purpose of the atonement of Christ."

The scriptures are filled with defining moments when someone who makes a mistake comes to feel honest humility and pure intent and ponders returning to the Lord. There is one lesson that is consistent in every one of these scriptural examples. Always, the Lord's arms are open. Always, He can look on the heart and find good therein.

I love the story of Jehoshaphat found in Second Chronicles.

The scriptures tell us that Jehoshaphat was a good man. He strengthened himself against the ways and the doings of the world and walked in the way his father had taught him. Because of his righteousness, great blessings came to Jehoshaphat, "and he had riches and honour in abundance. And his heart was lifted up in the ways of the Lord. . . . And

Jehoshaphat waxed great exceedingly; and he built in Judah castles ... and the men of war, mighty men of valour, were in Jerusalem" (2 Chronicles 17:5–6, 12–13).

At one point Jehoshaphat, king of Judah, joined with Ahab, king of Israel, to fight Syria. This was not a wise decision on Jehoshaphat's part, for King Ahab was a wicked man, a man who hated the Lord. Before making this alliance, Jehoshaphat neglected to ask the Lord, as had previously been his custom; instead he made the decision to join Ahab alone. Recognizing his mistake at the last minute when they were beyond the point of no return, Jehoshaphat asked King Ahab to inquire of his prophets whether they should go to battle. Ahab's prophets gathered, but they did not listen to the Lord. Instead, they foretold victory.

"But Jehoshaphat said, Is there not here *a prophet of the Lord* besides, that we might enquire of him?

"And the king of Israel said unto Jehoshaphat, There is yet one man, by whom we may enquire of the Lord: *but I hate him;* for he never prophesied good unto me, but always evil" (2 Chronicles 18:6–7; emphasis added).

Have you heard this sentiment before? Ahab didn't like what the prophet of the Lord had to say. It bothered him so much that he had grown to hate the prophet. However, I expect that out of respect for Jehoshaphat, and because he knew he needed Jehoshaphat and his army, King Ahab called for Micaiah, the prophet. Then Jehoshaphat and Ahab sat together on their thrones and waited to hear what Micaiah would say.

When the messenger went to get Micaiah, he said to him, "Behold, the words of the prophets declare good to the king with one assent; let thy word therefore, *I pray thee,* be like one of theirs, and speak thou good"

(2 Chronicles 18:12; emphasis added). I am sure this messenger was looking out for Micaiah as he begged him to simply say exactly what everyone else was saying. But Micaiah said, "As the Lord liveth, even what my God saith, that will I speak" (2 Chronicles 18:13).

When Micaiah arrived at the throne room, he prophesied that Ahab would die. Immediately Ahab turned to Jehoshaphat and said, "Did I not tell thee that he would not prophesy good unto me, but evil?" (2 Chronicles 18:17). Ahab was furious. He commanded that Micaiah be put in prison and fed the bread and water of affliction until Ahab returned back from the war in peace. Micaiah told him, "If thou certainly return in peace, then hath not the Lord spoken by me" (2 Chronicles 18:27).

So the two kings prepared for battle. Ahab must have been a little nervous, because he decided to disguise himself, though he told Jehoshaphat to wear the robes of a king. When the Syrians came to battle, they wanted only to destroy Ahab, the king of Israel. So when the captains saw Jehoshaphat dressed in royal robes, they surrounded him, thinking he was the king of Israel, "but Jehoshaphat cried out, and the Lord helped him; and God moved them to depart from him" (2 Chronicles 18:31). As the day went on, Ahab was wounded, and about the time the sun went down, he died.

An important lesson is taught within this account. Jehoshaphat had entered into a great undertaking without the sanction of the Lord. Having already entered into an alliance with a wicked man, it became troublesome for Jehoshaphat to inquire of the Lord, for regardless of what the prophet said, it was now too late to withdraw. "In truth, it was only what may always be expected when those who serve and love the Lord allow themselves to be entangled in alliances with ungodly men, where one step leads to another, and one inconsistency involves the next, till at last we recoil when it is too late to withdraw, and the only thing consistent is to be inconsistent in owning God where His will can no longer be obeyed. But even this is good, for it is the first step to repentance. And though we must suffer the punishment of our folly, yet God will hear a Jehoshaphat in the disastrous battle, when he crieth to Him, and give gracious deliverance" (Alfred Edersheim, *Bible History*).

When Jehoshaphat returned home, he spoke to one of his prophets whom he trusted. The prophet told him, "Shouldest thou help the ungodly, and love them that hate the Lord? Therefore *is* wrath upon thee from before the Lord. *Nevertheless there are good things found in thee,* in that thou . . . hast prepared thine heart to seek God" (2 Chronicles 19:2–3; emphasis added).

Sometimes our choices are going to be wrong. Like Jehoshaphat, we may find ourselves in a situation that we can't get out of on our own. At such a time, our first thought might be that we don't qualify for the grace the Lord extends to us, or perhaps we feel we are strong enough to walk the road alone. The Lord allows us to have choices. He will not force us to turn to Him. However, a day may come when we cry out for help. The Lord's response is certain every time. He will hear a Jehoshaphat. He knows there is good to be found in you because He knows your heart. In the disastrous battle, when you cry out to Him, He will be there.

ACT UPON THIS . . .
Read 2 Chronicles 17

There will be moments in each of our lives when we find ourselves in the middle of a disastrous battle. Making mistakes is the one part of life we can be certain of, but we must always remember, as Elder Jeffrey R. Holland has taught: "If anyone does not feel fully worthy . . . he can become worthy through repentance and the Atonement of the Lord Jesus Christ. The Savior wept and bled and died for you. He has given everything for your happiness and salvation. He certainly is not going to withhold help from you now!"

This week, learn something of the Atonement that you didn't know before. Then become more willing to accept help from the Lord.

Ponder . . .
Stretching

The winter solstice represents the moment in December when the nights become shorter and the days become longer. It is a time of hope, of reawakening, of change. I will never forget the winter solstice of December 1986.

On the eve of this winter solstice, my parents gathered our family together. It was four days before Christmas. We sat circled within our family room, the spirit of the upcoming celebration surrounding us. The tree was lit, and the anticipation that had been building since Thanksgiving filled the room. It is not unlike my mom to give an early Christmas present. Actually, it is one of her favorite things to do. So a growing expectation began filling our hearts.

My mother handed each of us a white journal. We knew it was special because our names had been embossed in gold writing on the cover. This was a permanent invitation to fill the pages inside with thoughts about the unknown journey that lay ahead. We sat with the books on our laps, waiting with expectation bursting, until finally she had us turn to the first page of our journals and read the poem that had been carefully pasted there.

STRETCHING
By Nancy Sorensen

No one promised this would be easy.
Change is never easy
but then,
neither is reaching
for a star.
But,
too much change at once
makes the stretch marks on my heart
gaping holes,
Through which the world can see
my tears
And even the hurt,
sometimes.
When I am done
with this change,
I wonder if I will be taller
from all this stretching?

I will be honest, I didn't know what to think. Immediately the room was filled with questions—we knew a change was coming, but we didn't know what it was. Expectation and anticipation immediately mixed with the intense fear of the unknown.

What was about to happen?

There are six children in my family. I am the oldest. I was sixteen years old at the time. My youngest sister was six. The journals lay forgotten on our laps; our eyes were focused now on our parents, all hearts leaping unrestrained. After what seemed like ages, my parents quieted us down and then had us turn to the next page. It was a message printed on letterhead stationery from The Church of Jesus Christ of Latter-day Saints. We only had to read a few lines before we realized my dad had been called to serve as a mission president. I have always found it interesting that a heart is capable of holding so many intense emotions at one time. It was as though we were all wrapped up in uncertainty, wonder, excitement, and fear. I will never forget the fear.

Change.

The room was filled with it. The possibility of it brought a flow of unending questions. The unexpectedness of it brought instantaneous nervous excitement. The uncertainty of it brought tears.

We turned to the next page of the journal. Here my mom had carefully written a scripture President Thomas S. Monson had quoted in their interview on December 9, 1986: "Your families are well; they are in mine hands, and I will do with them as seemeth me good; for in me there is all power. Therefore, follow me, and listen to the counsel which I shall give unto you" (Doctrine and Covenants 100:1–2).

Yes, a change was coming—one that would stretch us, that would cause tears to fall and even hurt to come. But one also that would lead us to know the Lord—that we were in His hands, that what He had in mind for us would be good, and that He had all power.

My first inscription in that journal was a dictionary definition. It reads, "Epiphany: a moment of intense emotion when a person reveals their true character."

We never know what the future holds in store for us. One thing is constantly certain, and that is the possibility of change. Often these changes are painful, as we are carefully refined and molded into what the Lord would have us become. Elder Richard G. Scott once said, "To get you from where you are to where He wants you to be requires a lot of stretching, and that generally entails discomfort and pain."

And so we stretch, and tears fall, and sometimes the hurt comes. And our stretching hearts reach out to God.

And we see His hand.

And we see His good.

And we see His power.

And we are taller.

PONDER THIS . . .

Read Joshua 3

"My call to you tonight is something of the call Joshua gave to an earlier generation . . . who needed to perform a miracle in their time. . . . Joshua said, 'Sanctify yourselves: for to morrow the Lord will do wonders among you.' [Joshua 3:5] . . . You must be ready and worthy to act. . . . The day may come—indeed, I am certain will come—when in an unexpected circumstance or a time of critical need . . . the future will be in your hands. Be ready when that day comes. Be strong. . . . I testify that the call in every age—and especially our age—is Joshua's call: 'Sanctify yourselves: for to morrow the Lord will do wonders among you'" (Elder Jeffrey R. Holland).

Do you believe God has wonders in store for you? Are you prepared to hear His call and follow where it leads? Is there a change in store for you? Will it require stretching?

I love the description of the Lord found in Psalm 77:14: "Thou art the God that doest wonders." This week, begin to make whatever change is required so that you will be prepared to experience God's wonders in your life.

Become . . .
A Masterpiece

One afternoon my sister-in-law picked up her four-week-old little girl and carried her from her crib to the changing table. Maezie had just woken from a nap, and her mother soothed her cries by whispering, "It's okay, little lady; we'll change your diaper, little lady." Her two-year-old son, Talmage, followed right on her heels. As she carefully laid little Maezie down to change her diaper, Talmage said, "No, Mom! *Her* is not a little lady, *her* is a princess." He had high expectations, not only for who she was but also for what she was destined to become.

Have you ever taken the time to consider who you are destined to become? Do you wonder what achievements or accomplishments will fill your life? Sometimes we lose sight of our true potential, setting up our own limitations instead of living up to the full measure of our creation (see Doctrine and Covenants 88:25).

I have noticed that even in the midst of our practicality, the nudging to become who we really are never stops. At certain stages of life, particularly in moments of change, it seems our soul longs to become something better. In quiet moments, do you ever feel a stirring within, a whisper quietly prompting that perhaps there is something more? As President Thomas S. Monson puts it, "In the private sanctuary of one's own conscience lies that spirit, that determination to cast off the old person and to measure up to the stature of true potential."

Who are you, really? What do you have the power to become? Is there something that stirs within you, waiting patiently for the opportunity to be revealed? Michelangelo, who was a master at taking a solid block of marble and making of it a masterpiece, is reported to have said, "In every block of marble I see a statue as plain as though it stood before me, shaped and perfect in attitude and action. I have only to hew away the rough walls that imprison the lovely apparition to reveal it to the other eyes as mine see it."

He had a gift. He was a master at taking something ordinary and turning it into an object of outstanding workmanship. On another occasion he is said to have explained, "I saw the angel in the marble and carved until I set him free."

Have you ever stopped to ponder what the Lord would make of your life if you allowed yourself to become His? What does He see in you? If you willingly placed yourself into the hands of the Master of creation to be molded and shaped, to have the rough edges hewn away, what would you become?

One quality I love about the Lord is that He "searcheth all hearts, and understandeth all the imaginations of the thoughts" (1 Chronicles 28:9). He knows who we are, but, more important, He knows who we can become. Through Him, all things are possible. Our life can become a masterpiece, if we just let the Master do His work.

The most important quality we can bring to the project is patience, calmness, and a perseverance to stay the course as we are molded, shaped, and refined. Becoming who we are meant to be can be a painful process. The journey is often filled with detours. The hewing can be painful. But in the quiet moments, the Spirit will whisper of our continued progress, and we will see glimpses of who it is we are becoming. We must hold onto these glimpses so that in the painful growing moments we can remember not only who we are—but who we are destined to become.

Elder Sterling W. Sill spoke of James McNeill Whistler, a famous American painter, who once painted a tiny picture of a spray of roses. "The artistry involved in the picture was magnificent. Never before, it seemed, had the art of man been able to execute quite so deftly a reproduction of the art of nature. The picture was the envy of the artists who saw it, the despair of the collectors who yearned to buy it. But Whistler refused steadfastly to sell it.

"'For,' he said, 'whenever I feel that my hand has lost its cunning, whenever I doubt my ability, I look at the little picture of the spray of roses and say to myself, "Whistler, you painted that. Your hand drew it. Your imagination conceived the colors. Your skill put the roses on the canvas." Then,' said he, 'I know that what I have done I can do again.'"

Have you had glimpses like that? Moments when you knew who you were and what you could become? Think of the moments in your life when you were the happiest. Think of the moments when you were content and at peace with who you were. Think of the moments when you experienced the outcome of something you had dreamed of, or planned for, or put all of your efforts toward. In those glimpses, in those moments, did you recognize the hand of the Master?

These are the moments we must remember. Then, in moments of discouragement, doubt, or despair, we can hold on to these glimpses, and those memories will help to steady our course, giving us strength to continue and determination to fulfill our dreams.

The scriptures are filled with accounts of people who have found great strength in a time of need by looking back on a moment where their testimony of the Lord was forged and fortified. It was this strength of character that allowed them to continue to give their lives to the Lord. The same can be true in our lives.

One of my favorite life quotes is another statement by James McNeill Whistler: "Hang on the walls of your mind the memory of

Become

Someone who sits at the feet of the Lord

Able to recognize the great things the Lord has done

Someone who moves forward, not backward

Humble enough to cry to the Lord in your disastrous battle

Willing to stretch

Taller

Moldable, pliable, workable

A masterpiece

Who you were meant to be

your successes. Take counsel of your strength, not your weakness. Think of the good jobs you have done. Think of the times when you rose above your average level of performance and carried out an idea or a dream or a desire for which you had deeply longed. Hang these pictures on the walls of your mind and look at them as you travel the roadway of life."

Think for a moment of the pictures that hang on the walls of your mind. Are they memories that include the Lord? It seems we can learn a great lesson from Whistler's example—within our view, both inside our mind and in front of our eyes, we need to place the glimpses and memories of the moments when the Lord molded us into something greater than we would have been on our own. Then, in the hard moments of our life, when thoughts of doubt creep alongside, we will be able to say, "I know that what I have done, I can do again."

For the Lord is capable of creating a masterpiece.

BECOME
Read Jeremiah 18:1–6

"Behold, as the clay is in the potter's hand, so are ye in mine hand" (Jeremiah 18:6). Have you ever stopped to ponder what the Lord would make of your life if you let Him? If He were to mold you in His hands, what could you become?

Solo Time
Become Who You Might Have Been

In the most difficult and discouraging days of World War II, Winston Churchill said to the people of England: "To every man there comes . . .

that special moment when he is figuratively tapped on the shoulder and offered the chance to do a special thing unique to him and fitted to his talent. What a tragedy if that moment finds him unprepared or unqualified for the work which would be his finest hour." What can you begin doing now to prepare for your chance? Have you learned to sit at the feet of the Lord so you will hear Him? Do you recognize the great things He has done in your past and believe He has more in store for your future? Are you willing to stretch? To cry out to Him for help? Do you believe Him when He says there is good to be found in thee?

Take a minute to study the following verse:

"And thou, Solomon my son, know thou the God of thy father, and serve him with a perfect heart and with a willing mind: for the Lord searcheth all hearts, and understandeth all the imaginations of the thoughts: if thou seek him, he will be found of thee" (1 Chronicles 28:9).

If God truly understands our imaginations, can we even begin to comprehend who we might become in His hands? When you think of who you might become, you must spend some time focusing on the imaginations of your heart.

There are four words that stand out to me as opposites in Churchill's quote—*special, unique, unprepared,* and *unqualified.* One thing of which I am certain is that each of us is unique. We have been given special gifts and talents that set us apart from each other. Some of these talents are easily recognizable. Others require seeking and sometimes great effort before they are made manifest.

Sometimes developing these talents requires a life change. We might have to give up old habits. We might have to set higher expectations for ourselves. We must be willing to explore the possibilities of our life, to uncover the talents that are special and unique to us. Then we must learn how to use them.

How disheartening would it be to realize, when called upon, that we are unprepared or unqualified for the moment at hand? The important task is to find out what your gifts are. Reviewing your patriarchal blessing, pondering the scriptures, or talking with people who know you well are some good places to start. Then become prepared and qualified by practicing using those gifts.

The Lord has a great work in store for you.

He will tap you on the shoulder.

Will you be ready?

What a great blessing it would be if you could respond by saying, "I have prepared. I am qualified."

Become Refined

*Do not question too much, dear friend, for the God
who ordained the beginning can safely be trusted with
the end, as well as with all that lies in between.*

—MYRTLE REED

Consider . . .
There Is Hope in Thine End

When my oldest son, Caleb, was a toddler, he wouldn't watch movies alone. It wasn't because he couldn't sit still; it was because he was so worried about what was happening that he wanted a constant play-by-play. He would frequently ask, "Mom, what's happening now?" If something went wrong in the story line, he would cry out, "Oh, no! What will they do?" My role was to play the part of commentator, reassuring him that everything would work out in the end.

It's funny how often my life mirrors Caleb's toddler stage. Almost every day I find myself on my knees asking, "What's happening now?" Particular dark moments in my life have led me to question, "Oh, no! What will we do?" I find myself turning to the Lord, seeking reassurance that everything will work out in the end.

The fifth step on the road to discipleship is to become refined. This principle often encompasses some of the most painful experiences of our lives. Have you ever had one of those life moments when you wonder if the Lord is aware of you and the situation you are currently in? Sometimes, when the journey seems to take longer than you had hoped and the destination becomes increasingly unclear, do you wonder if the Lord might have forgotten you?

I love the scriptures that testify of how aware the Lord is of the intricate details of our life, especially in the moments of our refinement. One of my favorite chapters in the scriptures teaches that the Lord keeps us in

His thoughts. I love knowing that the Lord not only watches over us but also thinks about us along the journey. This truth is taught in the book of Jeremiah.

In the twenty-ninth chapter of Jeremiah we read of a group of people who have not found favor with the Lord. Because of their disobedience, the Lord allows this group of people to be carried away captive from Jerusalem into Babylon. Our refining moments can come as a result of our own choices; they can also come through the process of mortality, by no choice or consequence of our own. Either way, the lesson we are about to learn from Jeremiah is applicable. The Lord counsels the people, "Build ye houses, and dwell in them; and plant gardens, and eat the fruit of them; Take ye wives, and beget sons and daughters; and take wives for your sons, and give your daughters to husbands, that they may bear sons and daughters; *that ye may be increased there, and not diminished*" (Jeremiah 29:5–6; emphasis added). Obviously these people are about to spend a lot of time in that place of refinement—enough time to build houses, plant gardens, marry, and raise children and grandchildren. This news must have been worrisome to the people, for immediately they knew that this refinement process wasn't going to last just a couple of years.

The Lord gave them some important counsel: through that period of trial He wanted them to experience an increase, and not to be diminished. Is the same lesson applicable in our own lives? Can we experience growth through trial? Can we experience an increase?

Then the Lord said, "Seek the peace of the city whither I have caused you to be carried away captives, and pray unto the Lord for it: for in the peace thereof shall ye have peace" (Jeremiah 29:7). The footnote for *peace* defines the Greek translation of the word as *contentment*. I find it interesting that the Lord counsels them to seek the peace of the city, to find contentment in the place of refinement. Knowing that this period of their lives would be challenging, the Lord encouraged them to pray to receive peace. How hard would it have been to find contentment within the captivity? It is difficult to be content with the place where you are when it's not the place where you want to be.

The last counsel the Lord gave Jeremiah's people at this time included a blessing: "For thus saith the Lord, That after seventy years be accomplished at Babylon I will visit you, and perform my good word toward you, in causing you to return to this place. *For I know the thoughts that I think toward you,* saith the Lord, thoughts of peace . . . *to give you an expected end.* Then shall ye call upon me, and ye shall go and pray unto me, and I will hearken unto you. And ye shall seek me, and find me, when ye shall search for me with *all* your heart. And I will be found of you" (Jeremiah 29:10–14; emphasis added).

Seventy years is a long time. The people were in a place that was far from home, held captive by an unfamiliar people. But the Lord did not leave them without hope—He gave them a wonderful promise. Even though they would experience that trial for seventy years, the Lord promised they would not be forgotten. He would keep them in His thoughts. He promised to send peace, to answer their prayers, and to always be found by them. There was only one condition on their part—they had to seek for Him with all their heart. Not just a part of the heart . . . He wanted all of it.

One of my favorite parts of this verse is found in the footnote of a word in the first sentence. It reads, "For I know the thoughts that I think toward you, . . . thoughts of peace . . . to give you an expected end" (Jeremiah 29:7). If you follow the footnote for *end* it leads to Jeremiah 31:17, which reads, "and there is hope in thine end."

What a wonderful promise to those in the midst of refinement—there is hope in the end.

Some months ago I was talking with a dear friend whose six-year-old son had been diagnosed with cancer. The diagnosis caused deep and heartfelt reflection. Many of our conversations were filled with those familiar questions: *What's happening,* and *Oh, no, what will we do?* One afternoon we were talking about how much her family was leaning on faith, and she asked, "But what do I do during the times when I don't have enough faith?"

It was one of those moments when you feel the Spirit whispering a response, and my answer was His, "On those days, you hope."

The journey ahead of this family is uncertain, the length completely undefined. My friend will have time to clean her house, plant her garden, and continue raising her children. In the midst of that, she will pray for peace to get through this place she doesn't want to be. Perhaps the contentment will come as she turns to the Lord with all her heart. Maybe she will be reminded of these words:

"I know the thoughts that I think toward you, saith the Lord . . .

Thoughts of peace . . .

To give you an *expected* end.

And there is hope in thine end . . ."

CONSIDER THIS . . .
Read Jeremiah 29

Have you learned to find contentment in the refining moments of your life? Does turning to the Lord with all of your heart help? Consider how it makes you feel to know that the Lord's thoughts are filled with your situation, that He has an expected end in mind for you, and that there will be hope in that end. Does it bring you peace?

Act . . .

A Land Choice above All Other Lands

I have always been intrigued with the journeying of the Lord's people. It does not matter how many times we read the accounts of these journeys in the scriptures; it seems at different times in life certain passages take on new meaning. Recently that happened for me. I was studying Ether, chapter one. I've read this account many times, because the story of the brother of Jared is one of my favorites, but this time I saw something new.

The brother of Jared was a large and mighty man. He was known as a man highly favored of the Lord. What does it mean to be highly favored of the Lord? More important, how does someone become known as a person who is highly favored of the Lord? The verse that follows this one makes me wonder if it was because he was recognized by others as someone who knew how to pray and receive answers from the Lord. Perhaps his gift of being able to *communicate* with the Lord through prayer, to hear and to receive answers, set him apart among his peers as being highly favored.

Jared came to his brother and said, "Cry unto the Lord, that he will not confound us that we may not understand our words" (Ether 1:34). So the brother of Jared cried unto the Lord, and his prayer was answered. Then Jared asked his brother to cry unto the Lord to see if He might turn away His anger from their friends, so they would be able to understand them. Again, the Lord answered his prayer and blessed not only the friends but also the friends' families. Then Jared approached his brother again and said, "Go and inquire of the Lord whether he will drive us out of the land, and if he will drive us out of the land, cry unto him whither we shall go. *And who knoweth but the Lord will carry us forth into a land which is choice above all the earth?*" (Ether 1:38; emphasis added).

The Lord answered the brother of Jared and told him to go into the valley that was northward, saying, "There will I meet thee, and I will go before thee into a land *which is choice above all the lands of the earth.* And there will I bless thee . . . and thus I will do unto thee because this long time ye have cried unto me" (Ether 1:42–43; emphasis added).

I love that in this time of great trial Jared didn't just ask his brother to pray, he told his brother to pray for the very best thing. The best-case scenario. Not just simply a different place—*a land choice above all the lands of the earth.*

I believe that all along the Lord had set aside for Jared and his brother the land that was choice above all the lands of the earth. But what if the brother of Jared had not prayed? What if he hadn't asked? The brother of Jared would never have been able to arrive at that place through his own knowledge. He had to be led by inspiration from the Lord through the process of prayer to find that choice land. I have often wondered if that land would have remained uninhabited, and if the brother of Jared and his family and friends would have stayed in the place where they were, with their language confounded, if the brother of Jared hadn't prayed. The lesson I learn from Jared in the midst of refinement is the importance of praying for good things to come.

Recently our family had a bit of a scare. My sister discovered a lump on the back of her eight-year-old son's arm. They went in for an X-ray and heard back from the radiologist almost immediately. The report used words like *aggressive* and *immediate concern*. The pediatrician pulled this anxious mother out of the room and into the hallway. He told her to prepare herself for a long haul. Both he and the radiologist felt like it would be one of two cancers: Ewing's sarcoma or osteosarcoma. Both are very aggressive and very scary. They were 95 percent sure of the diagnosis. My nephew, Ashton, was scheduled for an MRI the next morning and then an appointment with the oncology department at Primary Children's Medical Center.

We found out about the situation around lunchtime, and both Greg and I stopped what we were doing to have a prayer. I picked my girls up from school at two thirty. As we got in the car, I explained the situation and told them to pray for Ashton every time they remembered throughout the day. Grace asked what we were supposed to pray for. I told her I was praying for strength for their family and courage for Ashton. Grace said, "Well, can I just pray he doesn't have cancer?" I thought about it for a minute. (Yes, I am embarrassed to say that I stopped to consider if it was all right for her to pray for that.) Then I said, "Sure, you can pray for that until we find out what it is."

The next morning, Ashton went in for his MRI. He was covered from head to toe in sandbags and Styrofoam. Only his little face peeked out. Just before they put him in the machine, he turned to his mom and said, "This is going to be scary!" The test took forty-nine minutes. Ashton and his mom had been sitting in the waiting room for only a few minutes when the radiologist came out and told them that after looking at the report he felt that there was one other kind of tumor it might be—one that was benign. He said he would send the report to two more doctors for review and they would know for sure by late that afternoon. Later that day, when Ashton found out that the tumor on his bone really was benign and that he didn't have cancer, he turned to his mom and said, "I am a lucky boy."

On that day I learned a great lesson from eleven-year-old Grace. In the midst of a really scary situation, she prayed for the best-case scenario. She prayed for good things to come. Her request unto the Lord was limitless. I love the report of this situation that she wrote in a letter to her missionary brother, "Ashton almost got diagnosed with cancer but luckily it was just a B 9 or something." She had no idea of the particulars, but still she prayed for the very best thing, the situation choice above all others.

In the midst of our greatest trials, we must turn to the Lord, who is known as the high priest of good things to come (see Hebrews 9:11). We must open the lines of communication, ask for the best thing, and then commend ourselves to Him, placing our faith and our trust in His will, knowing that ultimately and eternally He knows what the very best thing is.

Sometimes that is easier said than done. I don't know if you are like me, but my choice would be to steer the boat, set the speed, and choose the destination. However, most of our journeys will not be like that. Ours is a river journey on a raft we do not steer. We have no idea as to the length of the journey or what the final destination will bring. The conditions of the river will also be out of our control. There will be still-water moments and white-water rapid experiences. Ours will be a journey much like that of the Jaredites we have just learned about, who climbed aboard vessels they could not steer to be taken to a destination they did not know. Still, they prayed for the best thing and then prepared for their journey, and "when they had done all these things they got aboard of their vessels or barges, and set forth into the sea, commending themselves unto the Lord their God" (Ether 6:4).

I am always intrigued by what happened next. "The Lord God caused that there should be a *furious* wind blow upon the face of the waters, *towards* the promised land; and thus they were *tossed* upon the waves of the sea before the wind" (Ether 6:5; emphasis added).

We must remember that just because they prayed for the best thing didn't mean the journey would be easy for them. The brother of Jared and his people were driven by furious winds, tossed upon the waves, and swallowed up in the depths of the sea. Has your journey ever included moments like those? But throughout the journey the Lord held in reserve for them great blessings—a land choice above all other lands.

This process of becoming refined will require us to commend ourselves unto the Lord, knowing that the ride may not be smooth, but knowing also that the Lord will direct us toward the promise He has in mind for us. We will have to let go of our plan and accept His. In so doing we begin the process of becoming who He wants us to be.

In the part of our journey that includes moments of refinement, we must remember to cry unto the Lord, to inquire of Him, and to pray for good things to come. We can't possibly imagine the blessings the Lord has in store for us. It is through prayer that we secure those blessings for ourselves and for others. It is through prayer that we come to know the Lord during the refining moments of our lives. Then we will recognize Him within the journey—for He will go before us, and there He will bless us.

ACT UPON THIS . . .
Read Ether 1

"Prayer is the act by which the will of the Father and the will of the child are brought into correspondence with each other. The object of prayer is not to change the will of God, but to secure for ourselves and for others blessings that God is already willing to grant, but that are made conditional on our asking for them. Blessings require some work or effort on our part before we can obtain them. Prayer is a form of work, and is an appointed means for obtaining the highest of all blessings" (Bible Dictionary, s.v. "Prayer").

This week, study the entry "Prayer" in the Bible Dictionary. You may discover insights about prayer that you might not have understood before. Find a way to apply the principles you learn to your personal prayers. Pray for good things to come.

Ponder . . .
Against Hope, Believe in Hope

On December 13, Jesse Caleb Richardson was born.
After fourteen years of waiting, of hoping, finally a baby. He was

early—too early, really. Seventeen weeks too early. Mother, healing from toxins, reeling from shock, willed him to live.

And she prayed.

Tiny as a dollar bill, smaller than a pound, Jesse fought for life. "He won't make it through the night," they said. But somehow, he did. "He won't live forty-eight hours," they cautioned. But somehow, he did.

And she prayed.

So many miracles in such a tiny boy. Hour after hour, day after day brought miracles. But a week and a day after he was born, things took a turn for the worse. Doctors rushed in, nurses hovered. Finally, after trying everything they knew, medical hands began unhooking baby Jesse, tiny and fragile, from the tubes and machines intertwined. Tenderly, a nurse placed Jesse into the longing arms of his mother for farewell.

And she prayed.

"Is there nothing else we can do?" she begged the doctor.

"There will be no more miracles today," he replied. "There is nothing else we can do." But deep inside her mother heart she knew he was wrong. There was something she could do.

She could hope.

Just as another parent had done thousands of years before her, "Who against hope believed in hope. . . . And being not weak in faith . . . he staggered not . . . but was strong in faith . . . being fully persuaded that, what [God] had promised, he was able also to perform" (Romans 4:18–21).

What God had promised
He was able *also*
To perform.

So prayer intertwined with faith intertwined with hope. Then heart beat strong, and lifeblood pumped. Tenderly nurse hands lifted baby tiny, fighting for life, from mother arms into waiting bed.

Tubes intertwined were fixed back into place. Hope abounded.

And she prayed gratitude.

Through hope, the Lord had sent another miracle. Through hope, an unspeakable gift. Through *that* hope, which sustains the soul in moments that would otherwise destroy us.

Against hope, believe in hope.

God doesn't just speak promises.

He is able *also* to perform them.

PONDER THIS . . .

Read Romans 4

"There may be times when we must make a courageous decision to hope even when everything around us contradicts this hope. Like Father Abraham, we will 'against hope [believe] in hope.' Or as one writer expressed, 'in the depth of winter, [we find] within [us] an invincible summer'" (Elder Dieter F. Uchtdorf).

This week, find the courage to have hope in Christ. Take a moment to write down the Lord's promises to you. They can be found in the scriptures and within your patriarchal blessing. Then search your heart. Do you believe the Lord is able to fulfill those promises in your life? Could you find the courage needed to hope for that realization?

Become . . .
Turned toward Him

One Sunday morning I received a phone call from my sister asking for advice. She quickly explained that her daughter Annie, who was four years old, had been in a sledding accident the day before. As she was coming up the hill, a man had crashed, slamming into Annie's head with his shoulder. At eight o'clock that night, Annie had started vomiting. She vomited through the night, and woke the next morning irritated and drowsy. My sister wondered if Annie had a concussion. I told her to drive straight to the hospital.

Once she arrived at the hospital, things began to look worse. Doctors accompanied Annie from the ER to the pediatric ICU, and they began to prep a room for emergency brain surgery. Just before they took her down for surgery, Annie became completely unresponsive. My sister was scared.

All of the sisters in my family gathered, because that is what we do. We filled a corner of the ICU waiting room, sitting next to my sister and her husband, trying to have hope. Finally the surgery was over. It had gone well, but the doctor informed my sister that they wouldn't know the extent of the damage until she woke up. He told us we could each take a visit into the ICU to see Annie.

I was last. As I stood to walk into the ICU, I reached under my chair for the small bag I had brought with me to the hospital. Several months before this accident happened, Annie had come to my house. It was October, and I had a bag of caramels on the counter that we were going to use for dipping apples but never had. She asked for a caramel and I gave her the whole bag to take home. After that, every time I saw her she would ask, "M, do you have a caramel for me?" So on the way up to the hospital that afternoon I had stopped and bought a bag of caramels. I knew they would make her happy.

I walked into the ICU and stood by Annie's bed, rubbing her hands and feet, saying her name, trying to wake her up. I talked to her about her cousins, her brothers and sisters, and some of her favorite things, but she wouldn't open her eyes. Finally it was time for me to go. As I prepared to leave, I leaned over close to her ear and whispered, "Annie, it's M, and I brought you some caramels."

Immediately her eyes popped open, she looked around the room until she found me, and then she asked, "Where are they? I want one right now." We all laughed, even the ICU nurse who was sitting outside the door. We were so happy to see that the old Annie was there, and that she was okay. She knew who she was, she knew who I was, and she knew she liked caramels. After a brain injury of that magnitude, it was quite a relief!

Several days later Annie came home from the hospital. She had a huge scar just above her ear that couldn't get wet, but she really wanted to wash and comb her hair. Her mom prepared the kitchen counter with towels, thinking she could carefully wash Annie's hair in the sink. Just as she was ready to begin, Annie said to her, "I don't want *you* to do it. I want *The One Who Brings Caramels* to do it." So my sister called and said, "You are going to have to come over and wash Annie's hair; she wants *you* to do it. And make sure you stop and pick up some caramels on your way."

As I drove over to Annie's house, I thought what a great name that was: *The One Who Brings Caramels.* I decided maybe I don't want to be called Emily Freeman anymore; *The One Who Brings Caramels* is a much better name.

Do you ever find yourself wishing that you knew someone like that? Someone who you could turn to in a time of need?

Perhaps, like Annie, we have a favorite aunt, or a spouse, or a friend who we know is always there for us. But sometimes our need is greater than for a dollar's worth of caramels. In times of adversity or uncertainty, where do we turn? In those moments when we feel heavyhearted, careworn, or weary, who is it that comforts and sustains us?

In those reaching moments, I find myself searching for The Giver of Every Good Gift, The High Priest of Good Things to Come, The One Who Orchestrates Miracles in the Ordinary Moments of Life.

He is Jesus Christ. I am drawn to Him. There is a place within my heart that only He can fill, a need within my soul that only He can succor, a longing that only He can soothe. In the midst of greatest adversity, in the moments of intense refining, it is to Him I turn—and He is there.

"Yet I am the Lord thy God from the land of Egypt, and thou shalt know no God but me: for there is no saviour beside me. I did know thee in the wilderness, in the land of great drought. According to their pasture, so were they filled" (Hosea 13:4–6).

In every Red Sea moment, in the furnace of affliction, when anguish fills my soul and fear rests in my heart, He is there. He always has been, and because of that I know He always will be.

Beside Him there is no Savior. He will not leave us to travel alone.

He knows our wildernesses, our times of drought, and our need for green pastures. He will part the sea, send the manna, and lead us to the still water that He has prepared. That is the way of the Lord.

In times of adversity or uncertainty, turn to Him. Cry unto Him.

He will bring comfort.

He will sustain you.

That is the way of the Lord.

BECOME . . .
Read Hosea 13:4–6

Viktor E. Frankl said, "What is to give light must endure burning." In the midst of greatest darkness, even a very small candle will provide a wide beam. So it is with the Lord in the midst of our greatest trials. Refining requires heat, but it also enables light. In your black moments, look for the light of the Lord. Consider this—is the burning worth it if within the process you come to know His light?

Become

Content with the situation you are in

Full of peace

Certain that there is hope in the end

Determined to pray for good things to come

Willing to commend yourself unto the Lord

Persuaded that God will fulfill all His promises

Hopeful

A believer in the high priest of good things to come

Refined

Solo Time
Become Refined

THE RED SEA PLACE
By Annie Johnson Flint

Have you come to the Red Sea place in your life,
Where, in spite of all you can do,
There is no way out, there is no way back,
There is no other way but through?
Then wait on the Lord with a trust serene
Till the night of your fear is gone;
He will send the wind, He will heap the floods,
When He says to your soul, "Go on."

And His hand will lead you through—clear through—
Ere the watery walls roll down,
No foe can reach you, no wave can touch,
No mightiest sea can drown;
The tossing billows may rear their crests,
Their foam at your feet may break,
But over their bed you shall walk dry shod
In the path that your Lord will make.

In the morning watch, 'neath the lifted cloud,
You shall see but the Lord alone,
When He leads you on from the place of the sea,

To a land that you have not known;
And your fears shall pass as your foes have passed,
You shall no more be afraid;
You shall sing His praise in a better place,
A place that His hand has made.

Sometimes the greatest strength through adversity comes from knowing the Lord is with us. He knows our name, He knows our situation, and He does not leave us to face it alone. In the times of refinement I have passed through, I have found comfort in gathering scriptures that testify that the Lord is aware of us and promises constantly to journey with us. This passage found in Isaiah 43 is one of my favorites:

"But now thus saith the Lord that created thee. . . . Fear not: for I have redeemed thee, I have called thee by name; thou art mine.

"When thou passest through the waters, I will be with thee; and through the rivers, they shall not overflow thee: when thou walkest through the fire, thou shalt not be burned; neither shall the flame kindle upon thee.

"For I am the Lord thy God, the Holy One of Israel, thy Saviour. . . . Since thou wast precious in my sight . . .

"I have loved thee. . . . Fear not: for I am with thee" (Isaiah 43:1–5).

Here are some other favorite verses you might consider studying:

Deuteronomy 2:7

Psalm 139:8–10

Jude 1:24–25

Philippians 4:12–13

Become His Instrument

*Our privilege and our responsibility . . . is to become
the most effective instruments we can be.*

—MARY ELLEN SMOOT

Consider . . .

Great Is the Work He Has in Mind for You

The missionary returned home from his two-year mission the day before his grandfather's funeral. The chapel was full. After his mother finished playing a musical number on the piano, he stood up to speak. Tearfully he began. He thanked his mother for the beautiful song she had played. He spoke of the time his mother had spent practicing and preparing for that moment, and of her desire to perform in celebration of her father's life. He spoke of the Spirit we had felt so strongly as the music filled the room, lifting us, bringing comfort and peace. Then he asked a very important question: What if the piano had not been in tune?

It would not have mattered how much practice had occurred, or even how much preparation had taken place—if the instrument had not been in tune, we would not have felt the Spirit there.

It was an impressive sermon, one that has occupied my mind. Throughout my life I, too, have longed to be an instrument in the Lord's hands. But I have never really thought about how important it is to *always* be in tune so that I will be prepared in the very moment the Lord needs me.

The last time I had my piano tuned, I watched for a while as the man worked. It is a tedious business, requiring all of the other strings to be muted, isolating just one string at a time to ensure that it gives the correct pitch. I found it interesting that the man didn't just tune the strings he thought I used the most. To get the instrument ready to play, he made sure every string was in tune.

The same is true in our lives. If we want to act as instruments in the Lord's hands, we must first work on being in tune. The sixth step on the road to discipleship is to become an instrument in the hands of the Lord. I love how this lesson is taught by the sons of Mosiah.

Before they left on their fourteen-year mission to the Lamanites, the sons of Mosiah spent some time in the wilderness. The scriptures teach us that "they fasted and prayed much that the Lord would grant unto them a portion of his Spirit to *go with them,* and *abide with them,* that they might be an instrument in the hands of God" (Alma 17:9; emphasis added). After many days the Lord spoke to them, saying, "Go forth . . . *be patient in long-suffering and afflictions,* that ye may show forth good examples unto them in me, *and I will make an instrument of thee in my hands*" (Alma 17:11; emphasis added). After they heard the promise of the Lord, their "hearts . . . took courage to go forth . . . for they supposed that great was the work which they had undertaken. And assuredly it was great" (Alma 17:12–14).

There are two lessons we learn from this scripture story. First, to become an instrument, we must pray that the Lord's Spirit will not only abide with us but also go with us wherever we serve. Second, sometimes it requires long-suffering and affliction before we can act as an instrument in the hands of the Lord.

The Spirit of the Lord is sensitive, which means that to allow it to *abide with us* and *to go with us* will require us to look at how we are living. To really be in tune, we must evaluate the music we listen to, the books or internet sites we read, the television shows and movies we choose to watch, and the conversations we participate in. We have to decide whether they invite or detract from the Spirit, and then we have to choose if those that are questionable are more important to us than keeping the Spirit is. It is true, being constantly in tune will require sacrifice on our part, but in the very moment when the Lord performs a great work through us, every sacrifice will become worth it.

Elder Dieter F. Uchtdorf has counseled, "In the end, the number of prayers we say may contribute to our happiness, but the number of prayers we answer may be of even greater importance. Let us open our eyes and see the heavy hearts, notice the loneliness and despair; let us feel the silent prayers of others around us, and let us be an instrument in the hands of the Lord to answer those prayers." Perhaps we could make a conscious effort every day to live in a way that will allow us to be more in tune—a way that will not offend the Spirit. We could choose to participate in activities that will allow the Spirit to be with us. We could listen and act upon promptings that come to us through impressions or prayer, or through our scripture reading that day.

Another key phrase in that verse counsels that Alma and the sons of Mosiah would need to be patient in long-suffering and afflictions before they could act as instruments in the hands of the Lord.

Can trials and tribulations teach us how to be a more effective instrument?

Four days before we were married, my husband-to-be, Greg, felt sick. Instead of a simple virus, the doctor found a tumor on Greg's thyroid. Worried that it might be cancer, he told us to see a specialist immediately after returning from our honeymoon. Sadly, the first four months of our marriage were filled with surgeries, doctors' appointments, and long nights in the hospital. What wasn't cancer turned into a staph infection, which led to months and months of recovery and unemployment.

The years that followed those first four months were not any easier. In between several miscarriages, we had four children. I was down in bed for each of the pregnancies. On the last pregnancy, I went into labor at seventeen weeks and spent the next five months on bed rest. Our second son spent the first six years of his life in and out of the emergency room. Between sleep apnea, tubes, stitches, broken bones, and finally a diagnosis of juvenile diabetes, it seemed that perhaps the hospital should just give us a permanent room there, including a plaque by the door with our name on it. During this process I struggled with my own health problems, including severe depression for a time. I can remember saying to Greg on our tenth anniversary, "My life was perfect until I met you—then everything went downhill." We laughed and laughed. Such was the state of our life.

Many people were led to us during those experiences. They were people who knew what it meant to "succor the weak, lift up the hands which hang down, and strengthen the feeble knees" (Doctrine and Covenants 81:5). In the midst of every trauma and every hospital visit, each time someone was an answer to our prayers, I received a prompting: *Remember this.* So I did. I committed to memory what it felt like to be discouraged, lonely, exhausted, frightened, and heartbroken, and then I remembered how it felt to be succored, lifted, comforted, and strengthened. I have drawn on the lessons I learned from those moments many times since then.

Some years ago I was called to serve as the Relief Society president in my ward. When I received the calling, I wondered what the Lord thought I had to offer the families in our ward. One unforgettable week the bishop and I visited seven different members of our ward in four different hospitals. One was in the newborn intensive care unit. There were several in the pediatric intensive care unit, one in the emergency room, another in the detox wing, and one more in a specialized unit I never even knew existed. Some stayed in the hospital for months. Others left those hospitals but came home with health challenges they struggled with for the rest of their lives.

Now, I had not been through the exact experiences of any of these families, but I knew what it was like to live in a hospital for lengths at a time. I could remember sacrificing everything for the health of a child. I knew the devastation of leaving the hospital knowing you were not better, and that you would struggle with that illness for the rest of your life. I knew what it was like to realize there were dreams you had but would never know, and what it felt like to let go of things you had always hoped for. Maybe I hadn't gone through the exact trials these families were facing, but because I had experienced moments that left me discouraged, lonely, and exhausted emotionally, I knew what it meant to succor, lift, and strengthen. I realized the Lord had placed me in that calling at that time for a reason. Because of my own trials and tribulations I could now act as His instrument.

One of the blessings that comes after much tribulation is the ability we are given to act as an instrument for the Lord. These sacred opportunities would not be ours if we had not experienced the adversity firsthand that would allow our heart to truly be in tune.

If we prepare ourselves, the Lord will use us in ways that we would not think of on our own. When we choose to become an instrument in

His hands and live so that we are in tune, we will begin to experience miracles within the ordinary moments of our life. Like Peter, I am "confident of this very thing, that he which hath begun a good work in you *will perform it*" (Philippians 1:6; emphasis added). We must come to believe that great is the work the Lord has in mind for us, and then let our hearts take courage. The touch of the Master's hand can do amazing things with an instrument that is in tune.

Then great will be the work that we are undertaking.

Assuredly, it will be great.

CONSIDER THIS . . .
Read Alma 17

Ammon taught, "Behold I say unto you, how great reason have we to rejoice; for could we have supposed when we started . . . that God would have granted unto us such great blessings? And now, I ask, what great blessings has he bestowed upon us? Can ye tell? *This* is the blessing which hath been bestowed upon us, *that we have been made instruments in the hands of God*" (Alma 26:1–3; emphasis added).

Becoming an instrument in the hands of the Lord can be a great blessing in our lives and in the lives of those we serve. One of the requirements for obtaining that blessing is to live in tune. As you strive to live more in tune, you might consider the personal experiences you have had that might benefit someone who is struggling right now. This week, try to find time to act upon any promptings you receive.

Act . . .

To What Lengths Would I Go?

One afternoon the Savior was teaching in a home. Having heard that the Savior was teaching there, a group of men brought their friend who lay sick with palsy on a bed. The home was full, and the doorway was crowded. It didn't take long before the four men realized they were not going to be able to get inside. But the men didn't give up. The scriptures tell us, "they sought means to bring him in, and to lay him before [the Lord]" (Luke 5:18). Giving up was not an option. Their intent was to bring their friend to Christ.

So they came up with a plan. "They went upon the housetop, and let him down through the tiling with his couch into the midst before Jesus" (Luke 5:19). Now, stop and consider this for a minute. How did the four men get that man *and* his couch onto the roof? It couldn't have been easy. I imagine there was a ladder involved and a lot of thought. Who would hold the man on the couch? There must have been someone on the roof to lift, and someone down below to support. There would have been someone who would be willing to add strength as the man ascended to the roof. Consider those four assignments—to lift, to support, to hold, and to strengthen. Now, we must also keep in mind that the roof was not the final destination. Once they got onto the roof, there was more work to be done. In Mark 2 we learn that the roof had to be uncovered and broken up, which would have required a lot of effort.

Sometimes when I read this chapter I stop and ask myself, *To what lengths would I go to bring a friend to Christ?*

Once they had lowered the man carefully into the room where Jesus was, a very interesting conversation took place. Both accounts in the New Testament phrase this conversation exactly the same way. We read, "When Jesus saw *their* faith, he said unto the sick of the palsy, Son, thy sins be forgiven thee" (Mark 2:5; emphasis added). Take note of the word *their*. Whose faith is the Savior talking about? The line doesn't read, "When Jesus saw *his* faith . . ." it reads, "When Jesus saw *their* faith." Is He talking about the four friends? The ones who lifted, supported, held onto, and strengthened their friend? Was it through both the great lengths of their effort and the great faith of these friends that the Lord was able to heal this man? Is the same true today?

There is much we can learn about being an instrument from this story. First, we must consider the true intent of the four men. They, in and of themselves, could not heal this man. They could not fix the ailment. They could not tell the man what to believe or how to live his life. Their task was simple and yet profound—their only responsibility was to bring their friend to Christ. They were not the healers or the teachers, but they could bring their friend to the One who could heal, to the One who could teach. That would require faith. It would also require lifting, supporting, strengthening, and holding on.

Sometimes I think we get confused. We become so intent on fixing the problem ourselves that we don't allow the Savior to do what He is best at—saving.

Many years ago I was driving to the temple, my heart filled to bursting with heavy thoughts. I had a sister whose family was carrying a heavy emotional burden that they didn't have strength to bear. We had gathered as a family to offer strength and support, but we couldn't fix the situation for them, and that was heartbreaking. Then my sister-in-law had called the day before to say that her husband had lost his job and they were certain to lose their home. She didn't know what to do. Oh, how I longed to be able to come up with a solution that would fix that problem, but I couldn't. I also had a dear friend who was struggling with a problem that had the potential to destroy her life and her family. We had prayed and fasted together, and yet I knew deep within my heart that I did not have the knowledge that would be needed to fix the challenge she was facing. I was discouraged, and I walked into the temple that morning with a heart that was heavy.

The temple was busy, so as I waited I turned to the scriptures hoping to find some counsel I could use in any of the situations I had been praying about. I turned to Doctrine and Covenants 76 and read, "Hear, O ye heavens, and give ear, O earth, and rejoice ye inhabitants thereof, for the Lord is God, *and beside him there is no Savior.* Great is his wisdom, marvelous are his ways, and the extent of his doings none can find out. His purposes fail not, neither are there any who can stay his hand" (Doctrine and Covenants 76:1–3; emphasis added).

Immediately I knew what I needed to do. My responsibility was not to fix the burdens these families were carrying; my responsibility was to help bring them to Christ. I could not save them, but He could. I knew the Savior would know what to do—He would know how to help heal their hearts. He could teach them and send them in the direction they needed to go. His purpose would not fail and His hand would not be stayed. Through His great wisdom and His marvelous ways He would do what was right in their lives. As an instrument in His hands I could lift, support, strengthen, and help them to hold on, and I could add my faith. The Savior would do the rest.

As an instrument, our most important role is to lead someone closer to the Lord. We can do that by sharing what we know of Him from the feelings within our hearts. Have you ever noticed that when you spend time with someone who loves the Lord, you come to know the Lord a little better? Somehow we come to better understand what He teaches, to feel how He loves; we even come to know His heart because we have come to know their heart. As His instrument, their words become His words, their actions become His actions, and through their love we are led to feel His.

Think of someone who has supported you in a time of trial. How did that person lift you, support you, strengthen you, or help you to hold on in that particular moment of your life? What can you learn from their example? What lengths were they willing to go to as they led you to know the Lord?

ACT UPON THIS . . .
Read Luke 5

John Taylor once said that Joseph Smith "told me never to arise in the morning without bowing before the Lord, and dedicating myself to him during that day." How different would our days be if we were to do that?

This week, prayerfully consider some of the ways you might act as an instrument. Remember, our job is not to fix someone's life or to save them from where they are—that is the Savior's job. Our job requires faith, lifting, supporting, strengthening, and holding on in some form or another as we lead our friends closer to Him.

Together, you and the Lord can decide what it is you might

do. How will you lift? How might you strengthen? How could you support? Do you know someone carrying a burden so heavy that you might help them hold on for a time?

To what lengths might you go to bring a friend to Christ?

Ponder . . .
Nevertheless, I Went Forth

One morning we stood at the upper rim of Sunrise Point overlooking Bryce Canyon. Morning light blanketed the peach, pink, and white statues rising up out of the rock. A trail led from where we stood down deep into the valley called Queen's Garden.

In those early hours the trail descended into soft morning sunshine with adventure waiting below. A morning hike appealed to me. However, I knew the going down meant coming up at some point. The ascent back up promised to be challenging, and the switchbacks grueling. By then the midmorning sun would be beating down.

Nevertheless, I went forth.

The hike down was filled with beauty, adventure, and intrigue, with moments of stillness and something new around every bend. As we had anticipated, the destination was worth arriving at. We found a resting point and from a log bench took a moment to admire a rock statue carved by nature to resemble a woman I greatly admire—Queen Victoria—standing high on a rocky peak, steady, solid, and sure.

We took in the great beauty that surrounded us and then turned for home. The climb strained against muscles seldom used and required endurance, patience, and strength from reservoirs I wasn't sure existed. Along the way, small glimpses of shade offered shelter from the intensifying heat—a needed break for relief and refuge. Finally, we stood at the upper rim of Sunrise Point again, and I pondered the experience.

The journey had been challenging.

Nevertheless, I went forth.

How often do we have life moments such as this? Nephi did. On a dark night, hidden without city walls, he was commanded to approach the house of an enemy. To go might mean not to come back. I am sure fear must have filled his heart. The adventure would be challenging, grueling—a dangerous encounter was certain. But Nephi was determined to do what he felt prompted to do. "And I was led by the Spirit, not knowing beforehand the things which I should do. *Nevertheless I went forth*" (1 Nephi 4:6–7; emphasis added).

Think of the Nevertheless moments of your life. Most often these moments include following promptings that often lead to situations unknown. What begins as an adventure often leads to moments of stillness. We are led to discover something new around every bend. Often we learn from those who have gone before, people we admire who are steady, solid, and sure.

Somehow we know at the beginning of each of these opportunities that they will require endurance and patience. Heartstrings will be strained. We will find strength from reservoirs we didn't know existed. Nevertheless, we go forth.

I will not forget a phone call I received as I drove toward home one afternoon. The news was devastating. A baby boy in our neighborhood who had fought valiantly against overwhelming odds was to return home to Heaven. While he slept, sustained by life support within his home, his family gathered to end their fast and find strength from reservoirs combined. *You need to go there.* The prompting was clear. Urgent. *But I am not family,* I argued. In my mind I went through a list of all the reasons why I shouldn't go.

Nevertheless, I went forth.

I rang the doorbell, and the mother and grandmother met me at the door. When I walked into the home, I immediately felt the Spirit of the Lord, which had become a constant companion there, offering strength, relief, refuge. Gratefully the tearful mother asked, "Can you hold him here in his room while we gather in the other room as a family?" And so I did. As she placed her sleeping son in my arms, I was grateful to be entrusted with such a sacred responsibility. For fifteen minutes I rocked Miles in the silence of his room. Sweet boy. Perfect. I held tiny fingers. I stroked soft pink cheeks. I was in the presence of a stalwart spirit— steady, solid, sure. This destination was worth arriving at. A resting point. A sacred experience graven in my heart.

When we are led by the Spirit, not knowing beforehand the things which we should do, great blessings await. Moments will be forever graven on our hearts.

Promptings will come.

You may question the timing.

You might wonder why or how.

Nevertheless, go forth.

Ponder this . . .

Read 1 Nephi 4

"The Lord knoweth them that are His . . . a vessel unto honour, sanctified and *meet for the master's use*" (2 Timothy 2:19, 21; emphasis added).

This week, work on listening to the promptings of the Holy Ghost and then learning to act upon them so that you might be more meet for the Master's use. Keep these words of President Spencer W. Kimball in mind: "[The Holy Ghost] comes a little at a time as you merit it. And as your life is in harmony, you gradually receive the Holy Ghost in a great measure."

Become . . .
In Tune

In the October 2009 general conference, Elder Richard G. Scott spoke of some of the conditions necessary to become an instrument of the Lord.

From us it requires:

- *Sincerity*
- *Purity of intent*
- *Love*
- *Prolonged, prayerful efforts*

We must keep in mind:

- *What we do does not need to be something obscure or unusual*
- *It does not need to impress*
- *It must be humble*

He suggested that as we receive promptings we should carefully write them down, asking, "Is there yet more to be given? Is there more I should know?" He taught us that "impressions of the Spirit can come in response to urgent prayer or unsolicited when needed."

When I think of these characteristics, I am reminded of a woman who knows what it is to act an as instrument by doing much good. Her name is Valerie Hawkins, and my favorite quality of hers is that somehow she knows what to do before you even think to ask.

When my father served as the mission president of the California Ventura Mission, Sister Hawkins's husband was serving as a stake president in the area. I will never forget two zone conferences my father held the first Christmas we were there. President Hawkins's stake was in charge of the first day, and another stake was in charge of the second day. When we showed up to the stake where President Hawkins presided, we knew immediately that a lot of time had been put into making sure the missionaries knew they were loved. Instead of lasagna, the staple meal of every zone conference, the women in this stake had prepared ham, potatoes, and salads—it was a real Christmas dinner. To top it off, Sister Hawkins had baked handmade Christmas sugar cookies, each carefully decorated. There was one plate for every companionship to take back to their apartment when they left.

As my parents prepared to leave, Sister Hawkins met my mom at the door. My mom told her, "This was so nice. I wish the missionaries we will see tomorrow were going to be this spoiled. Thank you for taking such good care of us."

The next morning, early, just as we were leaving for the next conference, my mom received a phone call. It was Sister Hawkins, asking if we could stop by her house on our way to the conference that would be held that day. When we arrived at her home, the entire family was waiting there. They had stayed up all night baking and decorating homemade sugar cookies for the missionaries who would be at the other conference that day. Sister Hawkins wanted to make sure that they too would feel spoiled.

Sister Hawkins is an instrument of the Lord. She is someone who is sincere, and she serves with purity of intent and a lot of love in her heart. Her efforts are prayerful. Her giving is not obscure or unusual; it is not meant to impress. Her service is humble, and because of that she is one who is able to do much good as an instrument in the hands of the Lord.

Become

In tune

Qualified to have the
Spirit go with you and
abide with you

Assured that great will be
the work you undertake

Willing to share what
you have learned
through tribulation

Sincere, prayerful, humble

Prepared for the moment

Willing to perform
the Lord's work

Meet for the Master's use

An instrument

BECOME . . .
*Read Elder Richard G. Scott's conference address, "To Acquire
Spiritual Guidance," Ensign, November 2009, 6–9.*

"And this is my glory, that perhaps I may be an instrument in
the hands of God . . . and this is my joy" (Alma 29:9).

Acting as an instrument in the hands of God can bring great
joy. As you experience these moments of joy, perhaps you might
write them down so that you will always remember them.

Solo Time
Become an Instrument

"Behold, I have created the smith that bloweth the coals in the fire,
and that bringeth forth an instrument for his work" (Isaiah 54:16).

Have you had the opportunity to watch a blacksmith at work? The
picture that remains vivid in my mind is how the intense heat from the
fire leaves its mark, for just an instant, on the tool being created. There,
where the black steel momentarily turns to burnt orange and fire red, the
metal can be shaped and molded, in an instant, for the work it is about
to perform. Each tool is individually crafted through this process for a
specific role.

Is the same true of our lives?

Whether we are tools molded by the Smith or instruments handcrafted by the Master, we are brought forth, if we are willing, to be
molded and handcrafted for His work.

As Mary Ellen Smoot said:

"Truly, we may each be an instrument in the hands of God. Happily, we need not all be the same kind of instrument. Just as the instruments in an orchestra differ in size, shape, and sound, we too are different from one another. We have different talents and inclinations, but just as the French horn cannot duplicate the sound of the piccolo, neither is it necessary for us to all serve the Lord in the same way. . . . Our privilege and our responsibility . . . is to become the most effective instruments we can be."

How can you become a more effective instrument in the hands of the Lord? What are some specific steps you learned from this section that could help you become more in tune?

Become Drawn to Him

All that he had intellectually was an unanswered why, but what he had spiritually was faith, and with that faith he pressed forward.

—ELDER TAD R. CALLISTER

Consider . . .
Being Filled to the Brim

Several years ago I was struggling with a Church assignment I had been given. Discussing the situation with a wise man who lives in my neighborhood, I asked for some advice. In response, he asked me two questions that gave me something to ponder. First he asked, "When was the last time you had an answer to your prayers?" I tried to think back over my week to remember when that might have been. Then he said, "If it wasn't in the last two days, you need to change the way you are praying." Next he asked, "When was the last time you received an answer through your scripture study?" Again my thoughts tried to think back over the scripture reading I had done recently. Again he counseled, "If it wasn't within the last week, you need to change the way you study the scriptures."

That was a life-altering learning experience that changed my relationship with the Lord. Since that moment, I have learned to approach my prayers and scripture study in an entirely different way. The change in my life has been profound. There is a powerful communication process we can draw upon when we pray and study the scriptures in this manner. The Lord will speak to us if we are patient enough to watch and listen for these personal moments of inspiration. Being willing to follow this counsel will open up a line of communication with the Lord that many of us have never experienced before.

The seventh step on the road to discipleship is to become drawn to Him. We do this through prayer and through scripture study. Studying the scriptures becomes a great resource as we strive to draw closer to the Lord because the stories in the scriptures are layered with meaning. This makes them an invaluable resource, for the verses within are able to teach us what we need to know from the Lord in the very moment we need it. Through that process we become drawn to Him.

A great example of this is found in the New Testament, in the story of the marriage in Cana of Galilee. You may be familiar with this story; it is the one where Mary, Christ's mother, is worried because they have run out of wine. Often we focus on the exchange that takes place between Christ and His mother—at least, that is what I have previously done. However, my favorite part of the story happens in the verses that follow that conversation.

I love to read these verses figuratively rather than literally. In my mind the water becomes reminiscent of the living water of the scriptures. The servants are symbolic of disciples of Christ. When I look at the story in this regard, it becomes a lesson in learning to love the scriptures and the power they have to draw us closer to Christ as we strive to become His disciples.

The first lesson takes place in the very beginning of the conversation. "His mother saith unto the *servants,* Whatsoever he saith unto you, do it" (John 2:5; emphasis added). If I want to be a servant, a disciple of Christ, I must do whatsoever He says. Knowing this, I look carefully at the next instruction He gives, "Jesus saith unto them, Fill the waterpots with water. And they filled them up to the brim" (John 2:7). Consider the instructions the Lord gave in light of your own relationship with Him. When you have the opportunity to fill your soul with living water, how much do you take? Just a drop or two? A bit? Or do you fill completely to the brim? Sometimes I wonder how my scripture study would differ if my goal was to be filled to the brim each time I finished reading.

"And he saith unto them, *Draw it now*, and bear unto the governor of the feast. *And they bare it*" (John 2:8; emphasis added). It is not enough to be filled to the brim; as servants of the Lord we must draw out from what we have filled and share it with others. There is great importance in bearing what we know of the scriptures to those who we associate with. The sharing requires us to draw out from our reservoir of knowledge. "The ruler of the feast had tasted the water that was made wine, and knew not whence it was: (but the servants which drew the water knew;)" (John 2:9). There is a profound lesson here—the servants did more than just draw out from what they had filled, they *knew* what they were sharing.

This moment was recorded in the scriptures as "the beginning of miracles" (John 2:11). I believe this is true in more than one regard. When we learn to love the scriptures, when we become filled to the brim with them, when we draw out and bear to others what we know, *this* is the beginning of miracles. Through this process we are drawn to the Lord. As we hear and recognize His voice, answers come, and we are led to become His disciples. We begin to experience miracles and to believe in Him because our life is filled with Him. Filled with His words.

To the brim.

CONSIDER THIS . . .
Read John 2

In speaking of the scriptures, Joseph Smith once said, "He who reads it oftenest will like it best." This week, as you read your scriptures, try something different. First, consider something in your life that requires an answer. In your personal prayers, ask that your eyes will be opened as you read the scriptures so you might see and recognize answers from the Lord. Become more aware of the promptings that come to you that are specific to your needs. Read often. As you do, you will begin to develop a greater love for the words of the Lord.

Act . . .

Day by Day, from the First Day unto the Last Day

Recently I was speaking to a group of women. I asked them to raise their hand if they had a favorite scripture. Every woman in the group raised her hand. I invited them to think about that scripture and explain why it was a favorite. The answers were thought-provoking:

"I found comfort from that scripture."

"It gave me strength to get through something hard."

"It was the answer to a question I was searching for."

I noticed a pattern: Each scripture had become a favorite because each woman had experienced something meaningful when she read it.

When I hear the phrase *personal scripture study,* one word always stands out to me—*personal.* We need to remember to make our scripture study personal. By so doing we can have a personal experience with the Lord every day.

I love the story of Ezra in the Old Testament. "Ezra had *prepared his heart* to seek the law of the Lord, and *to do it,* and to *teach*" (Ezra 7:10; emphasis added). There are three important steps we learn from this verse.

Becoming drawn to the Lord prepares our hearts to understand His words; then we must act on what we learn and teach what we know to others.

The scriptures explain that Ezra became a renowned teacher of the scriptures. Because Ezra possessed the wisdom of God, he was asked to teach all those who did not already know the laws of God. So Ezra went to Jerusalem to teach. "And he read therein before the street that was before the water gate from the morning until midday, before the men and the women, and those that could understand; and the ears of all the people were attentive unto the book of the law. And Ezra the scribe stood upon a pulpit of wood, which they had made for the purpose" (Nehemiah 8:3–4). As he read, he expanded the meaning and caused them to understand (see v. 8).

For seven days Ezra taught, "day by day, from the first day unto the last day" (Nehemiah 8:18). We learn that the people were attentive, they wept and prayed as they listened to the words, they understood what they were learning, and there was a very great gladness (see Nehemiah 8:3, 6, 9, 12, 17). Think for a minute how many hours Ezra read the scriptures to these people. Seven days, day by day. We are led to believe that the people were not only attentive but perhaps even excited to hear his words. More important, we know that listening to him teach from the scriptures made them happy.

I can't help but wonder what kind of a teacher Ezra must have been. Why was he such a good teacher? Ezra was drawn to the Lord, he was someone who loved the scriptures, and I am sure he considered it a great privilege to draw others closer to Christ. I want to love the scriptures like Ezra did. To weep when I read the words. To become more attentive and understand what I am learning. To find a very great gladness within. Ezra prepared his heart before he read—to seek the Lord, to follow Him, and to testify of Him. His actions played a significant role in changing not only his heart but also the hearts of others.

I want to be more like that.

ACT UPON THIS . . .
Read Nehemiah 8

In the book of Deuteronomy we are given counsel on how we might come to love the words of the Lord.

"And thou shalt love the Lord thy God with all thine heart, and with all thy soul, and with all thy might. And these words, which I command thee this day, shall be in thine heart: And thou shalt teach them diligently unto thy children, and shalt talk of them when thou sittest in thine house, and when thou walkest by the way, and when thou liest down, and when thou risest up. . . . And thou shalt write them upon the posts of thy house, and on thy gates. . . . Beware lest thou forget the Lord" (Deuteronomy 6:5–7, 9, 12).

Think about the scriptures—are you teaching them to your children? Do you talk about favorite verses in conversations within your home? Do you think of them as you are going about your day? Do you take the time to read before you go to sleep, or when you arise each morning? Have you written down favorite verses that you can look at often within your home? This week, implement one of these ideas into your life. Perhaps you will gain a greater appreciation for the words of the Lord as you study them and share them day by day.

Ponder...
Come with a Question

It was the Sunday before girls camp. Along with long packing lists and detailed rules, each girl was extended an invitation: *Come to girls camp with a question.* Look deep within your heart. Search your soul. When you arrive at girls camp this week, lugging suitcase and sleeping bag and pillow—bring with you also a question for the Lord.

We drove away from city loud and life pulsing to mountains quiet and moments of peace-filled inspiration. We pondered our questions. We studied the words of the Lord. We learned.

The first day, we wondered: How does an answer come from God? What of the asking?

We turned to His word and we were taught. "Desire of me in faith, with an honest heart, believing in the power of Jesus Christ" (Doctrine and Covenants 11:10).

Is it through the asking that we become drawn to the Lord? Because the scriptures are filled with asking...

"What lack I yet?" (Matthew 19:20). "How is it that thou ... askest drink of me?" (John 4:9). "Whence shall we buy bread, that these may eat?" (John 6:5). Each question turns hearts to Him, invoking a personal moment with the Lord. It was the question that led to the learning, which led to the understanding, which led to the knowing.

Is the same true now?

In the very moment of asking, we enter the grove, the place we have previously designed to be. We offer faith on bended knee. It is hard work, this learning to listen. The world does not allow for moments of silence. We are not used to this. We are familiar with having every empty space filled with noise. We must relearn the art of questioning and then of listening. For within the silence, there, answers can be found.

We have learned that we must trust the Spirit to teach us. How does it feel, this trust in the Spirit? It is a leading to do good, to walk humbly, to judge righteously. "This is my Spirit," says the Lord. To enlighten your mind. To fill your soul with joy. And then you shall know. By this you shall know. In faith. Believing (see Doctrine and Covenants 11:12–14).

But what if the answer is slow in coming?

"Hold your peace; study my word" (Doctrine and Covenants 11:22). Study His word. His answer is clear and consistent. "I speak unto all who have good desires" (Doctrine and Covenants 11:27).

I speak.

Unto all.

Study my word.

And so we studied. In a quiet hour, spread out across the meadow, with the creek flowing, and birds singing, and sun warming. Each in a place of her own, bent over scriptures, studying. Somewhere within that moment, the studying heart became Spirit-filled, and eyes were opened, and understanding began to flow. What once were complex words on holy paper became rungs on a ladder to higher knowledge, and we were led, drawn to Him.

As the last evening of girls camp fell upon us, stars sprinkled the heavens and flames danced. Sitting close around the fire's warmth, we began to share. In a sacred setting we heard the profound questions we had each packed in our heart and brought with us to camp.

Am I loved?

Does Heavenly Father know me?

Where do I go from here?

Is what I have always believed true?

Even a desperate cry for understanding, this question, just one word: "Why?"

Each question heartfelt, honest, meaningful. But more remarkable were the answers that had been given and received privately during the days and nights that made up girls camp. One by one. Through listening quietly. Through studying His word. Each gift a tender mercy as we drew closer to Him. He loves. He knows. There is a plan.

The girls spoke of learning. Of understanding. Of knowing.

His hand. Their life.

A private moment with the Lord.

Answers as they studied His word.

Ponder this journey toward discipleship. Look deep into your heart. Search your soul. Become drawn to Him. Then, consider trying the process yourself.

Come with a question.

Then turn to His word.

"My power which speaketh unto thee . . . behold, it is I that speak" (Doctrine and Covenants 11:10–11).

PONDER THIS . . .
Read Doctrine and Covenants 11

In speaking of the Lord, Elder James E. Talmage said, "Whither the people followed Him; there He taught them again."

When you have a question nestled deep in your heart,

ponder the advice from Elder Talmage—follow Him. Become drawn to Him. He will teach you; through the Spirit His answers will come. Sometimes the best place to find the Lord is in the scriptures. Take a moment this week to read Doctrine and Covenants chapter 11. Make a list of what you learn concerning asking questions and receiving answers. Come with a question. Then try to apply the lessons you learn from Doctrine and Covenants 11 to your asking.

Become . . .
Willing to Hold On

One year my sisters and I decided to take our kids skiing over the Christmas break. None of the dads could go, but for some reason that didn't worry us. My kids were between the ages of nine and seventeen, and they were all capable of skiing on their own, so I volunteered to help out with the younger kids.

When we got to the resort, the lines were really long. We had a pow-wow at the bottom of the hill and decided we wouldn't take the easy run; the line was too long for such a short run. Instead we would take the lift up to the part of the mountain that had a longer run. Everyone thought the kids could make it down.

I rode up the lift with my sister-in-law, Amy, and her son, Camden, who was four. Amy had never been skiing with Camden before, but her husband said Camden would be just fine. I knew we were in trouble when Camden started saying, "I can't get off, I can't get off, I can't get off," just as we got to the top of the lift. Amy and I carried him off the lift and then turned around to look down the mountain. The hill was a lot steeper than I had remembered.

We started off slowly, but it was still a disaster. Camden couldn't keep his skis together. Amy and I switched off trying to carry him down the mountain, but he was too heavy and the run was too steep. Finally, all three of us took off our skis, sat down on our bottoms, and slid down the hill. It took us an hour and a half to get to the bottom of the first run.

Once we reached the bottom, I ran to the rental shop. I explained our situation to the man there and asked him if he had any advice for teaching a four-year-old to ski. He gave me a nifty little rubber band to hook to Camden's skis. This simple device would hold the tips of his skis together and would somehow, magically, make it easier to get down the hill. So, armed with our purple rubber band, we headed up the hill again.

Don't worry, this time we chose the easy hill.

When we got off the lift, we hooked Camden's skis together. Then I took my own poles and held one on each hip, sticking out straight behind me. I put my skis together into the shape of a slice of pie, and then I told Camden to come right behind me and hold on as tightly as he could to my poles. With the fronts of his skis held together by the purple band and his hands holding on tightly to my poles, we started our second attempt to go down the mountain. This time we made it all the way down in under ten minutes. And so we went again, and then again.

The third time down, things were going really well until all of a sudden I found myself tangled up in a mess of skis, poles, and four-year-old arms and legs, tumbling down the mountain. We came to a stop, and as his mother tried to put us back together, I asked Camden what had gone wrong. He looked up at me with his innocent blue eyes and replied, "I was just trying to do a 360." I looked back at him in total disbelief and then answered, "We don't do 360s when we are holding on to each other's poles."

The next day was Sunday. In Gospel Doctrine class we were studying section 122 of the Doctrine and Covenants, and our teacher pointed out a verse I had never noticed before. We had just finished reading the part when Joseph Smith is in Liberty Jail and the Lord tells him all of the awful things that could happen, "If thou be cast into the deep; if the billowing surge conspire against thee . . . if the very jaws of hell shall gape open the mouth wide after thee . . . know . . . that all these things shall give thee experience, and shall be for thy good" (Doctrine and Covenants 122:7).

In other words, all of these learning experiences, all of this knowledge, even though it was hard, would be for his good. It didn't sound very good to me, and I was immediately reminded of our ski trip the day before and the moment when I looked down that huge, steep hill and knew that none of us had enough knowledge or experience to get us safely down. Then we read the verse I had never noticed before: "Therefore, *hold on thy way* . . . fear not what man can do, for God shall be with you forever and ever" (Doctrine and Covenants 122:9; emphasis added).

Hold on thy way. It's exactly what Camden did all the way down the hill: he held on to my poles, and he learned how to ski. When we have an experience where we feel like we don't have enough knowledge to make it through, all we need to do is follow that advice, hold on thy way.

Often moments of growth are preceded by moments of doubt. We question our ability to move forward. We wonder if we are strong enough. We fear the consequences of failure. In the moments when we are hardest on ourselves, we must draw closer to the Lord and hold on to what we already know. That is where we will find the strength to move forward into the unknown. Just as He did for Joseph Smith, the Lord will ensure that all our experiences will be for our good. They may not be experiences we would have chosen on our own, but they will help us to understand that the Lord is with us. Forever and ever.

Within this journey toward discipleship there will be moments when moving forward will require you to hold on to the truths you already know. Some of the most important truths are found in the words of the scriptures. Open your scriptures daily and immerse yourself in the words of the Lord. As you become drawn to Him through the scriptures, you will find verses you can cling to when life is hard.

BECOME . . .
Read Doctrine and Covenants 122

"Hold on thy way" (Doctrine and Covenants 122:9). Take a moment to make a list of what you know for sure. What knowledge can you hold on to right now? List

Become

Filled to the brim

Willing to draw out and share with others

Prepared to seek the words of the Lord, to live them, and to teach them

Intent on studying day by day

Someone who comes with a question

Stronger from holding on

Immersed in the scriptures

Drawn to Him

simple truths that bring you strength. Include verses of scripture that fortify your belief. You might start with one or two items. Remember to add to the list as your testimony grows.

Solo Time
Become Drawn to Him

"Then said he unto them, Therefore every scribe which is instructed unto the kingdom of heaven is like unto a man that is an householder, which bringeth forth out of his treasure things new and old" (Matthew 13:52).

The scriptures are much like a treasure chest. Sometimes we turn to them to find comfort from *old* scriptures that we have loved and held on to. Other times we turn to a verse or chapter we have read a hundred times and are led to find something *new*. Has this been true in your life?

Take a moment to glance through your scriptures. Can you find verses you have marked or notes in the margin that define lessons that are precious to you?

I have had the opportunity in my life to meet a handful of people who consider their scriptures to be their greatest treasure—an elder from the backwoods of Virginia, a woman from Sierra Leone, a man who has dedicated his life to building the Lord's kingdom. How do I know their scriptures are a treasure to them? I can tell by the way they hold them in their hands. I can hear it in their voices as they speak about them. I can see it as they turn the pages to testify of what is found therein. Their reliance upon the word of the Lord is the very essence of who they have become. They are constantly drawn to Him.

Elder Carlos E. Asay said: "I fear that many of us rush about from day to day taking for granted the holy scriptures. We scramble to honor appointments with physicians, lawyers, and businessmen. Yet we think nothing of postponing interviews with Deity—postponing scripture study. Little wonder we develop anemic souls and lose our direction in living. How much better it would be if we planned and held sacred fifteen or twenty minutes a day for reading the scriptures. Such interviews with Deity would help us recognize his voice and enable us to receive guidance in all of our affairs. We must look to God through the scriptures."

How can you strengthen your study habits? How might you make your reading more meaningful? More personal? Consider what changes you would like to make to your personal scripture study. Write down what you feel inspired to do.

THE EIGHTH MONTH

Become a True Follower

True discipleship is for volunteers only. Only volunteers will trust the Guide sufficiently to follow Him in the dangerous ascent which only He can lead.

—ELDER NEAL A. MAXWELL

Consider . . .

Are You Almost Persuaded or Altogether Committed?

One of my least favorite teenage phases is the "almost" phase. My oldest son, Caleb, was expert at this phase. It went something like this. I would text, "Are you coming home?" His reply? "Almost." My question, "Have you finished your homework?" His reply, "Almost." Me, "Is your room clean?" Him, "Almost." I learned that "almost" meant he had completed about 97 percent of the job—he cleaned his entire room but forgot to make the bed; he emptied the kitchen garbage but forgot to put in a new bag. His theory was that "almost" was good enough—"I almost made it home by midnight."

One week I became tired of the almost phase, so I told Caleb that if he wanted to play the almost game I could play it too. I would *almost* cook his chicken for dinner, I would *almost* dry his clothes, and I would *almost* drop him off at school. It didn't take long before *almost* was no longer his word of choice.

As recorded in Acts, chapter 26, Paul was speaking to King Agrippa and Festus about his current situation. Things didn't look good for Paul. The Jews were asking for his death. As he spoke to these two men, Paul bore a powerful testimony of the Savior. Through the process, the king's heart was softened, and he said to Paul, "*Almost* thou persuadest me to be a Christian" (Acts 26:28; emphasis added). Paul replied, "I would to God, that not only thou, but also all that hear me this day, were both *almost,* and *altogether* such as I am" (Acts 26:29; emphasis added). It was as if he were saying that *almost* was not enough; the next step was getting to *altogether*. There is a difference between being *almost* persuaded and *altogether* committed.

What does this difference look like in our lives today? How many times have we thought to ourselves, "I almost read my scriptures today," or "I almost remembered my morning prayers"? Perhaps we can think of this word as it applies to our service, "I almost called her," or "I almost did my visiting teaching last month."

What would it take for us to become altogether committed to the Lord?

In our family we have a job chart that illustrates this almost and altogether principle. The left side of the chart lists responsibilities. The right side lists privileges. Each set of privileges is linked to a set of responsibilities. There are three levels on the chart: level one, level two, and level three. To move up a level, you must live the responsibilities on the current level you are on for two days. If you fail at a set of responsibilities, then you move down a level.

The responsibilities for level one are simple: be a member of our family and live in our home. The privileges for this responsibility are food, clothing, shelter, and love.

The responsibilities for level two are a bit more complex. You are required to have a good attitude all day, make your bed, clean your room, pick up after yourself, practice music thirty minutes a day, request permission for all privileges, do one job from Mom, have respect, attend school, complete homework, and go to bed by nine o'clock P.M. If you do all of these things, the privileges are as follows: You can watch one hour of TV, play on the computer for thirty minutes, use a cell phone if you are thirteen or older, play with friends within our neighborhood, and participate in one sport.

My favorite level is the last one, level three. This time I will start by listing the privileges that go with this level: You can participate in all level-two privileges, plus you can go out of the neighborhood with friends (such as to a movie or snowboarding). You qualify for a late night past the nine o'clock curfew. You can participate in additional sports, and (this is my kids' favorite) you can ask to negotiate once if the answer is no.

Now, what do you think the responsibilities are to qualify for these privileges?

It is actually surprisingly simple. You just have to demonstrate level-two behavior independently for three days. The key word is *independently*. That means no one reminds you to make your bed or clean your room. You take care of practicing the piano or another instrument all by yourself. Your homework is done, and you get yourself to bed. You are no longer *almost* done with all of your jobs; you have become altogether committed—so much so, that no one needs to remind you what to do. Living responsibly has become a part of who you are.

Could the same be true as we attempt to live the Christian life? Rather than being almost persuaded to live as we should, could we become altogether committed so that living as Christ would have us live would eventually become a part of who we are?

Throughout the scriptures, the Lord has given us small lists of jobs we can work on. What if we were to take one quality at a time, put it up somewhere where we could look at it daily, and work on it until eventually it became who we are?

For example, I love the list found in 1 Thessalonians 5:11–22:

- Comfort yourselves together
- Edify one another
- Know them which labour among you
- Esteem them very highly
- Be at peace among yourselves
- Warn them that are unruly
- Comfort the feebleminded (faint-hearted, despondent)
- Support the weak
- Be patient toward all men
- Ever follow that which is good
- Rejoice evermore
- Pray without ceasing
- In every thing give thanks
- Quench not the Spirit
- Despise not prophesyings
- Prove all things
- Hold fast that which is good
- Abstain from the appearance of evil

It's quite a list! It might take some time to make all of those things part of who we are. But the Lord's job chart is much like my family's—the responsibilities come with a privilege, or, in other words, a blessing. In this case, the blessing is found at the end of the chapter, at the very bottom of the list: "And the very God of peace sanctify you wholly; and I pray God your whole spirit and soul and body be preserved blameless unto the coming of our Lord Jesus Christ. Faithful is he that calleth you, who also will do it" (1 Thessalonians 5:23–24).

The eighth step on the journey toward discipleship is to become a true follower of the Lord. This principle includes moving past being almost persuaded and becoming altogether committed to Him. Great privileges are associated with this kind of commitment. There is nothing expected of a true follower that does not qualify for the Lord's blessing in return.

CONSIDER THIS . . .
Read 1 Thessalonians 5

"We become what we want to be by consistently being what we want to become" (Elder Richard G. Scott). Consider making a list of some of the characteristics of a true follower you would most like to become. Then, work on becoming more like the characteristics on your list. You might be surprised by who you are becoming through your consistent efforts.

Act . . .
Offer Your Whole Soul

It was the middle of July. The very middle. It was the part of summer when the Popsicle begins melting before you can even unwrap it from the package. I was straightening the house when my six-year-old daughter, Meg, came in and asked if she could teach my three-year-old, Grace, how to ride a bicycle without the training wheels on. Grace had begged for weeks to learn how and then had taken a serious fall, leaving her with cuts on her knees and elbows and no inclination to ever ride a two-wheeler again. Not wanting to put a damper on Grace's newly lit enthusiasm, I told Megan that would be fine.

After about twenty minutes, I took a peek out of the front door just in time to see Megan running as fast as she possibly could, trying to catch up to Grace, who was riding like the wind, confidence filling the smile that took up her entire face. I couldn't help but laugh out loud at the sight. Megan was jumping up and down with the excitement of great accomplishment as Grace turned the little bike around, pedaling with all her might. But that was not what made me laugh. It was the sight of Grace's red face dripping with beads of sweat because she was clothed from head to toe in her pink winter snowsuit.

In an effort to ensure that Grace would not suffer a single cut, her brilliant sister had dressed her in snow pants, a parka, and a little pair of gloves to protect her hands. Every inch of her body was covered and protected in case of a fall. Never mind that it was ninety-five degrees outside; Megan was not going to let fear keep Grace from accomplishing what she most wanted to do. It took us several days, and a mysterious disappearance of the pink snowsuit, before we could finally talk Grace into riding her bike in summer attire.

What is it that holds you back from the things that you most want to do? Is it fear of disappointment? Worry that you might get hurt? Doubt that you might not be strong enough? Concern that what you receive in the end won't be what you had anticipated when you began?

It is disheartening to me that we sometimes set aside what matters most because we let doubt, discouragement, or failure persuade us that it is no longer important to us. President Thomas S. Monson has counseled, "I plead with you not to let those most important things pass you by."

Instead, he encourages, "may we fill our days—as much as we can—with those things which matter most."

I love reading through the Book of Mormon and watching the process each writer went through as he or she became a true follower of the Lord. There are lessons we can learn from their journeys. Their examples can become a pattern for us as we strive to follow the Lord.

In the book of Omni we read the testimony of Amaleki. He encourages, "And now, my beloved brethren, I would that ye should come unto Christ, who is the Holy One of Israel. . . . Yea, come unto him, and *offer your whole souls* as an offering unto him, and continue in fasting and praying, and endure to the end" (Omni 1:26; emphasis added). The lesson I learn from Amaleki is to offer my whole soul. Every bit. To hold nothing back from this journey toward discipleship.

Caleb, my oldest son, serving a mission in Serbia, wrote in one letter to us about the stripling warriors: "Somehow these guys beat the odds. They did what everyone else would call impossible. Going to battle and not losing a single man? No way. But they did it. They beat the odds. It says in these verses that they had exceeding faith—and because of that they did not fear, they were obedient to every command, and they never doubted. It also says that their minds were firm—they did not waver or falter. I've thought a lot about what it means to have a firm mind. I think it means controlled, tempered, and directed to a purpose (a united purpose). They also put their trust in God continually—not just sometimes, not just when they were fighting, or when they needed help, *always*. Because they did these things, they saw a miracle. Through their faith in Christ, which their mothers had taught them, they beat the odds."

Helaman records, "And we do justly ascribe it to the miraculous power of God, *because of their exceeding faith* in that which they had been taught to believe. . . . Now this was the faith of these of whom I have spoken; they are young, and their minds are firm, and they do put their trust in God continually" (Alma 57:26, 27; emphasis added).

Think of the words *exceeding faith*. The definition for *exceeding* is "going over the expected limit." How often do we set limits on ourselves? But the stripling warriors did not. Instead they exceeded the expected limit, and miracles came.

May we heed the advice of our dear prophet, President Monson, and "fill our days—as much as we can—with those things which matter most." This week, try not to let the most important things pass you by. Become a true follower. Be diligent in personal prayer and scripture study. Don't let anything dampen your enthusiasm. Offer your whole soul. Don't set any limits on yourself. Have exceeding faith. Go over the expected limit. Refuse to let fear keep you from accomplishing what you most want to do. If you have to, try wearing a pink snowsuit. It could work!

ACT UPON THIS . . .
Read Omni 1:26 and Alma 57

"We must not give up hope," says President Dallin H. Oaks. "We must not stop striving. We are children of God, and it is possible for us to become what our Heavenly Father would have us become." Just like Grace, we may run into some challenges along this journey. The important thing is to get back up and try again. How would offering your whole soul to becoming a true follower make a difference?

Ponder . . .

He Kept Back Nothing

In the book of Acts we read of a man named Ananias and his wife, Sapphira, who were members of the Church. They sold a piece of property and promised to lay the money they earned from that property at the feet of the Apostles. However, at the last minute they decided to keep back a portion instead of giving all.

Compare that with the pattern of discipleship characterized in the life of Paul. He served the Lord with all humility, with many tears, with love in his heart. He walked from house to house, gathering with true followers in upper chambers. Lights burned as he talked a long while, often until midnight. Bound in the Spirit he went, so that he might finish his course with joy. At all seasons, night and day, with tears.

This heart of a humble disciple held much. "Remember the words of the Lord Jesus," he taught, "It is more blessed to give than to receive" (Acts 20:35). Paul knew this, and knowing, he gave. At all seasons. For three years.

Then, heart breaking, he explained that he must leave. Bonds and afflictions waited for him. An angel told him he would not see these people again. "And when he had thus spoken, he kneeled down, and prayed with them all. And they all wept sore, and fell on Paul's neck, and kissed him, sorrowing most of all for the words which he spake, that they should see his face no more" (Acts 20:36–38).

No more the midnight gatherings.

No more the talking a long while.

No more the embracing.

Now, just the tears.

He said to them, "Ye know, from the first day that I came into Asia, after what manner I have been with you at all seasons. Serving the Lord with all humility . . . and with many tears . . . *and how I kept back nothing*" (Acts 20:18–20; emphasis added).

From the first day . . . how I kept back nothing.

The midnights. The tears. The talking a long while.

There is a difference between giving and giving all, between one who keeps back a portion and one who keeps back nothing.

Paul knew about these differences.

They are the characteristics of a true follower of Christ.

His life was filled with sacrifice, with giving all, every day and every night.

He kept back nothing.

PONDER THIS . . .
Read Acts 20

As you read this chapter in Acts, write down the ways in which Paul served. How was he a true follower of the Lord? Have you experienced the difference between keeping back a portion and keeping back nothing in your life? What have you learned?

Become . . .
Zealously Affected in a Good Thing

Eddie Aikau was a lifeguard and surfer in Hawaii. He saved many lives and was famous for his unfailing courage to surf the most formidable waves. He is known as the first lifeguard at Waimea Bay, and because he was willing to brave waves that often reached thirty feet high or more, not one life was lost during his service. In 1978, Eddie joined a thirty-day canoe voyage as a crew member. During the journey, the canoe capsized. Eddie volunteered to leave the others and go for help, paddling on his surfboard to Lanai. He was never seen again.

In his memory, a Big Wave Invitational is held in Hawaii. The condition for this surfing competition is that the open-ocean swells must reach a minimum of twenty feet, which translates to a thirty-foot wave face height. The T-shirts from this event include a three-word phrase, "Eddie would go." The phrase originated from the first Invitational. With huge waves and extremely dangerous conditions, the organizers gathered together to decide if the contest should be held. A man named Mark Foo looked out at the waves and said, "Eddie would go."

Mac Simpson explains, "Aikau was a legend on the North Shore, pulling people out of waves that no one else would dare to. That's where the saying came from—Eddie would go, when no one else would or could. Only Eddie dared."

I love the thought of that motto: *Eddie would go.*

One of my favorite Book of Mormon heroes possessed this same quality. If I were to give you the reference 1 Nephi 3:7, what is the first thing that pops into your head? For many of us, a familiar verse of scripture will come to mind, "I will go and do the things which the Lord hath commanded, for I know that the Lord giveth no commandments unto the children of men, save he shall prepare a way for them that they may accomplish the thing which he commandeth them" (1 Nephi 3:7).

Rather than focus on all of the amazing truths that are found in this verse, I want to focus on three words—*I will go.* Consider those three words in relation to the situation Nephi was in. There was a long journey involved. Nephi would have to go up against a man who was much more powerful than he. There was a possibility of great danger. What type of person commits to something like this? Those three words tell us something important about Nephi's character. This wasn't a simple request from a parent to a responsible teenage son, "Hey, will you go pick up some bread at the store?" This was a request that would lead to life-altering consequences, depending on how things played out. And yet Nephi answered simply, "I will go."

The footnote for that verse describes characteristics that defined Nephi's life—obedience, faith, loyalty. It did not matter if the task ahead was daunting, or if he might lose his life in the pursuit—this hero was obedient, faithful, and loyal. The theme of his life could be summed up in three words, *I will go.*

It takes courage to become a true follower. Commitment. Conviction. The scriptures teach us, "It is good to be zealously affected always in a good thing, and not only when I am present with you" (Galatians 4:18). Eddie Aikau could be described as someone who was zealously affected in a good thing. So could Nephi. Not just some of the time—always.

Sometimes when I question if I should attend a Church event, I think to myself, "Nephi would go." Visiting or home teaching? "Nephi would go." Attend the temple this month? "Nephi would go."

Our history includes great heroes, the likes of Nephi—men who were obedient, loyal, and faithful. Full of courage. Committed. True followers whose conviction allowed them to face obstacles that were daunting. Perhaps next time you are asked to participate in something that will allow you to become a true follower of the Lord, you could answer simply, "I will go."

BECOME . . .
Read Acts 5:1–12 and Acts 20

"Preach the word; be instant in season, out of season; reprove, rebuke, exhort with all longsuffering and doctrine. . . . Watch thou in all things, endure afflictions, . . . *make full proof of thy ministry*" (2 Timothy 4:2, 5; emphasis added).

What does it mean to "be instant" in season and out of season? Could it suggest that we are ready to teach of Christ at all times and in all things and in all places? How would

Become

Altogether committed

Willing to offer your whole soul

*Determined to exceed
the expected limit*

Someone who keeps back nothing

*Zealously affected always
in a good thing*

Full proof of thy ministry

Willing to go

A true follower

your life be different if you were to live in such a way that you made "full proof of thy ministry" daily? This week, hold nothing back from becoming a true follower of the Lord. When the opportunity arises to act as a true follower, let your first response be, "I will go."

Solo Time
Become a True Follower

"Behold, I am a disciple of Jesus Christ, the Son of God. I have been called of him to declare his word among his people, that they might have everlasting life" (3 Nephi 5:13). Have you had opportunities in your life to act as a disciple or a true follower of Jesus Christ? Could you make a commitment to become a true follower all the days of your life?

As President Gordon B. Hinckley said, "We of this generation are the end harvest of all that has gone before. It is not enough to simply be known as a member of this Church. A solemn obligation rests upon us. Let us face it and work at it. *We must live as true followers* of the Christ." What do you think the difference is between being known as a member of this Church and living as a true follower of the Christ?

Become a Succorer of Many

I'm glad to think that I've helped you a little when you came to a hard place, for the most any one of us may do for another is to smooth the road.

—MYRTLE REED

Consider . . .
Being Moved with Compassion

Both of my sons are in the moment of transition where they are about to leap from children into men, and they will become what they will spend the rest of their life doing. One wants to be an orthodontist, the other an emergency room doctor. In recent conversations, my husband and I have suggested the great benefit of shadowing a master of each profession. "Just spend a day," we counseled, "so you will know what you are getting into."

The advice led me to wonder what it might have been like to follow in the shadow of the Savior for just one day to learn the trade He was Master of—succoring. Perhaps we could choose the day described in Matthew, chapter nine. This day began as the Savior left a ship and entered into his own city. He spent the morning teaching and healed a man sick of the palsy. As He left that place, He saw a man called Matthew and extended an invitation, "Follow me" (Matthew 9:9). In the next account, Jesus took a moment to sit and eat. It is not surprising that His disciples surrounded him during that meal, but it *is* surprising that publicans and sinners also joined Him. This meal led to a conversation with the Pharisees, who questioned His choice of friends. While the Savior spoke to them, a ruler named Jairus came and asked the Lord if He would come heal his daughter, who was near death. On the way to the home of Jairus, the Savior walked down a crowded street. Here, a woman who had been sick for twelve years came behind Him and touched His garment.

Stopping, the Savior carefully studied the crowd, taking the time to find the woman. And when she came to Him, fearing, trembling, knowing, He blessed her, saying, "Thy faith hath made thee whole" (Matthew 9:22). Finally, Jesus arrived at the ruler's home. He passed through a room of people who laughed Him to scorn, entered the room of Jairus's daughter, and raised her from the dead. Leaving the home, He was met by two blind men, and, asking them if they believed, he touched their eyes, and they were healed. From there He was approached by others who brought unto Him a dumb man, and He cast out the devil.

The chapter ends with a verse that is a perfect definition of how the Savior's days were filled: "And Jesus went about all the cities and villages, teaching in their synagogues, and preaching the gospel of the kingdom, and healing every sickness and every disease among the people. But when he saw the multitudes, he was *moved with compassion* on them, because they fainted, and were scattered abroad, as sheep having no shepherd. Then saith he unto his disciples, The harvest truly is plenteous, but the labourers are few; *Pray ye therefore the Lord of the harvest, that he will send forth labourers into his harvest*" (Matthew 9:35–38; emphasis added).

Sometimes, when my day seems crazy with unexpected moments that are not my own, I think of this chapter in Matthew. I can't find record of even one moment when the Savior had time to Himself. Perhaps some of His appointments were fixed, but for the most part it seems that He allowed Himself to be available to whoever needed Him, whenever they needed Him. He knows what it is to succor.

The ninth principle on this journey toward discipleship is to become a succorer of many. We find a perfect definition of what this principle is as we study the example of the Savior given in Matthew, chapter nine. His day was filled with teaching and healing. He ate lunch with His friends, but He also invited those who were in need of a friend to join with them. He was kind to His enemies. He left what He was doing to answer a desperate cry for help. He took the time to focus on the one in the midst of the multitude. He was not angered by those who mocked Him, but continued in the Spirit, healing and teaching. He was moved with compassion. I love this thought of being *moved with compassion.* Is that what moves us through each day? Compassion?

Sister Bonnie D. Parkin said: "Most ministering opportunities are spontaneous, not planned in advance. Much of the Savior's ministering seemed almost incidental, happening while He was on His way to somewhere else—while He was doing something else. He gave us the example of ministering *as He went.*"

Consider the magnitude of the events that occurred in that one day, and how many lives were changed by the Master. His day was filled with healing, teaching, training up disciples, and raising from the dead. His focus was on ministering—He was moved with compassion. His day was filled with giving, filled with service. I have come to believe His service first was what allowed hearts to open in the end. Perhaps it was the service that allowed the opportunity for the teaching. Could the same be true now? Do we remember to serve before we teach?

My heart is pricked by the request of the Savior in the very last verse of this chapter, "The laborers are few; pray ye . . . that he will send forth laborers" (Matthew 9:37–38). The ninth principle on the journey toward discipleship includes learning to labor like Christ did—to be moved with compassion, to minister as we go. To become a succorer of many. Could we learn to become the laborers He prayed for?

"Just as ministering doesn't always need to be planned, it doesn't need to be spectacular," Sister Parkin continued. "It is something we can do every day in natural, comfortable ways. . . . We can offer a daily prayer that enlists the help of the Lord Jesus Christ as we ask: 'Help me to be the answer to someone's prayer today.' The Lord consistently answers this prayer as we tune our eyes and ears to discerning the needs of those around us. . . . Asking to be an answer to someone's prayer has a powerful impact. There are sacred, quiet experiences for those who participate with the Lord in answering prayers. As we go about listening, watching, and feeling for the answer to those prayers—even in the midst of our busy schedules—I testify that our earthly ministry unfolds by revelation and divine empowerment. Our testimonies, faith, and feelings of connectedness to the Lord expand in amazing, unexpected ways."

Then we become His laborers, serving in His name, moved with compassion.

CONSIDER THIS . . .
Read Matthew 9

"Keep yourselves in the love of God, looking for the mercy of our Lord Jesus Christ unto eternal life. *And of some have compassion, making a difference*" (Jude 1:21–22; emphasis added). Consider how having compassion might make a difference in the life of someone you are close to this week. Could you devote one day this week for incidental ministering—allowing compassion to happen while you are on your way to somewhere else? Become moved with compassion. Discover what it means to *minister as you go.*

Act . . .
A Wise Heart

One day when I was studying my scriptures I came across the phrase "wise hearted" (Exodus 36:1). I was immediately intrigued. I prayed that the Lord would teach my heart that principle—I really wanted to understand.

The Lord has this way of teaching us that I am slowly coming to recognize. It requires prayer. It requires scripture study. It requires each of us to act on promptings in behalf of another.

The Lord has often taught my heart through everyday experiences. One such lesson was contained in a pound of butter.

One night I had the opportunity to discuss sacred topics with a group of women. We spoke of hope, trust, faith, optimism, and prosperity. As the topic turned to prosperity, one of the women asked, "What is prosperity? What does it mean in your life?" I said the first thing that came to mind, "Prosperity is when you go to the grocery store and you don't have to spend time looking at the price of every brand of butter to find the cheapest one."

That might have been a trivial description, but each of us could relate to having financial burdens. We spoke of all the things we would focus on if money and professions and expenses didn't have to occupy so much of our minds.

The next morning, I felt like having warm bread and butter for breakfast. I pulled out the bread and then opened the fridge only to realize

I was completely out of butter. I couldn't help but be reminded of our conversation the night before.

I put *pick up butter* on my list of things to do.

Within the hour, someone knocked on my front door. It was one of the friends I had been with the night before. She stood there on my porch with a pound of butter tied up with white tulle. "I just felt prompted to bring this over this morning," she said simply, "and to say the Lord wants you to have prosperity."

I was momentarily speechless. And then I said, "How did you know I needed butter?" Which was as ridiculously trivial as the definition of prosperity I had given the night before.

"I didn't know," she said. "I just woke up at four o'clock this morning and felt a prompting that you needed butter. This morning. Before I did anything else with my day."

The funny thing is, I could have totally made it through the day without the butter. I would have picked some up that afternoon. As I tried to figure out the urgency of the four A.M. prompting, I realized . . . it wasn't about the butter.

It was about the lesson.

Because just after the butter came, I sat down to study what it meant to have a wise heart. "And they came, every one whose heart stirred him up, and every one whom his spirit made willing, and they brought the Lord's offering" (Exodus 35:21). I followed the footnote for the word *offering,* and it said *generosity.* "And they brought the Lord's generosity to the work." "And they came, both men and women, as many as were willing hearted . . . Them hath he filled with wisdom of heart . . . and every wise hearted man, in whose heart the Lord had put wisdom, even every one whose heart stirred him up to come unto the work to do it" (Exodus 35:22, 35; 36:2).

I finished reading and remembered my friend. The one whose heart had been stirred up. The one whose spirit was willing. The one who brought the Lord's generosity. The one whom the Lord had filled with wisdom of heart.

She who had a willing heart.

She who didn't think it might be odd to drop off a pound of butter to someone who was perfectly capable of obtaining her own, but took the wisdom of the Lord in her heart and then acted.

Through her willing and wise heart—and through a pound of butter—I learned an extremely powerful lesson about succoring. Her generous act took five minutes out of her day, but it made all the difference in mine. She became the answer to the prayer I had prayed before I went to bed. The Lord taught me, through her, about what it meant to have a wise heart.

One of my favorite lessons from that chapter in Exodus describes what happened as the people of Israel lived in the spirit of having a wise heart. "The people bring much more than enough for the service of the work. . . . For the stuff they had was sufficient for all the work . . . and too much" (Exodus 36:5, 7). I love that their giving was more than enough, and too much—two characteristics of the generosity that comes from a wise heart.

Perhaps right now, this very moment, you could ask the Lord for a wise heart. Maybe you could ask that you might be the means of extending the Lord's generosity to someone, somehow, today. It doesn't have to be outlandish. A stick of butter can be life changing. Trust me.

As you strive to become a succorer of many, ask to be made wise hearted. Let your heart be stirred up, and let your spirit be made willing.

ACT UPON THIS . . .

Read President Henry B. Eyring's conference address,
"Opportunities to Do Good," Ensign, *May 2011, 22–26.*

"May I invite you to take the next few seconds, no matter where you are, and offer a prayer. . . . Think about who you could help. Now, if you saw a face or thought of a name, would you offer another prayer and ask our Heavenly Father what He specifically wants you to do for that person? Write it down. Would you be willing in the next week to act upon your promptings?" (Mary Ellen Smoot).

"You could, this moment, begin to think of those for whom you bear responsibility. If you do, and do it with the intent to serve them, a face or name will come to you. If you do something today and make some attempt to help that person come unto Christ, I cannot promise you a miracle, but I can promise you this: you will feel the influence of the Holy Ghost helping you, and you will feel approval. You will know that, *for at least those minutes,* the power of the Holy Ghost was with you" (President Henry B. Eyring).

Ponder . . .
Good Measure, Shaken Down,
Pressed Together, and Running Over

How much are you willing to give?

Your whole heart?

Some of your heart?

A portion of your heart?

All of your time?

Some of your time?

A portion of your time?

Everything you have?

Some of what you have?

A portion of what you have?

Is there a difference between giving all, giving some, and giving a portion?

To truly succor, we must learn how to measure what we are willing to give.

The Lord says, "Give, and it shall be given unto you; good measure, pressed down, and shaken together, and running over. . . . For with the same measure that ye mete withal it shall be measured to you again" (Luke 6:38).

I think of canning wheat. I fill the ten-inch round can with hard brown kernels to the rim, but this is not enough. If I *shake* the wheat together, if I *press it down,* there is always room for more. The good measure, the most that can fill the can, requires the shaking together. It requires the pressing down. I don't want just a portion; I want the running over.

Now my thoughts fill with giving and I begin to understand that this is not just the way of my wheat, stored up and waiting—it is also the way of my heart. For it is within the good measuring, the shaken-down-and-pressed-together moments that my heart runneth over. Those are the moments of succor. The dictionary explains that the word *succor* comes from the Latin *succurrere,* "to run to the rescue." This running over, this running to rescue requires every bit of the heart, holding nothing back.

There are different kinds of giving—giving of our heart, giving of our time, giving of what we have. This kind of giving requires learning. Daily, it is a process for me. The lessons come through the shaking together and the pressing down, and I soon begin to understand that measuring with *good* measure is harder than it first appears. Through the process I have learned that there is one kind of giving that requires the whole of us.

FORGIVENESS FLOUR
By Marguerite Stewart

When I went to the door, at the whisper of knocking,
I saw Simeon Gantner's daughter, Kathleen, standing
There, in her shawl and her shame, sent to ask
"Forgiveness Flour" for her bread. "Forgiveness Flour,"
We call it in our corner. If one has erred, one
Is sent to ask for flour of his neighbors. If they loan it
To him, that means he can stay, but if they refuse, he had
Best take himself off. I looked at Kathleen . . .
What a jewel of a daughter, though not much like her

Father, more's the pity. "I'll give you flour,"
Said, and went to measure it. Measuring was the rub.
If I gave too much, neighbors would think I made sin
Easy, but if I gave too little, they would label me
"Close." While I stood measuring, Joel, my husband
Came in from the mill, a great bag of flour on his
Shoulder, and seeing her there, shrinking in the
Doorway, he tossed the bag at her feet. "Here, take
All of it." And so she had flour enough for many loaves,
While I stood measuring.

There is giving in for*giving.* The lesson is contained right there inside the word, a giving. The same is true right there inside the heart, for to forgive, one must give—without measure. To truly become a succorer of many, one must learn what it is to forgive.

We have a great example in Philemon, who, having been wronged by Onesimus, his slave, was asked to take him back in a letter from Paul. It wasn't the taking back that would be hard, it was the forgiving that would require the heart, for Onesimus had left under conditions that weren't pleasant for either man involved.

But Paul trusted in Philemon's heart, that he would take Onesimus back, not as a servant, but as a brother. Knowing it would be hard, Paul asked of Philemon, as our Older Brother asks of each of us, "If he hath wronged thee, or oweth thee ought, put that on mine account . . . I will repay it" (Philemon 1:18–19).

I will pay the debt, if he hath wronged thee. Put that on mine account. I will repay it.

The Lord asks us to forgive, knowing it will require us to give.

Give a little in our stubbornness.

Give a little in our proud stance.

Give a little in our adherence to what we think is right, to how it is, to why we were wronged.

Give, without measuring.

Shaken together, pressed down, and running over.

Yield.

"For love's sake I rather beseech thee . . ." (Philemon 1:9).

For love's sake.

So, with great hope in us, He watches for this giving, this for*giving.*

"Having confidence . . . *knowing that thou wilt also do more than I say*" (Philemon 1:21; emphasis added).

And so we fill our hearts to the brim, but this is not enough. The good measure, the most that can fill the heart, requires the shaking together. It requires the pressing down. Just a portion of forgiveness will not give the running over.

He has confidence that we will do more than He says. Without measure.

That is the way of for*giving.*

PONDER THIS . . .
Read Philemon 1

"In the day of my trouble I sought the Lord: my sore ran in the night, and ceased not: *my soul refused to be comforted*" (Psalm 77:2; emphasis added). Sometimes succoring requires us to forgive. Such was the case with the father of the prodigal son; it was also the case with Alma the Elder. What if those boys had been raised by fathers who could not give their hearts in forgiveness? Would the moment of succor have been as sweet?

Is there someone you hold resentment toward? Let your soul refuse to be comforted. Give without measure, until love runneth over—until you can forgive. The Lord has confidence in you. Do more than He says. Pressed down and shaken together.

This week give the good measure.

Become . . .
A Succorer of Many

In the book of Romans we read of a woman named Phebe. Not much is mentioned about her; in fact, only two verses speak of her. But within those two verses we learn what an amazing person she must have been.

"I commend unto you Phebe our sister, which is a servant of the church which is at Cenchrea: That ye receive her in the Lord, as becometh saints, and that ye assist her in whatsoever business she hath need of you: for she hath been a succourer of many, and of myself also" (Romans 16:1–2). Perhaps, if we were to look carefully at our own lives, we might see a resemblance to the life of Phebe. She was a sister and a servant in the Church. But there is more to Phebe's life than just those two sentiments. We are led to understand that she was a sister, a servant, *and* a succorer of many. My favorite description of her is one that comes from assumption on my part. I love Paul's counsel, "assist her in whatsoever business she hath need of you." As a sister, a servant, and a succorer of many, Phebe must have been very busy. Paul noted and appreciated her effort, and he asked that others would assist her in her service. What a remarkable woman she must have been; what a great compliment to be known as a succorer of many.

I think of Phebe and I want to know more. How does this succoring work? I am reminded of a line from a favorite hymn, "As thy days may demand, so thy succor shall be." From this line we come to understand that the succor is given according to what the day demands. Do you know what it is to ache? To yearn for something that is unobtainable? Have you felt a weight so heavy you have not had strength enough to bear it? Has sleepless night after sleepless night ever left you emotionally exhausted? In the darkest moments of your life, have you ever thought there might be nowhere else to turn? If so, then your heart has been taught. Through your own personal experience, your days have demanded that you learn powerful lessons in succoring.

Would you now be willing to succor someone whose day demands aching? What if the day demands mourning? Perhaps you know someone whose day demands a burden beyond their ability to bear. You have been there before—what would have brought you comfort, peace, or strength? We may not know just what it is someone else is going through, but chances are we have felt many of the same emotions. We become a succorer, a means of help, when we walk beside another and smooth the road ahead.

In my life it has been my great blessing to be surrounded by many women such as Phebe. Sisters, servants, succorers. These women have a gift for looking outside of themselves to see how they might bless the life of another.

Their succoring has made itself manifest in their way of life. In times of distress they are women of the covenant—comforting those in need of comfort, mourning with those who mourn, bearing burdens that cannot be shouldered alone.

Their giving is not constrained by hours or time. They are on call whenever they are needed, no matter the inconvenience to their own pursuits. Leaving behind a project, giving up an entire afternoon, going without sleep or food or privilege, they give what is needed most when it is most needed.

Their love is unconditional. Their service is not limited to those acts that will bear the greatest dividend. They see with the Savior's eyes, they love with the heart of the Lord. No person is of lesser consequence. No deed is undeserving of their time. Theirs is not to judge the necessity, for if there is a need, no matter how small, somehow they know how to fill it.

Their service knows no bounds. They are not caught up in casseroles or calendared visits. Instead, they care, and because of the caring, they serve. To one, a visit; to another, a phone call. One may need a listening ear and a word of encouragement; another, a shoulder to cry on. Some require time and effort in their behalf; others, just to be remembered along the way. These succorers know, and, as sisters, they serve.

Some serve out of duty; some serve out of love. It is as we progress from one level to the next that we learn charity—the pure love of Christ, the love that cannot fail.

"And he will take upon him their infirmities, that his bowels may be filled with mercy, according to the flesh, that he may know according to the flesh how to succor his people according to their infirmities" (Alma 7:12).

He, knowing how to succor, He, a succorer of many, asks us to succor also.

To help. To run to.

"Succor those that stand in need of your succor" (Mosiah 4:16).

"Succor the weak, lift up the hands which hang down, and strengthen the feeble knees" (Doctrine and Covenants 81:5).

He needs our help.

And so we open our hearts.

And we serve.

And we become the laborers He prayed for, succorers of many.

And through the process we become His.

BECOME . . .
Read Romans 16:1–2

"For though I be free from all men, yet have I made myself *servant unto all,* that I might gain the more. And unto the Jews *I became as a Jew,* that I might gain the Jews; to them that are under the law, *as under the law,* that I might gain them that are under the law; To them that are without law, *as without law,* (being not without law to God, but under the law to Christ,) that I might gain them that are without law. To the weak *became I as weak,* that I might gain the weak: *I am made all things to all men,* that I might *by all means* save some" (1 Corinthians 9:19–22; emphasis added).

Become

Moved with compassion

The laborer He prayed for

Stirred up with a wise and willing heart

A giver with good measure

Forgiving

Someone who will do more than is asked

A servant unto all

A succorer of many

Paul knew what it meant to succor as the days may demand. He was a servant unto all and became whatever the people were in need of so that he might bring them to Christ. Think about your ability to succor those you love. Look within your circle of influence and find someone who needs to be loved; then try to serve them in whatever way their day demands. This week, serve by all means.

Solo Time
Become a Succorer of Many

"And charity suffereth long, and is kind, and envieth not, and is not puffed up, seeketh not her own, is not easily provoked, thinketh no evil, and rejoiceth not in iniquity but rejoiceth in the truth, beareth all things, believeth all things, hopeth all things, endureth all things. Wherefore, my beloved brethren, if ye have not charity, ye are nothing, for charity never faileth. Wherefore, cleave unto charity, which is the greatest of all, for all things must fail—but charity is the pure love of Christ, and it endureth forever; and whoso is found possessed of it at the last day, it shall be well with him" (Moroni 7:45–47).

President Dallin H. Oaks said this about the preceding passage of scripture: "The reason charity never fails and the reason charity is greater than even the most significant acts of goodness he cited is that charity, 'the pure love of Christ' (Moro. 7:47), is not an act but a condition or state of being. Charity is attained through a succession of acts that result in a conversion. Charity is something one becomes."

Think of someone you are acquainted with who lives with charity. Try to pinpoint some of the qualities or characteristics they have that help you to see charity in their countenance. I love the lesson taught in the following story from Sister Bonnie D. Parkin about what it means to have charity in the ordinary course of a day.

"My daughter-in-law's mother, Susan, was a wonderful seamstress. President [Spencer W.] Kimball lived in their ward. One Sunday, Susan noticed that he had a new suit. Her father had recently returned from a trip to New York and had brought her some exquisite silk fabric. Susan thought that fabric would make a handsome tie to go with President Kimball's new suit. So on Monday she made the tie. She wrapped it in tissue paper and walked up the block to President Kimball's home.

"On her way to the front door, she suddenly stopped and thought, 'Who am I to make a tie for the prophet? He probably has plenty of them.' Deciding she had made a mistake, she turned to leave.

"Just then Sister Kimball opened the front door and said, 'Oh, Susan!'

"Stumbling all over herself, Susan said, 'I saw President Kimball in his new suit on Sunday. Dad just brought me some silk from New York . . . and so I made him a tie.'

"Before Susan could continue, Sister Kimball stopped her, took hold of her shoulders, and said: 'Susan, never suppress a generous thought.'"

A succorer of many is someone who knows what it means to have charity. Consider the importance of the lesson President Oaks taught, that charity is something one becomes. How can applying Camilla Kimball's advice to never suppress a generous thought help you to become someone who lives with charity?

Become His Warrior

The kingdom of God is like a besieged city surrounded on all sides by death. Each man has his place on the wall to defend and no one can stand where another stands, but nothing prevents us from calling encouragement to one another.

—MARTIN LUTHER

Consider . . .
Who Is Your Captain?

Several years ago my husband, Greg, and I decided we wanted to have a family mission statement. We gathered our children together and told them we were searching for a word or phrase that would define our family—not just who we were but who we wanted to become. The discussions were passionate because each of our children had in mind what they wanted our word to exemplify. At the end of several weeks we had narrowed it down: We wanted to be known as a family who was forever strong and valiant in our testimony of Christ. Now we just had to find a word or a phrase that defined that.

Not long after we began our search, a man spoke in sacrament meeting about the courage it takes to live in our dispensation. He quoted the scripture found in Matthew 24:24, "If it were possible, they shall deceive the very elect." Then he said it would require valor to make it safely through this time. I knew immediately that was the word we were looking for: *valor.*

That week in family home evening we studied the word in detail. In the Topical Guide there are five words listed after *Valor* as cross-references: *Apathy, Courage, Diligent, Loyalty,* and *Valiant.* The last four made sense to me, but I couldn't figure out the correlation between apathy and valor. As I studied further, I began to understand. I believe it is because one who is apathetic is the exact opposite of one who has valor.

In the book of Deuteronomy, it is recorded that Israel made a covenant with the Lord. The covenant would require courage, valiance, diligence, and loyalty. Moses said, "Ye stand this day *all of you* before the Lord your God; your captains of your tribes, your elders, and your officers, with all the men of Israel, your little ones, your wives, and the stranger that is in thy camp; from the hewer of thy wood unto the drawer of thy water: That thou shouldest enter into a covenant with the Lord thy God" (Deuteronomy 29:10–12; emphasis added). This covenant would include everyone—from the captain of the tribe to the drawer of the water, both men and women, from the eldest to the little ones.

Moses explained what the covenant would entail, "That he may establish thee today for a people unto himself, *and that he may be unto thee a God,* as he hath said unto thee, and as he hath sworn unto thy fathers, to Abraham to Isaac, and to Jacob" (Deuteronomy 29:13). God wanted a people who were willing to become His, but more important, He wanted to become their God. Not a spiritual figure to be worshipped from a distance, instead He wanted to be a guiding influence, an integral part of their life, reachable. The Lord wanted to be Israel's God—to guide and protect them, to comfort and sustain them, to lead them to the Promised Land. And yet, in place of a living God, they frequently turned to idols of "wood and stone, silver and gold" (Deuteronomy 29:17). I have often wondered why it was so hard for Israel to live up to that covenant. Why would they choose a God they could not speak to, one that was incapable of providing succor, direction, or redemption?

Moses worried "lest there should be among you man, or woman, or family, or tribe, whose heart *turneth away this day from the Lord* our God, to go and serve the gods of these nations; lest there should be among you a root that beareth gall and wormwood" (Deuteronomy 29:18; emphasis added).

Is this what apathy is—a turning away from God? I see the same circumstance in our world today. It seems that for some, life's greatest pursuit is to obtain more and more of the things that cannot satisfy. From homes built of wood and stone, to happiness purchased with gold and silver, to friends that simply want to eat, drink, and be merry, sometimes our every thought becomes consumed with wanting, even longing after more. What we worship most can often be determined by where we spend most of our time. We experience apathy when our God, who is living, is slowly replaced by cold items, which are not capable of feeling after us.

Like the people who lived in the time of Moses, we can find it just as easy to turn from the Lord. Then roots, which once were firm and planted, become bitter and poisoned, like gall and wormwood.

One of the plagues of the last days is described in the book of Revelation, "And the third angel sounded, and there fell a great star from heaven, burning as it were a lamp, and it fell upon the third part of the rivers, and upon the fountains of waters; and the name of the star is called Wormwood: and the third part of the waters became wormwood; and many men died of the waters, because they were made bitter" (Revelation 8:10–11).

Just as a drop of poison can destroy many waters, killing and making bitter all who drink from them, apathy can do the same for our hearts. Then, what was once strong becomes bitter, and even dead to what once sustained growth. When we become as wormwood, we suffer a spiritual death. Turning away from His living water, we are made bitter toward the Lord. This is the poison of apathy.

The tenth principle on the journey toward discipleship is to become a warrior for the Lord. This will require a decision between these two characteristics—apathy and valor. The Lord has made His feelings clear, "So then because thou art lukewarm, and neither cold nor hot, I will spue thee out of my mouth" (Revelation 3:16). To be on the Lord's side we cannot be lukewarm or apathetic; instead we must be people who are courageous, valiant, diligent, and loyal to what we believe. We cannot be caught up in idols of wood or stone, silver or gold. We must beware of apathy and become warriors of valor.

To be known as a warrior of Christ, one must first determine the answer to this question:

Who is your captain—or, in other words, Who is your God?

When we consider the battle that wages all around us, it brings great comfort to know God is on our side, and that He is more than a god of wood or stone standing frozen and aloof. This is a battle in which prisoners include friends and family who are held captive by an enemy who takes away freedoms and removes one's ability to choose. To conquer an enemy who poisons with apathy, we need a God who will fight—not just for us, but with us. We must become valiant in our belief in Him.

CONSIDER THIS . . .
Read Deuteronomy 29

When I think of valor in the battle against the adversary, I am reminded of verses three and four of the hymn "For All the Saints":

Thou art our rock, our fortress, and our might;
Thou, Lord, our captain in the well-fought fight;
Thou, in the darkness drear, our one true light. . . .

And when the strife is fierce, the warfare long,
Steals on the ear the distant triumph song,
And hearts are brave again, and arms are strong.

When we choose the Lord as our captain, our heart can be brave again, and arms again strong. This week, consider how you might serve Him with more valor.

Act . . .
As a Good Soldier of Christ

In the book of Ezekiel, the Lord speaks of the great battle of the last days. He is worried that the world will not prepare sufficiently to be protected. "Ye have not gone up into the gaps, neither made up the hedge for the house of Israel to stand in the battle in the day of the Lord" (Ezekiel 13:5). Because of the lack of protection, and in order to make up for the gaps, Ezekiel explains, "And I sought for a man among them, that should make up the hedge, and stand in the gap before me for the land . . . but I found none" (Ezekiel 22:30).

This scripture haunts me—why could he not find a man to stand in the gap? We live in the era Ezekiel prophesied of. The battle rages fiercely around us, and I can clearly see the gaps in the hedge. Who will be ready, prepared, and protected to fill the gaps and make up the hedge? The Lord has given great counsel in this regard.

"Be strong in the Lord, and in the power of his might. Put on the whole armour of God, *that ye may be able to stand* against the wiles of the devil. . . . Wherefore take unto you the whole armour of God, that ye may be able to withstand in the evil day, and having done all, to stand. Stand therefore, having your loins girt about with truth, and having on the breastplate of righteousness; and your feet shod with the preparation of the gospel of peace; Above all, taking the shield of faith, wherewith ye shall be able to quench all the fiery darts of the wicked. And take the helmet of salvation, and the sword of the Spirit, which is the word of God" (Ephesians 6:10–17; emphasis added).

When we question who will stand in the gap, perhaps we might remember this scripture—put on the whole armor, that you might be able to stand. Is your armor on? The armor the Lord has provided for His Saints living in the last days is unique in the fact that it can be personally designed and fitted with each warrior in mind, specific to the gap in the hedge that we will be assigned to fill. President Boyd K. Packer teaches that "it is meant to be handcrafted in the home and fitted to each individual."

With that in mind, think for a moment of your weaknesses, and then consider your strengths. How can the armor of God be handcrafted and fitted to become more of a protection to you personally? Elder James E. Talmage explained that the armor is important, but "the man within may be vulnerable if he can be reached." That is why it is essential that we take upon us the *whole* armor, not just the parts we think we need. At the end of verse 13 there is an interesting phrase, "having done all, to stand." To me, *having done all* means taking upon us the whole armor, or the full protection of the Lord. We cannot fill the gap without being fully prepared and wholly protected.

When I think of a soldier who has *done all* in preparing to fulfill his duty, I am reminded of the conditions required for those who guard the Tomb of the Unknown Soldier. The requirement includes the soldier's commitment never to do anything to disgrace the uniform for the rest of his life. During his time off, the soldier studies the 175 most notable people who have been laid to rest in Arlington National Cemetery. He memorizes who they were and where they are interred. Every guard spends five hours a day getting his uniform ready. There are no folds, wrinkles, lint, or stains on the uniform. Each day when the soldier reports for duty he knows he has done all, such is his esteem for his responsibility.

Perhaps having done all means we are willing, just as the soldier described above, to consider each piece of the Lord's combat equipment on a regular basis. It is essential that each piece of equipment becomes familiar to us, for God gives the full resource of protection to those who follow Him. The scripture in Ephesians speaks of six levels of protection: truth, righteousness, preparation in the gospel, faith, salvation, and the Spirit, which is the word of God. Now, consider your own situation. Are you implementing all six levels of protection into your life daily? Does the communication you allow into your mind invite truth, righteousness, and the Spirit? Are you setting aside time every day to study the gospel, to read the word of God, to understand salvation? If these six pieces of armor are to be our greatest protection, it becomes vital to implement them into our daily routine.

Notice that the Lord's armor for those living in the last days is spiritual. This is a spiritual war we are waging, and every day we lose numbers to the other side. That is why daily reinforcing our spiritual armor is so essential to filling our gap in the hedge.

Have you ever taken the time to notice that the armor of the Lord is mainly centered on a frontal attack? It consists of a covering for the loins, a shield, a helmet, shoes, a sword, and a breastplate. What happens if the enemy comes from behind? In Isaiah 58:8 we find the answer, "and *thy righteousness* shall go *before* thee; the glory of the Lord shall be thy *rearward*" (emphasis added). The footnote for *rearward* explains that it means *rearguard.* The Lord will not leave us to fight the battle alone. He has promised to guard us from the things we don't foresee. He has our back.

The world we live in is dangerous, the battle rages all around us, but as Saints we are encouraged to "endure hardness, as a good soldier of Jesus Christ" (2 Timothy 2:3). Becoming a good soldier of Jesus Christ will require us to put on the full protection of the Lord as we prepare to fill in the gaps and make up the hedge. We must surround ourselves with that which builds truth, increases righteousness, and solidifies our preparation in the gospel. We must handcraft and fit our armor with faith, focused on salvation, as we are led by the Spirit. Then we can fill our place in the gap, standing in righteousness, knowing the Lord is behind us.

Act upon this . . .
Read 1 Nephi 3 and 4

"May I say once more to the youth of the Church—prepare, believe, be ready, have faith. Do not say or do or be that which would limit your service or render you ineffective in the kingdom of God. Be ready when your call comes, for surely it will come. Keep your gospel shoes on, or, as Paul wrote to the Ephesians, 'Stand therefore, having . . . your feet shod with the preparation of the gospel of peace' (Ephesians 6:14–15). The Lord would say to you tonight what the angel said long ago to Simon Peter:

'Arise. . . . Bind on thy sandals. . . . Follow me.' (Acts 12:7–8)"
(President Howard W. Hunter).

Consider the six levels of protection spoken of in Ephesians.
Could you choose one area of protection to work on this week?
How might you handcraft and fit each piece of the armor de-
scribed in this section to offer you the best protection?

Ponder . . .
And He Did Raise the Standard

Spring sun sparkles across the parking lot, warming asphalt, glinting
off windshields, brightening the smiles of young students running to the
school. I watch them come, laden with lunch and backpacks heavy, leaving safety of car for safety of school.

I stand on white stark lines striped on black pavement, red stop sign
in hand. My job ensures safety. On these mornings, mine are the eyes of a
hawk. Watching cars, watching sidewalks, watching children come.

The school lies quiet, waiting. The parking lot is chaos organized.
Moving tires, running feet, coming and going, without end. In the midst
I see the science teacher walking. Then I see him stop. He stands between
parked cars, and students running, and traffic flowing. Still.

What is he doing? I wonder. He must have forgotten something in
his car. Still, he stands. Waiting. He must be trying to decide if he should
go back to his car, I think to myself. The parking lot revolves around him.
Still. He waits.

I look more closely now.

He's fixed on something. Focused. Waiting.

I draw my eyes away from traffic streaming, students walking, to see. There, behind me, star-spangled, red-and-white-striped canvas, carefully unfolded and rope strung, rises up the mast.

I look back at the science teacher. Yes. He is watching. Standing tall. Now I see hand over heart. Silent. Still. Sacred. Until the flag is fully raised.

The students run, the traffic flows, and finally the science teacher walks into the school.

I say nothing. But I have learned.

Some have greater respect. Some live to a higher standard. When something is most sacred, some honor it at all costs.

Like a man who spoke of liberty. Who raised a standard in a situation that was exceedingly precarious and dangerous. Whose actions came as a result of the corruption caused by one very wicked man who wanted to destroy the very foundation of liberty.

This chief commander "rent his coat; and he took a piece thereof, and wrote upon it—In memory of our God, our religion, and freedom, and our peace, our wives, and our children" (Alma 46:12). In memory of everything that was sacred.

He took this torn fabric and carefully stretched it out and fastened it upon the end of a pole.

He called it the Title of Liberty.

Then he put on his headplate and his breastplate, his shield and his armor, and bowed himself to the earth.

And he prayed mightily.

Then, after pouring out his soul to God, he went forth among the people, waving the flag and crying with a loud voice: "Whosoever will maintain this title upon the land, let them come forth in the strength of the Lord, and enter into a covenant that they will maintain their rights, and their religion, that the Lord may bless them" (Alma 46:20).

And the people came running.

"And he did raise the standard . . . in whatsoever place he did enter" (Alma 62:4).

He raised the standard.

Some have a greater respect. Some live to a higher standard. When something is most sacred, some honor it at all costs.

A captain of great courage. Certain. Always.

I want to stand with him.

PONDER THIS . . .
Read Alma 62

> *O thou Rock of our salvation,*
> *Jesus, Savior of the world,*
> *In our poor and lowly station*
> *We thy banner have unfurled.*
> *Gather round the standard bearer;*
> *Gather round in strength of youth.*
> *Ev'ry day the prospect's fairer*
> *While we're battling for the truth.*

What does it mean to gather round the standard bearer? Can you think of someone in your life you look up to? What is it about their standards that you admire most? Have they come to know their Captain? Do they point you to Him?

Become . . .

The Battle Is Not Yours, but God's

"Once there was a ship . . . sinking in mid-ocean, surrounded by fog. It had drifted far out of its course, and collided with a derelict. The captain ordered the band to play, the officers put on their dress uniforms and their white gloves." And so they played, on into the night, until "another ship, also drifting, signalled in answer to the music and all were saved" (Myrtle Reed).

I love the message of this story. When all seemed lost, with the ship completely off course, sinking, surrounded by fog, the captain did not quit. His inspiration and direction led to the rescue of the entire crew. Rather than giving up, the captain put on his white gloves and ordered out the band.

There are some who, when all of life seems to combine against them, lower their flags in defeat. Abandoning hope, they no longer await the clear signal that promises safety. But there are others who approach life with white gloves on and flags flying. These know what it means to order out the band. What is it that allows us to continue to fight for the kingdom even in the very moment we question our belief? To put on our white gloves with flags flying? What is the signal for which we play our battle song? The answer can be found in Second Chronicles.

King Jehoshaphat was a man who understood the importance of the condition of the heart. He was a man who prepared his heart to seek the

Lord. Because his heart was thus prepared, Jehoshaphat was able to experience a great miracle.

During his reign, a great multitude came against him from beyond the sea. Jehoshaphat was scared, but he did the most important thing: he "set himself to seek the Lord" (2 Chronicles 20:3). In this moment of great need, he did what he had always done—he prepared his heart to seek God.

During this time he proclaimed a fast throughout all the land, and then he stood in front of the house of the Lord and prayed, remembering a covenant the Lord had made with them. "If, when evil cometh upon us, as the sword, judgment, or pestilence, or famine, we stand before this house, and in thy presence, (for thy name is in this house,) and cry unto thee in our affliction, then thou wilt hear and help.... O our God, ... we have no might against this great company that cometh against us; *neither know we what to do: but our eyes are upon thee*" (2 Chronicles 20:9, 12; emphasis added).

How many times in our own lives have we, each of us, approached the Lord in our affliction, begging that He will hear and help, explaining, *"I know not what to do."* In these moments, when what is against us seems mightier than we are, how often is our first inclination to focus our eyes upon the Lord? Perhaps we look to our own strength first. Maybe we are good at problem solving. Too many times our first course of action is a practical one rather than a spiritual one. What was it that prompted Jehoshaphat to look immediately to the Lord?

Perhaps it was because he had prepared his heart to seek God. First. Always.

And so King Jehoshaphat petitioned the Lord in all of Israel's behalf. "And all Judah stood before the Lord, with their little ones, their wives, and their children. Then . . . came the Spirit of the Lord in the midst of the congregation; And he said, Hearken ye, all Judah, and ye inhabitants of Jerusalem, and thou king Jehoshaphat, Thus saith the Lord unto you, Be not afraid nor dismayed by reason of this great multitude; *for the battle is not yours, but God's*" (2 Chronicles 20:13–15; emphasis added).

Think of the greatest trial you face right now; consider your multitude of burdens. Have you taken the time to prepare your heart to seek God? In the hour of greatest indecision, is your first choice to look to the Lord? Our God is great. He is mightier than any multitude of burdens we could ever face. Only He can fight our battles, because only He knows what it will take to conquer them. With a heart that is prepared we will be able to heed the final counsel the Lord gave to King Jehoshaphat, "to morrow go out against them: for the Lord will be with you" (2 Chronicles 20:17). Then we will recognize the Spirit of the Lord as it descends upon us, and we will feel His calming words, "the battle is not yours, but God's."

Sometimes, as God's warriors, all that is required of us is to stand before His house, in His presence, and cry unto Him. He will hear and help. This is what makes our courage strong—the knowledge that the Lord is with us. This battle is not ours, but His.

President Ezra Taft Benson counseled the Saints who would live in the last days: "The final outcome is certain—the forces of righteousness will finally win. What remains to be seen is where each of us personally, now and in the future, will stand in this fight—and how tall we will stand. . . . Great battles can make great heroes, but heroes will make great battle. You will never have a better opportunity to be a greater hero in a more crucial battle than in the battle you will face today and in the immediate future. Be warned that some of the greatest battles you will face will be fought within the silent chambers of your own soul. . . . Fortunately for us, we have the privilege of fighting under the Lord's banner. . . . He wants to help us win every battle, be it personal or public."

I love what happened as the enemy approached Jehoshaphat's people that next day. "They rose early in the morning . . . and as they went forth, Jehoshaphat stood and said, Hear me, O Judah . . . Believe in the Lord your God, so shall ye be established; believe his prophets, so shall ye prosper. And when he had consulted with the people, *he appointed singers unto the Lord* . . . that should praise the beauty of holiness, *as they went out before the army,* and to say, Praise the Lord; for his mercy endureth forever" (2 Chronicles 20:21; emphasis added).

Jehoshaphat called out the band. When our trials seem to overtake us, in the moments when we find ourselves overwhelmed by the multitude of our burdens, perhaps it would help if we were to consider this example.

We must raise the banner, put on our white gloves, order out the band, and then remember—the battle is not ours, but God's.

And He is with us.

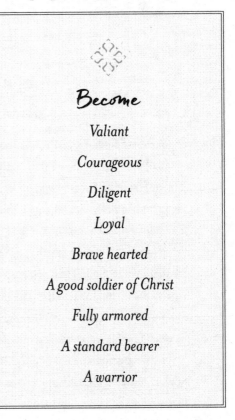

Become

Valiant

Courageous

Diligent

Loyal

Brave hearted

A good soldier of Christ

Fully armored

A standard bearer

A warrior

BECOME . . .
Read 2 Chronicles 20

"Ye shall not fear them: for the Lord your God he shall fight for you" (Deuteronomy 3:22).

Have you ever faced something bigger than you? Do you know what it feels like when the odds are against you? Where do you turn in the very moment that requires courage strong and a heart brave? In a place unfamiliar when direction is unsure, what is the clear signal that beckons you on?

Solo Time
Become a Warrior

"If God be for us, who can be against us? . . . Who shall separate us from the love of Christ? shall tribulation, or distress, or persecution, or famine, or nakedness, or peril, or sword? . . . Nay, in all these things we are *more than conquerors* through him that loved us. For I am persuaded, that neither death, nor life, nor angels, nor principalities, nor powers, nor things present, nor things to come, nor height, nor depth, nor any other creature, shall be able to separate us from the love of God, which is in Christ Jesus our Lord" (Romans 8:31, 35, 37–39; emphasis added). The footnote for the phrase *more than conquerors* offers the Greek translation as *abundantly victorious*.

Is there anything that could separate you from Christ? Could adversity? Doubt? Lack of hope? Discouragement? Fear? Sin? Consider the pattern of your life right now. What currently separates you from your love of the Lord? If we wish to become abundantly victorious, this scripture is clear—we cannot allow anything to separate us from our love of the Lord.

A good example of this is found in the third chapter of First Nephi, when Nephi and his brothers are sent back to obtain the plates. The first attempt to retrieve the plates had been for Laman to simply ask Laban for the plates, which made Laban so mad he tried to kill Laman. Next they gathered together all of their gold, silver, and precious things. This time Laban tried to kill all of them as he took possession of their belongings. But still Nephi wasn't ready to give in, which made his brothers angry.

Laman and Lemuel began to murmur, saying, "How is it possible that the Lord will deliver Laban into our hands? Behold, he is *a mighty man,* and he can command fifty, yea, even he can slay fifty; *then why not us?"* (1 Nephi 3:31; emphasis added). And Nephi responded, "Let us go up again unto Jerusalem, and let us be faithful in keeping the commandments of the Lord; for behold *he is mightier* than all the earth, *then why not mightier* than Laban and his fifty, yea, or even his tens of thousands? ... Wherefore can you doubt? ... The Lord is able to deliver us" (1 Nephi 4:1, 3; emphasis added).

I love the exchange between these brothers. Sometimes, when I am about to face something that is bigger than all of my resources, I quote bits of this exchange to myself, "*How is it possible?"* I say, "This has gone wrong in every way, then *why not for me?"* And then I reply to myself, "*He is mightier* than all the earth, *then why not mightier* than this? Wherefore can you doubt? The Lord is able to deliver you."

Then why not us?

Then why not mightier?

Nephi refused to let anything separate him from the love of the Lord, and he became abundantly victorious. In moments when the battle rages fierce on every side, we can remind ourselves, "He is mightier than all the earth . . . then why not mightier than this?"

THE ELEVENTH MONTH

Become His Witness

And Joshua said unto the people,
ye are witnesses . . . that ye have chosen you the Lord,
to serve him. And they said, We are witnesses.

—JOSHUA 24:22

Consider . . .
Settle It in Your Heart

Atestimony is an interesting thing because it is so individual. It is made up of one-on-one experiences unique to each of us. Therefore, what you believe and what I believe won't ever be exactly the same because each of our lives and our experiences are so different. A testimony can be strong, forged in moments of definition, a witness of truths never to be forgotten. A testimony can be fragile, requiring intimate care and dedication. Here is a truth that is simple but profound: No one can take your testimony from you, but you can choose to let it go.

In Luke 21 we read of a conversation between the Savior and His Apostles. He spoke about the journey ahead. It was one that would require great courage. He said: "They shall lay their hand on you, and persecute you, delivering you up to the synagogues, and into prisons, being brought before kings and rulers for my name's sake. And it shall turn to you for a testimony. *Settle it therefore in your hearts,* not to meditate before what ye shall answer: For I will give you . . . wisdom" (Luke 21:12–15; emphasis added).

Within those verses the Lord gave His Apostles some profound advice. First, their journey was going to be hard. Second, it would become a testimony to them. Last, their commitment to the Lord needed to be settled in their hearts. This settling process is important. It is what helps to get us through the hardest times.

Experience has led me to understand that during the hardest

moments of our lives, the Lord often sends wisdom. We are taught things we might not otherwise have learned. We need to settle these moments in our hearts and never forget them. They can turn to us for a testimony if we choose—a lifeline, a source of strength beyond our own, something to hold on to. They become a witness.

In our ward family, over a two-year period, five babies were born into five different homes. Each of these babies had severe health challenges. All of them were unique. Jesse Caleb Richardson was born prematurely at twenty-three weeks gestation. Miles Fotheringham was born with a rare disorder that would not allow him to breathe on his own. Susie Allen was born without kidneys. Annie Grace Sabin was born with a severe heart defect. And because of a lack of amniotic fluid in the womb, Cade Bennett was born with lungs that were not developed enough to sustain life.

Our ward prayed for these tiny babies, and we saw miracles. The journey was hard, but we were given wisdom from the Lord. We gave, keeping back nothing in hours and hours of service to each of these families. Along the way we saw the hand of the Lord, and we settled that witness in our hearts.

It was a trying time.

Within those two years we lost all five babies, and yet we gained a deeper testimony of the Lord. Those days of trial turned to us for a testimony. That testimony was particularly manifest in the mothers of those tiny babies.

I watched these mothers become sanctified as they prayed for miracles and then yielded their hearts to the will of the Lord. I watched them become consecrated as they set their own lives on hold, sacrificing everything to the calling of mother. Every time I see these mothers, I see the testimony that burns in their eyes, witnessing that they have come to know the Lord in a very personal and individual way. Their trial turned to testimony, and they settled it in their hearts. Never to be forgotten. Always to be remembered. A witness.

I was invited to speak at the funeral of one of these babies. As I prepared my remarks, I spoke to the parents about their feelings looking back over the past year and a half of their life. We spoke of moments that were precious. We spoke of great sacrifice. We spoke of miracles. Looking back over the previous year, we wondered how they had found the strength to make it through. "Do you think you would be able to do it again?" I asked.

"No, never," was the mother's honest reply.

"But would you ever give up the testimony of the Lord you gained from this experience?" I wondered aloud.

Her response was exactly the same, "No, never."

I have learned that it is in the *no, never* moments of our life, the moments of the greatest sacrifice, that our testimony of the Lord becomes the most precious to us. We must remember to settle that testimony in our hearts.

"Here then is a great truth. In the pain, the agony, and the heroic endeavors of life, we pass through a refiner's fire, and the insignificant and the unimportant in our lives can melt away like dross and make our faith bright, intact, and strong. In this way the divine image can be mirrored from the soul. It is part of the purging toll exacted of some to become acquainted with God" (President James E. Faust).

The eleventh principle on the journey toward discipleship is to become a witness, to obtain a testimony. A testimony becomes a lifeline, a source of strength, something we can hold on to, when we settle it in our hearts as we become acquainted with the Lord. We don't have to wait until we know all there is to know before we make time for this settling; we can do it line upon line, precept upon precept, from the first day to the last day. The process will take time. It will require studying, learning, and trusting. Some kinds of knowledge will be gathered in moments of adversity, others in moments of gratitude or great joy. Each piece will become precious to us. Each must be settled in our hearts—settled in the very moment, not at the end, but as we go along.

There is one thing nestled deep within my heart that has changed my life completely. No matter what happens, I've already decided on this one thing. It's settled. I believe in Jesus Christ. I just do. I may not know everything about Him. But I want to. There are questions I have that I don't understand right now, but I hope to understand them one day. As I look back on pivotal moments in my life, I realize that they have been life-altering purely because they have led me to know one thing for sure—Jesus is the Christ, the Son of God, the Holy One of Israel. I know He lives. I know He loves me. It is one truth of which I am certain.

I have settled it in my heart.

CONSIDER THIS . . .
Read Luke 21

"It is not even enough for us to be *convinced* of the gospel; we must act and think so that we are *converted* by it. In contrast to the institutions of the world, which teach us to *know* something, the gospel of Jesus Christ challenges us to *become* something" (Dallin H. Oaks).

Consider the difference between being convinced and being converted. The conversion process takes place every time we settle a belief into our hearts. Have you become convinced, or have you become converted? Which one would you like to be?

Act . . .
Sirs, Ye Should Have Hearkened unto Me

One of the most important aspects of standing as a witness is learning to become absolutely steadfast in what we believe. Perhaps the easiest way to become steadfast as a witness is to anchor our testimony in the Lord. One of the best lessons on testimony anchors is found in Acts 27. This is, by far, my favorite story in the book of Acts. The heading explains that Paul, in a perilous voyage, traveled to Rome.

The season was late fall, sometime in the middle of October. Winter was fast approaching, and "sailing was now dangerous" (Acts 27:9). With what must have taken great courage, Paul, who was a prisoner, approached the centurion, saying, "Sirs, I perceive that this voyage will be with hurt and much damage, not only of the lading and ship, but also of our lives" (v. 10). But his advice was not heeded—"Nevertheless the centurion believed the master and the owner of the ship, more than those things which were spoken by Paul" (v. 11). The master felt that the haven they were in was not a good place to winter; he wanted to try to make it to Crete. Because the south wind blew softly, he felt confident in his decision and began the journey.

Not long after the journey started, they encountered a tempestuous wind called Euroclydon, known and feared for its destructive power. The storm became so powerful that the ship could not be steered, and the captain finally had to let go of the controls and let the ship steer itself. As the storm intensified, the men began undergirding the ship, tying it together with rope so that it wouldn't break apart in the storm.

On the second day of the storm they lightened the ship, throwing overboard everything they could do without. On the third day they threw out the tackling. Several days went by under complete and heavy cloud cover so dense they could not see sun or stars. They had lost the power to navigate, and, the scriptures tell us, "all hope that we should be saved was then taken away" (Acts 27:20).

I love what happens next. It seems Paul, who had known all along what was going to happen, waited patiently until this point. "But *after long abstinence* Paul stood forth in the midst of them, and said, Sirs, ye should have hearkened unto me" (Acts 27:21; emphasis added). I always get a giggle out of this told-you-so moment. But I also recognize that his hesitation and patience were an important part of the lesson that was about to come. During the days of storm these men had let go of their excess baggage, they had secured what was most important, and they had lost all ability to rely on their own strength or intelligence in navigating their course. Just when it seemed all hope was lost, in the moment of greatest humility, Paul began to teach. His sermon was a powerful one.

"Now I exhort you to be of good cheer: for there shall be no loss of *any man's* life among you, but of the ship. For there stood by me this night the angel of God, *whose I am, and whom I serve,* saying, Fear not, Paul; *thou must be brought* before Caesar: and, lo, God hath given thee all them that sail with thee. Wherefore, sirs, be of good cheer: *for I believe*

God, that it shall be even as it was told me. Howbeit we must be cast upon *a certain island"* (Acts 27:22–26; emphasis added).

Within this sermon Paul teaches four important lessons. I call them anchor points. First, he testified of his trust in God, "whose I am, and whom I serve." Second, he explained how the angel told him, "Thou *must* be brought before Caesar." God had a purpose in mind for him, and Paul knew it would come to pass. Third, he said, "Be of good cheer: for *I believe God,* that it shall be even as it was told me." Faith in God was something Paul would not turn his back on. Last, he said, "we must be cast upon a *certain* island." Paul knew that God knew what the end would be, that they were in God's hands and known of Him.

When we find ourselves on a perilous journey, I wonder if we could learn from these four anchor points: to trust God whom we serve, to know that He has a purpose for us, to have absolute faith in Him, and to know He is mindful of us.

You might be wondering why I call these anchor points. It is because of what happens next. When the fourteenth night came, the men began to worry that they were close to shore. Fearing that they might hit rocks, "they cast *four* anchors out . . . and wished for the day" (Acts 27:29; emphasis added).

Just as Paul had done with his four anchors spiritually, in the midst of the storm and the doubt, they cast out four anchors and waited for light to come. As they waited for the light, several more lessons were learned. First, some of the men tried to escape by the lifeboat. They were discovered, and Paul told them, "Except these abide in the ship, ye cannot be saved" (Acts 27:31). They could not rely on their own strength or timing; they had to be patient with God's timing. In an effort to make this extremely clear, the lifeboat was thrown overboard. Second, they took meat and bread, and gave thanks. During this time of waiting they gathered strength, and because they recognized it, they were able to thank God for it. Last, they threw everything off the ship, placing their full trust in God's plan.

When it was day they took up the anchors and *committed* themselves unto the sea. It wasn't until they had completely entrusted themselves into the hands of the Lord that they took up the anchors. Then, they "hoised up the mainsail to the wind, and made toward shore. And falling into a place where two seas met, they ran the ship aground; and the forepart stuck fast and remained unmoveable. . . . And so it came to pass, that they escaped *all safe* to land" (Acts 27:40–41, 44; emphasis added).

There is a great lesson on anchor points that can be learned from this chapter. When we find ourselves on a perilous journey, we too can cast out our four anchors and wish for light to come. We place our trust in God and let Him determine His purpose for us. This requires faith in Him and an understanding that He knows the end from the beginning and is mindful of us along the way. While our anchors are set we must let go of anything that might be holding us back and gather strength from Him with gratitude, rather than relying on our own strength. Then, when we are ready, we must commit ourselves into His hands, trusting that He will lead us exactly where we need to go.

These anchor points can become a testimony to us, steadfast and immovable. They are four anchors we can cast out during any life storm we might face while we wish for the day.

Trust God.

Believe He has a purpose for you.

Have absolute faith in Him.

Know that He is ever mindful of you.

ACT UPON THIS . . .

Read Acts 27

"We might have a strong consolation, who have fled for refuge to lay hold upon the hope set before us: Which hope we have as an anchor of the soul, both sure and steadfast . . . even Jesus" (Hebrews 6:18–20). There are many anchor points we can hold onto, but the surest is the Lord Jesus Christ. How does your testimony of Him give you hope? Is your testimony of Christ an anchor to your soul? Why?

Ponder . . .

Anchor Points as Witnesses

Setting an anchor is not a one-man job. As a boat pulls to shore, each fills an assignment prearranged. One steadies and guides the boat. Another readies the rope—untangling, tying knots strong. Several leave the boat, their sight focused on the shore. Shovels in hand, they dig holes in deep sand, casting dirt to the side relentlessly until finally anchors are set, knots secured, ropes tightened, and dirt replaced. Metal stakes angled from sand to shore are pounded above each anchor deep into solid ground.

I wonder why.

It seems so much time has been set apart to secure the anchors. I have checked the forecast. The weather man calls for clear skies. Sun. Perhaps this lengthy process is a waste of time.

Perhaps.

But on the third day in the midst of a beautiful afternoon the wind picks up. Suddenly.

From every direction men come running. Yelling. I feel the ship tugging against ropes taut, listing into the fury, turning from the safety of the shore. Calmly the captain reaches for controls. Within moments the boat is righted and secured. Again, all is well.

But how was it done?

"Why," I ask, "was it so easy to right the boat against wind powerful and waves formidable?" The reply remains vivid in my memory still, "Because the anchors did not fail."

It is general conference weekend when I receive a phone call from a friend. His daughter, Isabelle, is having trouble with her eyes and experiencing trembling in her hand.

She is eleven.

The doctor has found a tumor. Cancer.

"How is she?" I ask.

"Brave," her father replies.

"Are you okay?" I question. "How will you get through?"

"We will hold on to our anchor points," he replies.

What are these anchor points? I wonder.

"It is the times in our life we can look back on and know for certain God was aware of us," he explains, "the moments when we saw His hand in our life. We write them down in a journal for times such as these. Then, in the hardest moments, we have something to hold on to. A testimony that is sure. "

Anchor points.

Anchors that will not fail.

What are your anchor points? What do you know for sure? Think back on your life to moments when you have been guided and steadied. The untangling. Sight focused on the goal.

Sure, you might chalk it up to coincidence, but think about that moment when you were impressed to walk outside and you happened upon a friend who needed you just then. Could that have been God's hand?

A witness. An anchor point.

And if there is that one, are there others? The sunset after your sister died. The phone call. The way that job lined up. The story you heard in church. The scripture that stood out to you this morning—the one you needed to read right then.

Whispers from heaven. Answers. Anchor points.

If they have been there before, they will be there again.

Perhaps it is worth the time to set the anchors.

Perhaps it is time.

PONDER THIS . . .
Read Ether 12:4

"Wherefore, whoso believeth in God might with surety hope for a better world . . . which hope cometh of faith, maketh an anchor to the souls of men" (Ether 12:4).

What are your spiritual anchors? Take some time this week to write them down.

Become . . .

Compassed About with So Great a Cloud of Witnesses

My favorite part of the eleventh chapter of Hebrews is actually found in chapter twelve.

The eleventh chapter of Hebrews is a list of heroes, people of great faith, men and women who understood the substance of things hoped for, the evidence of things not seen.

We read of Caleb and Joshua, who obtained a good report. Of Abel, Enoch, and Noah, who understood that "he that cometh to God must believe that he is, and that he is a rewarder of them that diligently seek him" (Hebrews 11:6). We read of Abraham, who obeyed, not knowing whither he went, and Sarah, who received strength because she judged him faithful who had promised. "These all died in faith, not having received the promises, but having seen them afar off, *and were persuaded of them, and embraced them*" (Hebrews 11:13; emphasis added). I want to be known as someone like that, one who is not only persuaded of God's promises but embraces them.

The verses talk of Isaac, Jacob, Joseph, and Moses. The walls of Jericho falling down, and Rahab, who perished not. Great men the likes of Gideon, Barak, Samson, Jephthae, David, and Samuel, "who through faith subdued kingdoms, wrought righteousness, obtained promises, stopped the mouths of lions, quenched the violence of fire, escaped the edge of the sword, out of weakness were made strong, waxed valiant in fight, . . . [and] women [who] received their dead raised to life again" (Hebrews 11:33–35).

We read of heroes who were tortured. Others suffered trials of cruel mockings, bonds, scourgings, imprisonment. They were sawn asunder, stoned, tempted, slain, left destitute, tormented, and afflicted.

This is a chapter that describes noble and valiant people. The stories and images contained within are filled with power. And yet, it is the first three verses of chapter twelve that make me love chapter eleven most. The first line reads, "Wherefore seeing we also are compassed about with so great a cloud of witnesses . . ." What is this cloud of witnesses? It's everyone we just read about in chapter eleven. "Wherefore seeing we also are compassed about with so great a cloud of witnesses, *let us lay aside every weight* . . . and let us run with patience the race that is *set before us*" (Hebrews 12:1; emphasis added).

This verse gives counsel to those who find themselves weary and faint. The instruction is clear—it is because we are compassed about by so great a cloud of witnesses that we are able to lay aside every weight. Think about those who have gone before you. Remember their stories of faith. When you set out to run the race before you, remember, you are compassed about by a great cloud of witnesses, both within the scriptures and within your own circle of influence. There you will find strength enough to lay aside every weight, strength to continue your own journey with patience.

Take a moment to consider the witnesses in your life. Who are they? Why do you consider them to be witnesses? Consider their testimonies and learn from them. Gather the strength you need from the witness they declare.

Perhaps there will be days when you wonder, moments when you question all you know. Maybe this cloud of witnesses will not be enough. In verse two of chapter 12 we are given counsel for times such as this. We are told we must look "unto Jesus the author and finisher of our faith; who for the joy that was set before him endured the cross. . . . *Consider him* that endured such contradiction of sinners against himself, *lest ye be wearied and faint in your minds*" (Hebrews 12:2–3; emphasis added).

On those days that are particularly difficult, *consider Him.* The Author and the Finisher. The One who knows the end from the beginning and all of the moments in between. The One who endured opposition. The One who endured the cross, for the joy that was set before Him.

Were *you* the joy that was set before Him?

If you are His joy, will He ever turn His back on you? Will He let you struggle through this on your own? In the moments when doubt fills your heart, "Consider how great things he hath done for you" (1 Samuel 12:24). In the moments when you question all you know, consider Him who said, "I will also ease the burdens which are put upon your shoulders, that even you cannot feel them upon your backs, even while you are in bondage; *and this will I do that ye may stand as witnesses for me hereafter,* and that ye may know of a surety that I, the Lord God, do visit my people in their afflictions" (Mosiah 24:14; emphasis added).

The testimony comes after the burdens, after the bondage, after the afflictions.

Then, you will stand as a witness.

Then, you will know of a surety.

If you are weary . . .

Consider Him.

Then stand as His witness.

He needs you.

BECOME . . .

Read Hebrews 11 and 12

The scriptures are filled with witnesses—people who have written down their testimonies of the evidence of the Lord's hand in their life. In essence, the standard works could be considered a book of evidences.

Perhaps you might consider keeping your own "book of evidences"—a book in which you record your own witness of the hand of the Lord in your life. To begin with, you might ponder the witnesses who surround you, both from within the scriptures and from your life. Make a list of their names and the reason each is a witness to you of the Lord's dealings with His people. How have they strengthened you? What can you learn from their example? Once you have written down what you have learned from the meaningful experiences of others, you could begin writing a record of your own personal experiences—the moments when you have seen the hand of the Lord in your life. A book of evidences. A cloud of witnesses.

Become

Settled

A believer

Converted

Anchored in Christ

Compassed about
by witnesses

The joy that was
set before Him

A witness

Solo Time
Become a Witness

Is there a process we go through to anchor our testimonies before we become witnesses of Christ?

I love the example found in Joshua 24.

In this chapter, it is recorded that Joshua gathered all of the tribes of Israel with their elders, judges, and officers. Then he explained a commitment that needed to be made. This commitment would require a choice. The people had to choose the God in which they would believe. Joshua told them first of their fathers who served other gods, idols made of stone and wood that were incapable of feeling after them. Then he reminded them of the great blessings and miracles that had come to the children of Israel from the Lord God of Israel. He spoke of the flood, the birth of Isaac, the plagues in Egypt and how the Lord brought them out, the parting of the Red Sea, the wandering through the wilderness, and the fighting and possession of the land, "for which ye did not labour, and cities which ye built not, and ye dwell in them. . . . Now therefore fear the Lord, and serve him in sincerity and in truth: and put away the gods which your fathers served on the other side of the flood, and in Egypt; and serve ye the Lord" (Joshua 24:13–14).

Joshua spoke of anchor points, of moments in the journey when the people had witnessed the hand of the Lord. He reminded them of the miracles that came to a people who chose to serve a living God. His goal was to ensure the people were anchored in the Lord before he extended them an invitation.

What follows next is the famous verse we are all so familiar with: "Choose you this day whom ye will serve . . . but as for me and my house, we will serve the Lord" (Joshua 24:15).

The children of Israel had to choose between two very different types of God. The gods of idolatry were cold and unfeeling. They demanded sacrifice but offered nothing lasting in return. The blessings the people sought after from these gods were those that fulfilled needs of immediate gratification—for example, maybe the right sacrifice in behalf of a certain god would lead to rain. Maybe.

Joshua believed in a different God. His God provided healing, direction, deliverance, sustenance, great miracles, even strength. The God of Joshua would communicate with His followers. He was a living God with the ability to become an integral part of their lives, if only they would let Him.

From this chapter we begin to realize that the process of making the commitment to choose to believe in the Lord required several steps. First, the people were required to make a conscious choice—to choose the Lord God over gods of idolatry. This choice required commitment and a willingness to keep the commandments of the God they chose.

Second, in order to help them make the choice, the people needed to be reminded of the times they had seen His hand in their lives. Recognizing these moments enabled the people to have anchor points— experiences that became a testimony to them of the reality of a living God.

Lastly, the people entered into a covenant to follow the Lord, the God of Israel.

After going through these three steps, the people answered, "therefore will we also serve the Lord; for he is our God" (Joshua 24:18).

"And Joshua said unto the people, Ye are witnesses against yourselves that ye have chosen you the Lord, to serve him. And they said, We are witnesses" (Joshua 24:22).

Have you gone through the process of becoming a witness? Have there been moments in your life when you have chosen the Lord over something else? Do you remember the times when you recognized His hand in your life? Have these moments become anchor points to you? Have you covenanted to follow Him?

I love the scripture found in Isaiah that reads, "Ye are my witnesses, saith the Lord, and my servant whom I have chosen: that ye may know and believe me, and understand that I am he . . . I, even I, am the Lord; and beside me there is no saviour" (Isaiah 43:10–11).

THE TWELFTH MONTH

Become Holy

Earth's crammed with heaven,
And every common bush afire with God;
But only he who sees, takes off his shoes . . .

—Elizabeth Barrett Browning

Consider . . .
Turning Aside to See

In the book of Exodus we read the story of Moses and the burning bush. "And the angel of the Lord appeared unto him in a flame of fire out of the midst of a bush: and he looked, and, behold, the bush burned with fire, and the bush was not consumed. And Moses said, *I will now turn aside, and see this great sight,* why the bush is not burnt. And when the Lord *saw* that he *turned aside to see,* God called unto him out of the midst of the bush, and said, Moses, Moses. And he said, Here am I. And he said, Draw not nigh hither: put off thy shoes from off they feet, for the place whereon thou standest is holy ground. Moreover he said, I am the God of thy father, the God of Abraham, the God of Isaac, and the God of Jacob. . . . I have surely seen the affliction of my people . . . and have heard their cry. . . . *I know their sorrows;* and I am come down to deliver them" (Exodus 3:2–8; emphasis added).

There is a great lesson contained within these verses. Notice that it wasn't until after Moses turned aside to see the great sight that the place where he stood became holy unto him. He stopped what he was doing, laid aside the task he was focused on, and took a moment to find the glory of God in the midst of the ordinary details of his day. He noticed the miracle in the midst of the mundane.

Have you learned to do that?

As Elizabeth Barrett Browning wrote, "Every common bush [is] afire with God, / But only he who sees, takes off his shoes." *Only he who sees.*

The Lord is everywhere. His mercies and His miracles surround us, but not everyone turns aside to see the great sight—not everyone takes off his or her shoes.

The question then becomes, what is it that we are so fixed on that we have lost focus on the holy in our lives?

For a moment try to imagine the scene of Bethesda. Five porches filled to bursting with multitudes of people surrounded a pool of water. The blind, halt, and withered were gathered there, waiting. The water in the pool before them had the potential to offer healing if the conditions were right. The waiting was done out of necessity, for at a certain season the water would be touched by an angel, troubled, and the first person to enter the water would be made whole. The conditions had to be perfect for the healing to take place. So, eyes fixed on the water, drawn to the potential for healing, they waited—all hoping, but each knowing that only one would be healed.

On a certain Sabbath, the Lord came to the pool and saw those who waited there. He noticed a man who had been afflicted for thirty-eight years. "When Jesus saw him lie, *and knew that he had been now a long time in that case,* he saith unto him, Wilt thou be made whole? The impotent man answered him, Sir, I have no man, when the water is troubled, to put me into the pool: but while I am coming, another steppeth down before me" (John 5:6–7; emphasis added).

It seems that having his focus fixed completely on the water wasn't working. Sadly, he was fixed on something that could not offer the blessing of which he was in desperate need. "Jesus recognized in the man a fit subject for a blessing, and said to him: 'wilt thou be made whole?'

The question was so simple as almost to appear superfluous. Of course the man wanted to be made well, and on the small chance of being able to reach the water at the right moment was patiently and eagerly waiting. There was a purpose, however, in these as in all words of the Master. *The man's attention was drawn to Him, fixed upon Him"* (Elder James E. Talmage).

For the first time, the man's eyes once drawn to and fixed on water that could not heal had turned to the Lord, who could. The holy in the midst of the mundane. He turned aside, and He saw it. "Jesus saith unto him, Rise, take up thy bed, and walk. And immediately the man was made whole" (John 5:8–9).

"It was Jesus, which had made him whole" (John 5:15).

The lesson captured within this story is taught over and over again in the life of the Lord. The miracle, the tender behind the mercy, comes after we are drawn to *Him,* after we are fixed on *Him.* John makes it clear—it was not the water, it was the Lord who had made him whole. When we shift our eyes from what occupies our attention and focus instead on the Lord, we will discover the holy within the ordinary moments of our lives. We must be willing to turn aside to see.

I have discovered Him during Sunday service, in the soft breathing of a child sleeping in mother's arms, safe. In one line of a hymn that captures the witness of my heart. In the welcome of a congregation held together by covenant to bear burdens, mourn together, and comfort—always comfort.

I have felt Him behind prison walls, as youth bound together by decisions once made and now regretted yearn for something more.

I have recognized Him in quiet chapels built into hospital halls.

I have witnessed the power of His love surrounding a circle of trust shared by those bound by addictions. His love beckons and they answer. It calls and they come.

I have seen Him reflected in the heart of one who abandons what is wanted most to give what is needed more.

We can find Him everywhere—within the walls of a church, a hospital, even a prison. In our own homes, when we want to know more of the Lord we can discover Him in the scriptures, in moments of prayer, in the words of a child. It is in those sacred moments that we truly become drawn to Him—fixed on Him. It is discovering Jesus, finding holy moments daily, that will make us whole.

The twelfth principle on the path to discipleship is to become holy. In order to do this we might have to lay aside the task we are focused on to look for the glory of God in the ordinary details of each day. We must learn to turn aside to witness the miracle in the midst of the mundane.

The Lord is everywhere. His mercies and His miracles surround us. Turn aside to see the great sight.

Take off your shoes.

CONSIDER THIS . . .
Read Exodus 3:2–8 and John 5

Experiencing holy moments in our day might require us to turn aside so we might see them. Try this experiment: Every day this week, let your eyes be open to discover a miracle, a tender mercy, or a holy moment in your day. Write it down. See if you can turn aside and see the great sight wherein the Lord can be found. Watch for the holy.

Act . . .
The Challenge

One Saturday evening I was studying the life events of John Moyle, a pioneer from Alpine, Utah. Greg was lying on the couch, Josh and Grace were each fixing a bowl of cereal, and Meg and some friends who had become bored with their evening adventures had gathered around the kitchen table to see what I was studying. I explained what I was learning about John Moyle. His was a very personal journey to know the Lord. It entailed a sacrifice acceptable, a testimony forged, and a life consecrated. His story taught holiness. Meg and her friends wanted to hear the story, and so I shared it with them, as related by Elder Jeffrey R. Holland:

"John R. Moyle lived in Alpine, Utah, about 22 miles as the crow flies to the Salt Lake Temple, where he was the chief superintendent of masonry during its construction. To make certain he was always at work by 8:00 A.M., Brother Moyle would start walking about 2:00 on Monday mornings. He would finish his work week at 5:00 P.M. on Friday and then start the walk home, arriving there shortly before midnight. Each week he would repeat that schedule for the entire time he served on the construction of the temple.

"Once when he was home on the weekend, one of his cows bolted during milking and kicked Brother Moyle in the leg, shattering the bone just below the knee. With no better medical help than they had in such rural circumstances, his family and friends took a door off the hinges and strapped him onto that makeshift operating table. They then took the bucksaw they had been using to cut branches from a nearby tree and amputated his leg just a few inches below the knee.

"When against all medical likelihood the leg finally started to heal, Brother Moyle took a piece of wood and carved an artificial leg. First he walked in the house. Then he walked around the yard. Finally he ventured out about his property. When he felt he could stand the pain, he strapped on his leg, walked the 22 miles to the Salt Lake Temple, climbed the scaffolding, and with a chisel in his hand hammered out the declaration 'Holiness to the Lord.'"

The watershed moment of Brother Moyle's life, told through the words of Elder Holland, left an impression on my heart so powerful and so compelling that the idea for an adventure began to unfold. As I finished, I said, halfway serious, "I think I'm going to do that . . . walk to the Salt Lake Temple." Immediately Josh chimed in, "My seminary teacher is going to do that. You should do it with him . . . you could go together." I said that might be a little awkward, but Josh announced that he would come with us. Instantly Meg and all her friends were committed. "Are you in?" I asked Greg. His response: "Probably." (That's the answer he gives to every adventure I propose; I'm pretty sure he said that when we talked about getting married . . .) It was unanimous.

The next morning I got a call from the mother of one of Megan's friends. "I heard you are doing a marathon or a triathlon or something . . ." I started laughing and explained the conversation from the night before. Her response was as immediate as all those from the night before in the kitchen, "We want to come." Before long there were eighty-five people who wanted to join the temple walk challenge, this twenty-two-mile journey toward holiness.

The experience was unforgettable. We trained physically for sixteen weeks, but we also trained spiritually. We studied sanctification. We studied consecration. We learned what it meant to become holy. Then we gathered together at 5:30 A.M. on Memorial Day. Before we started walking, we read a quote from J. Golden Kimball, who said, "When I think about the temple, every stone in it is a sermon to me. It tells of suffering, it tells of sacrifice, it preaches, every rock in it, preaches a discourse." I thought of the story of Brother Moyle. I knew of the sacrifice Brother Moyle had made to chisel those words in the stone. I was reminded of the suffering. That stone, high up on the Salt Lake Temple, has the power to remind me of the sermon of John Moyle's life: "Holiness to the Lord." Before we took the first step on our temple walk, we spoke of what it meant to suffer and to sacrifice to know the Lord. At the very beginning of our journey toward holiness we each asked ourselves, "What is *my* sermon?"

Seventeen miles into the walk we stopped for lunch. We were exhausted. Shoes came off, and blisters were popped. Muscles were stretched. We geared up for the portion that remained. Giving up was not an option, but we knew the last miles would be the hardest; these were the miles that would require the most sacrifice. We turned to Doctrine and Covenants 124, "If ye labor with all your might, I will consecrate that spot that it shall be made holy" (Doctrine and Covenants 124:44). For the most part we walked in silence. Our thoughts turned to what it meant to be holy.

The Bible Dictionary explains that, according to the Old Testament, things that were holy "were set apart for a sacred purpose." Is that what holiness is? Something set apart for a sacred purpose. I thought about my own life. What is the sacred purpose of my life? If I want to become more holy, I need to figure out what I have been set apart to do. Brigham Young said, "Every moment of my life must be holiness to the Lord . . ." In other words, every moment of my life must be set apart to the Lord. Every moment of my life must be consecrated to the Lord. I begin to understand that there is a difference between desire and consecration. When we learn to recognize and then live that difference, we start on the journey toward becoming holy.

When we started walking at 5:30 that morning, snow was falling and slush covered the ground. Throughout the day we walked under cloud-covered skies. But that afternoon, around 2:30 P.M., as we turned down the alley west of the Lion House, something remarkable happened. The sun came out. I will never forget turning to face the temple and looking up to see the words glinting in gold, sparkling in the sun, "Holiness to the Lord."

Suddenly it became clear to me that the exact moment when John Moyle chiseled the words "Holiness to the Lord" on the granite stone was not the most important part of his journey. The most important part of his journey happened in the moments of sacrifice along the way when the name of the Lord was carefully chiseled into his heart. His life was a journey that began with desire and, through consecration, ended with holiness.

That is what I hope my life journey will be.

ACT UPON THIS . . .
Read the entry under "Holiness" in the Bible Dictionary

"Consecration is not resignation or a mindless caving in. Rather, it is a deliberate expanding outward, making us more honest when we say, 'More used would I be' ("More Holiness

Give Me," *1985, Hymns,* no. 131). Consecration, likewise, is not shoulder-shrugging acceptance, but, instead, shoulder-squaring to better bear the yoke. . . . Consecration is thus both a principle and a process, and it is not tied to a single moment. Instead, it is freely given, drop by drop, until the cup of consecration brims and finally runs over" (Elder Neal A. Maxwell).

What does consecration mean to you? Spend some time this week studying the scriptures under "Consecration" in the Topical Guide. Then, try living your life in Holiness to the Lord, set apart to the Lord, consecrated to the Lord.

Ponder . . .

We Become Holy as We Become His

Journal entry May 30, 2011:

"The morning breaks, meadowlarks sing, and snow falls. At the other end of the valley the end awaits, a light amidst the gray. Eyes try to measure the distance of a goal vision can't comprehend. And yet something compels us forward."

What is it that compels us?

Is it what compelled Brother Moyle to go for twenty years, and then, at the age of seventy-seven, across twenty-two miles, limping?

Perhaps.

I am reminded of his sermon, Holiness to the Lord, lived every day of his life.

Did it come as an answer through the raindrops, and as healing through his tears?

Did his sacrifice lead to his sanctification?

Because somewhere between desire and consecration he came to know the Lord.

Was it on the first journey westward walking on feet sore and weary?

Or the fifty-third twenty-two-mile walk?

Or strapped to the door with courage strong and a bucksaw waiting?

I think I felt the stirring of it at mile one, the desire to be part of something that would require all of me. It was there again at mile three when we talked about stones that speak of sacrifice, sermons to be remembered. Then again, during the last seven miles. A sacrifice endured. But we kept back nothing, and our thoughts filled with holiness as we walked.

At mile twenty-two I wondered how he did it, week after week, month after month, year after year.

Not almost, but altogether. John would go.

His life was Holiness to the Lord.

Set apart to the Lord.

Consecrated to the Lord.

A man to be remembered.

A moment never to be forgotten.

It's a long, long way to walk.

But I realize now that the journey is as important as the destination.

The journey is where we come to know the Lord.

We become holy

As we become His.

PONDER THIS . . .

Read 3 Nephi 27:33

"And it came to pass that when Jesus had ended these sayings he said unto his disciples: Enter ye in at the strait gate; for strait is the gate, and narrow is the way . . . *and few there be that find it*" (3 Nephi 27:33; emphasis added).

The pattern toward discipleship is often described in terms of a journey in which we are asked to enter in at the strait gate and walk the narrow way. I find it interesting that He cautions us, "few there be that find it." Why do you think so few walk the pathway of discipleship? I wonder if it is because that journey entails sacrifice. Think of the disciples you have been privileged to meet in your life, people such as John Moyle. What can you learn from the journey they have walked that might help you to walk through the strait gate and along the narrow way? How will their example lead you to be more holy?

Become . . .
One Who Loves Much

There are few stories in the scriptures that are as tender as the account recorded in Luke chapter seven. "A woman in the city, which was a sinner, when she knew that Jesus sat at meat in the Pharisee's house, brought an alabaster box of ointment" (Luke 7:37). Immediately we are led to understand two things about this woman—she knew where to go to find the Lord, and her intent was to honor Him with a heartfelt offering that would require humility and love.

When she entered the home she stood behind the Lord, "weeping, and began to wash his feet with tears, and did wipe them with the hairs of her head, and kissed his feet, and anointed them with the ointment" (Luke 7:38). The Pharisee watched her humble service with eyes of condemnation, saying within himself, "This man, if he were a prophet, would have known *what manner of woman this is* that touched him: for she is a sinner" (Luke 7:39; emphasis added).

As was often the case with the Pharisees, the man had underestimated the Lord. The Savior knew exactly not only *who* this woman was but also what *manner* of woman she was. More important, He knew her heart.

For just a moment try to picture this situation in your mind. Jesus was seated at the table. On one side sat a man whose religious party prided itself on strict observance of the law. His heart was filled with keeping ceremonial rules and maintaining spiritual pride. On his other side knelt a woman whose life to that point had followed a path of mistakes and misturns. Broken and weeping, her heart was full as she offered a tribute to the Lord who knew her for who she really was.

Consider the condition of those two hearts—"which one of them will love him most?" (Luke 7:42).

Carefully the Lord tried to open the eyes of the Pharisee by saying, "Seest thou this woman?" (Luke 7:44). Do you *really* see her? "I entered thine house, thou gavest me no water for my feet: but *she hath washed my feet with tears,* and wiped them with the hairs of her head. Thou gavest me no kiss: but this woman since the time I came in *hath not ceased to kiss my feet.* My head with oil thou didst not anoint: but this woman *hath anointed my feet with ointment.* Wherefore I say unto thee, Her sins, which are many, are forgiven; *for she loved much:* but to whom little is forgiven, *the same* loveth little" (Luke 7:44–47; emphasis added).

In her adoration, this humble woman washed the feet of the Lord with her tears and then anointed them with an expensive ointment purchased for the purpose of honoring Him. From the Bible Dictionary we come to understand that "the English word *Christ* is from a Greek word meaning *anointed,* and is the equivalent of *Messiah,* which is from a Hebrew and Aramaic term meaning *anointed."* Perhaps this woman's humble offering, her tribute of anointing the Lord's feet, was an outward expression of her heartfelt testimony. She *knew* her Savior. She believed in Him as Jesus Christ the Holy One of Israel, the Messiah, the Son of God. She recognized Him as the Anointed One—He who had come to preach good tidings and to bind up the brokenhearted. The One who would proclaim liberty to the captives and open the prisons of those who were bound. He who would offer comfort to all that mourn, who would give unto them beauty for ashes, and the oil of joy for mourning. The Savior who would bring the garment of praise for the spirit of heaviness (see Isaiah 61:1–3).

What set this woman apart can be defined with three simple words: "she loved much" (Luke 7:47). She loved the Lord. Her heart was filled to overflowing with adoration for Him, and that sentiment dictated her actions.

Is the same true of us?

What is your offering to the Lord?

When was the last time you poured from the alabaster flask?

When I was pregnant with my last daughter, Grace, I began to experience complications. I went into preterm labor at seventeen weeks and spent six months down flat in bed, only getting up once a week to go to the doctor. Because of the severe restrictions placed upon me, I could not attend church for those six months. During that time the Young Men in our ward brought the sacrament into my home.

There, in my living room, they would kneel beside my sofa table, which had been draped with a white linen cloth. On that table they carefully placed *one* piece of bread and *one* cup of water. One. In that moment it became clear to me how individual the Atonement really is. *I* was the brokenhearted. *I* was the one held captive. *I* was the one seeking comfort. He was *my* Savior, *my* Messiah, the Anointed One who promised, "yet will I not forget thee. Behold, I have graven thee upon the palms of my hands" (Isaiah 49:15–16). It was just as Ammon had testified, "Behold, they are in the hands of the Lord . . . and they are his" (Alma 26:7). I was in His hands.

In that moment I knew what it meant to love much.

He knows what manner of woman I am—He knows my heart. Because of that knowing, He became my Savior—healing, making whole again, holding my life in His hands. His promise is clear, "Fear not, little children, *for you are mine*" (Doctrine and Covenants 50:41; emphasis added). It is a truth that is simple but profound—and it is found again in the book of First Corinthians, "Ye are Christ's, and Christ is God's" (1 Corinthians 3:23).

You are Christ's. In moments when you question all you know, remember those words. In moments when you feel alone or frightened, whisper that simple phrase. In moments when you face something that seems bigger than you, consider the promise those three words testify of. You are Christ's. You are. His.

He will not forget you. He will not forsake you. "The keeper of the gate is the Holy One of Israel; and he employeth no servant there" (2 Nephi 9:41). He is there. Always. Constant. Forever. Bringing peace. Bringing comfort. Bringing hope. He has graven you on the palms of His hands because you are precious to Him, because you are worth it, because you are His.

When we truly begin to understand the magnitude of this gift, we understand the heart of the woman with the alabaster flask, the woman who loved much. I want to love the Savior as she did. I want to honor Him with my actions. I want to pour daily from the alabaster flask. Through that process, I hope to become holy—to become His.

With all my heart,
for all my days.

BECOME . . .
Read Luke 7

Think about your journey and the invitations that have been extended to you along the way. What are the parts of this experience that have been the most meaningful? Has your relationship with the

Become

Someone who
notices the holy

Fixed upon Him

Set apart to the Lord

Consecrated to the Lord

Holiness to the Lord

One who loves much

Humble enough to pour
from the alabaster flask

Holy

Lord changed? Is your journey leading you to become more holy? Closer to becoming His?

As you ponder, perhaps you could take a moment to write down your testimony of this journey and who you have become. Include your thoughts and feelings about your relationship with the Lord.

Solo Time
Becoming His

You hold in your hands a journey that is almost finished. I wonder if you would mind pausing for a moment to look back? It is no surprise that every ending starts with a beginning. We must remember it is the journey that captures the learning in between.

How do we best capture the learning in between?

By retracing each step.

Perhaps, just now, we could study a few small glimpses of the journey of those who have gone before. Maybe their lessons will feel similar to ours. Some of these glimpses include stories from disciples that we have studied within the pages of this book; other glimpses come from stories within the scriptures. The experiences that have been chosen are meant to act as a reminder of the pathway we have walked, the lessons we have learned together, the disciples we are becoming.

I turn to holy words on gilded pages. I see glimpses of disciples who have known the Lord. I try to discover memories of my journey within each of their steps.

It is the first month . . .

And I look upon Jesus where He walks, and I hear Him speak, and I follow. "What seek ye?" He questions (John 1:38). My heart ponders and I realize there is a longing within to know Him. He invites, "Come and see" (John 1:39). So I leave behind what once consumed me.

Slowly, I become more, and in the process I discover He is my everything.

It is the second month . . .

And I am dressed in fine linen, and it is evening, and I find myself intrigued by a Master who is good. I wonder *what good thing I should do,* and I ask, "What lack I yet?" (Matthew 19:20). I learn from the lesson of the young man with great possessions and pray that my heart will soften.

I become willing, and in the process I discover He is my constant guide.

It is the third month . . .

And I bring precious stones, and gold from the furnace, and I refine silver. Then I gather ore, and make a bellows to blow the fire, and from the ore I make tools (see 1 Nephi 17). I discover the Lord has a great work in mind for me. I know that He can instruct me, that I too might build. So I bring my finest.

I become a builder in His kingdom, and in the process I discover He is my cornerstone.

It is the fourth month . . .

And I am one who has journeyed into a far country, and wasted my substance, and lived blindly, and I find myself wanting. I know what it is to feed swine; I know what it feels like to have spent all. I look back and recognize the moments when I finally came to myself (see Luke 15).

I was not always who I might have been, but through the process I discover He is my second chance.

It is the fifth month . . .

And it has been years, and I have spent all that I have, and I am not better—but worse. From the press I reach to Him, longing to touch His robe, to be made whole. In that moment I come fearing and trembling, knowing (see Mark 5:25–28).

I become His brokenhearted, and in the process I discover He is my healing balm.

It is the sixth month . . .

And I am in the wilderness, and I have been patient in longsuffering, and I have fasted and prayed much. I learn what it means to live in tune, and my heart takes courage, and I suppose that what I am about to undertake is a great work (see Alma 17).

I become an instrument in His hands, and in the process I discover He is the symphony of my life.

It is the seventh month . . .

And I am walking along the road, and my eyes are holden, and perhaps I, too, am slow of heart to believe. The day is far spent, and yet, I beg of the Lord to abide with me. My heart burns as He talks with me by the way and each time the scriptures are opened (see Luke 24).

I become drawn to Him, and in the process I discover He is the source of my sure word.

It is the eighth month . . .

And I am walking down a dusty pathway, and I have come from Samaria, and I need to draw water. I know not what I worship until my heart is opened, and I believe. Recognizing the Christ, I leave behind my water pot—choosing to serve with humility, to keep back nothing (see John 4; Acts 20).

I become His obedient follower, and in the process I discover He is the pathway home.

It is the ninth month . . .

And I journey from Jerusalem to Jericho by chance, and I see, and I look, and I cross the road. Within the moment I learn compassion, and I take care, and I show mercy—for He has taught me, "Go, and do thou likewise" (Luke 10).

I become a succorer of many, and in the process I discover that He is love unconditional.

It is the tenth month . . .

And I have rent my coat in memory of my God, and my religion, and my freedom. I fasten on my headplate, and my breastplate, and my shield, and I gird my armor about my loins, and I pray mightily unto God. I raise the standard in whatsoever place I enter because I am a true believer of Christ (see Alma 46).

I become His valiant warrior, and in the process I discover He is my brave rearguard.

It is the eleventh month . . .

And I see wind boisterous, and the darkness of the fourth watch, and I am afraid. He beckons, and I learn that walking as His witness will require me to step out of the boat. So, I focus my eyes on Him and I come down out of the ship (see Matthew 14).

I become His steadfast witness, and in the process I discover He is my sure anchor.

It is the twelfth month . . .

And I have learned the wisdom of turning aside from the mundane to see the great sight, and I recognize holy ground, and I take off my shoes. There, in bare feet, I stand as His disciple. Set apart. Consecrated. One who loves much (see Exodus 3; Luke 7).

I become holy, and in the process I discover He is my burning bush.

Now my heart fills with gratitude,

And I look up, and I see His hand, and I know for certain.

There is One who is my everything, in whom I can always trust.

There is One whose guidance is constant.

There is One who will instruct me in a great work.

There is One who offers a second chance.

There is One who brings the healing balm.

There is One who orchestrates my life.

There is One whose word is sure.

There is One who marks the pathway home.

There is One whose love is unconditional.

There is One who guards bravely against defeat.

There is One who anchors my soul.

There is One who burns in every bush.

And I am becoming His.

The Journey Ahead

The last chapter of this book would not be complete without touching upon the most important principle of this journey: How can we truly become His unless we are known of Him?

This principle is the *summum bonum* of it all.

It is taught beautifully in the book of Moses, in the moment when Enoch steps back and realizes how large the universe is compared to how small each human being is, when he comes to understand that somehow the Lord is capable of loving each individual personally. "Were it possible that man could number the particles of the earth, yea, millions of earths like this, it would not be a beginning to the number of thy creations . . . *and yet thou art there*" (Moses 7:30; emphasis added).

I had the opportunity to sit in a Relief Society class where the teacher held up a glass jar filled to the brim with white sugar—the particles of the earth. She asked if someone would be willing to count each particle while she was teaching. We all laughed. Then she asked us how the Lord could really know each one of us. In that moment I felt small. Insignificant.

Forgotten. She asked us to turn to Moses and we read, "All things are numbered unto me, *for they are mine, and I know them*" (Moses 1:35; emphasis added).

Immediately my mind was filled with the moments in my life when I have been distinctly aware that the Lord knew me individually and personally. The tender-mercy moments that have taught me, without fail, that He is there.

Several years ago our stake president invited each of the families in our stake to purchase a picture of the Savior to hang in our homes. He told us not to buy just any picture; instead we were to find a picture that strengthened our testimony of the Lord. Perhaps the painting would portray the way we thought the Savior looked, or maybe the illustration represented one of our favorite stories of the Savior. The important thing was that every time we looked at it, our testimony would be strengthened.

Greg and I determined that we wanted to do this for each of our children. We set aside a night just before Christmas to go shopping for pictures of the Savior. Each of our children would choose his or her own picture, and as a gift we would frame the pictures and hang them in their bedrooms.

Josh chose a painting of the Second Coming. Meg chose a scene where the Lord was throwing a young girl into the air and catching her again. Grace chose a pastel rendition of the Savior sitting surrounded by children. Caleb knew exactly what picture he wanted, but we could not find it. He wanted a painting of the story found in Matthew 14, when Peter walks on the water to Christ. However, he didn't want Peter to be walking on the water; he wanted the moment when Peter was *drowning* in the water, and the Savior reached out His hand to rescue him. Caleb was thirteen years old at the time, so *of course* he wanted the most dramatic part of the story to be depicted. He would not settle for anything else.

We couldn't find a painting like that anywhere. I searched and searched, browsing the Internet, combing through every art book I could find. Then, finally, the week before Christmas, I stumbled upon a really expensive book of artwork that included the exact picture Caleb had described. I bought the *whole book* so I could rip out the one picture to have it framed. Just before we framed the pictures, we had each of our children write in his or her own handwriting at the bottom of the picture, "I am a disciple of Jesus Christ. Christmas 2004."

Those pictures had hung in my children's rooms for six years when, in August 2010, Caleb left on a two-year mission to Croatia. In the first letter he sent from the Missionary Training Center, he wrote, "I am the only missionary in the whole MTC learning Croatian." Lucky for me I was not quick to put two and two together. For ten blissful weeks it did not dawn on me that if you are the *only* missionary in the MTC learning Croatian, then you are probably the *only* missionary in the MTC going to Croatia.

When realization finally dawned, I panicked! "They can't send Caleb all the way to Croatia by himself," I told Greg, "There's no way they would send a missionary somewhere alone." Greg just smiled. Caleb called from the airport to check in as he was leaving. A nice couple from the MTC had dropped him off at the curb of the Salt Lake International Airport. Sure enough, he was traveling alone. He thought it was hilarious that people kept asking where his companion was. I did not find it nearly as amusing. I told him to call us when he arrived in Paris *after* he found his connecting flight to Slovenia. (I didn't want him to miss the plane because he was talking to his mother.) We hung up, and I started to pray. I prayed that the Lord would be mindful of Caleb, that He would not lose track of him, that Caleb would be known and remembered of the Lord throughout his journey. I must have said that prayer a hundred times.

Caleb was supposed to call at 3:45 A.M. From 3:45 A.M. to 4:30 A.M. I watched the phone and willed it to ring. And I prayed. Finally it rang. "Sorry, Mom! I went to find the plane like you told me, but I couldn't find it anywhere. I made sure I had the right gate and then went back again. Still, no plane. I must have been too early. I walked all the way to the end of the gate to make sure it wasn't there. While I was down there someone locked the gate shut, since they weren't currently using it, and I got stuck inside!" Caleb quickly explained.

"How did you get out?" I panicked.

"I found a cleaning lady, pointed to the lock, and said the only French word I know, *merci*. Finally she let me out."

At least he had made it safely as far as Paris. As soon as we hung up from that conversation, I started to pray again that the Lord would be mindful of Caleb, that He would not lose track of him, that Caleb would be known and remembered of the Lord throughout his journey. I figured if I didn't hear from the mission president, it meant Caleb had arrived safely in Croatia.

I spent the entire first week of Caleb's mission doing what every missionary mom does—I prayed. I pled with the Lord for his safety. I asked that he would be assigned to a companion who would teach him well. I knew that the mission encompassed seven countries, with only forty-four missionaries. This meant Caleb and his companion might serve in a country separate from the mission president or any other elders. I prayed that he would never feel alone. Constantly my heart uttered the prayer that

I had prayed throughout Caleb's journey, that the Lord would be mindful of Caleb, that He would not lose track of him, that Caleb would be known and remembered of the Lord along the way.

A week later Caleb wrote home. In his letter he wrote, "Last Wednesday was zone meeting. It was super awesome! I got to meet all the Croatian missionaries. President Hill had me stand and bear my testimony. Then after that President Hill talked a little about when I walked through the doors of the Slovenian Airport all by myself. *He likened me to Peter walking on water when he saw Christ*" (emphasis added).

Now, the mission president did not know that was Caleb's favorite scripture story—but the Lord did. He honored Caleb's commitment to serve Him in a way that was personal to Caleb. My son *was* known and remembered of the Lord.

When we become altogether committed to knowing and loving the Lord, we begin to understand how altogether committed He is to knowing and loving us.

In the moments when we wonder if the Lord is mindful of us, the moments when we wonder if He is aware of us and our situation, we must watch for His hand in our lives. It is in those tender-mercy moments that we come to realize an important truth—we are known and remembered of the Lord on every step of this journey.

He forgets not His own.

Perhaps that is the greatest blessing of Becoming His. We can look to Him in the middle moments of every long and difficult journey. We can lean on Him when we are tired and in need of a rest. We can turn to Him when we just want to laugh a little or cry a little. We can allow Him to fill the empty places when we yearn for something more. And when we find ourselves in deep trouble and we are looking for courage, when our hearts are weary or despairing and we are looking for strength to go on, we will find in Him a true friend, a constant companion, and a source of strength beyond our own.

Although you have reached the end of this book, I must remind you that this is not the end of the road, nor is it the conclusion of this journey. Those who have read the books I have written previous to this one know that I hate endings. Because of that, it is my hope that this chapter will not be viewed as a conclusion, but rather as a pause on our journey—a moment where we catch our breath and then move forward along the pathway ahead.

It has been a privilege to walk this path together with you for a time. Now we part ways, knowing not what the road ahead will bring. Life has taught me that there is more than one path to the top of every mountain and that our lives will bring unique experiences that will, in the end, lead us to know the Lord in very individual and personal ways. Perhaps along this journey our paths will cross again. If you would like to, you can stop by and visit at www.dailyclosertochrist.com, I hope you do. I would love to have the opportunity to hear from you and speak of miracles, and of mercies, and of the true Friend with whom we travel—a constant companion who has promised that we need never walk alone.

As you prepare to take your next step, I leave you with the Lord's blessing given to the children of Israel.

On this wise ye shall bless the children
of Israel, saying unto them,
The Lord bless thee, and keep thee:
The Lord make his face shine upon thee,
and be gracious unto thee:
The Lord lift up his countenance upon thee,
and give thee peace.
. . . put my name upon the children of Israel;
and I will bless them.

—NUMBERS 6:23–27

. . . for they are mine and I know them.

—MOSES 1:35

Notes

FRONTISPIECE

The first step on the path . . .

    Dieter F. Uchtdorf, "The Way of the Disciple," *Ensign*, May 2009, 77.

JUST A LITTLE BOOK

"What would you do . . .

    Myrtle Reed, *Flower of the Dusk* (New York: G.P. Putnam's Sons, 1908), 32–33.

THE BEGINNING

We do not really grasp . . .

    Truman G. Madsen, "The Savior, the Sacrament, and Self-Worth," in *The Arms of His Love: Talks from the 1999 Women's Conference Sponsored by Brigham Young University and the Relief Society* (Salt Lake City: Bookcraft, 2000), 246.

"The first step to finding faith . . .

    Robert D. Hales, "Finding Faith in the Lord Jesus Christ," *Ensign*, November 2004, 72; emphasis added.

"necessity to not only express but to do . . .

    David A. Bednar, "Ask in Faith," *Ensign*, May 2008, 94–95; emphasis added.

"Let us study the ways of the Lord . . .

> Gordon B. Hinckley, "A Time of New Beginnings," *Ensign*, May 2000, 87; emphasis added.

"Now is the time . . .

> Dallin H. Oaks, "The Challenge to Become," *Ensign*, November 2000, 33; emphasis added.

THE FIRST MONTH: BECOME MORE

Down in the wild garden . . .

> Myrtle Reed, *Old Rose and Silver* (New York: Grosset & Dunlap, 1902), 86.

"With this commitment . . .

> Neil L. Andersen, "The Joy of Becoming Clean," *Ensign*, April 1995, 52; emphasis added.

"To comprehend the works of Christ . . .

> James E. Talmage, *Jesus the Christ* (Salt Lake City: Deseret Book, 1982), 140–42.

"Welcome the task . . .

> Louise Yates Robison, as quoted in Janet Peterson and LaRene Gaunt, *Elect Ladies: Presidents of the Relief Society* (Salt Lake City: Deseret Book, 1990), 124.

"Men and women who turn . . .

> Ezra Taft Benson, "Jesus Christ—Gifts and Expectations," *Ensign*, December 1988, 4.

"The virtues expressed . . .

> H. David Burton, "More Holiness Give Me," *Ensign*, November 2004, 99.

"They rose to that height . . .

> Myrtle Reed, *Lavender and Old Lace* (New York: Grosset & Dunlap, 1902), 220.

THE SECOND MONTH: BECOME WILLING

A cathedral without windows . . .

> James L. Gordon, as quoted by David O. McKay, in Conference Report, October 1952, 12.

"It is significant that when we partake . . .

> Dallin H. Oaks, "Taking upon Us the Name of Jesus Christ," *Ensign*, May 1985, 81–83; emphasis added.

"Maintain your personal journals . . .

Spencer W. Kimball, "Listen to the Prophets," *Ensign*, May 1978, 77.

"a curse on all . . .

Bible Dictionary, s.v. "Haggai," 698.

"The submission of one's will . . .

Neal A. Maxwell, "'Swallowed Up in the Will of the Father,'" *Ensign*, November 1995, 24.

"Could you turn one of these women away . . .

Joseph Fielding Smith, *Teachings of Presidents of the Church: Joseph F. Smith* (Salt Lake City: The Church of Jesus Christ of Latter-day Saints, 1998), 189.

THE THIRD MONTH: BECOME A BUILDER

That which I *have* . . .

Dallin H. Oaks, "The Challenge to Become," *Ensign*, November 2000, 32.

"All that I have . . .

Dallin H. Oaks, "The Challenge to Become," *Ensign*, November 2000, 32.

An old man, going a lone highway . . .

"The Bridge Builder," by Will Allen Dromgoole, in James Dalton Morrison, ed., *Masterpieces of Religious Verse* (New York: Harper, 1948), 342.

"But as the walls of the city . . .

Dieter F. Uchtdorf, "We Are Doing a Great Work and Cannot Come Down," *Ensign*, May 2009, 61.

THE FOURTH MONTH: BECOME WHO YOU MIGHT HAVE BEEN

a legion conveys the idea . . .

See Alfred Edersheim, *The Life and Times of Jesus the Messiah,* accessed online at http://www.ccel.org/ccel/edersheim/lifetimes.viii.xxv.html.

"Such was to become his life-work . . .

Alfred Edersheim, *The Life and Times of Jesus the Messiah,* accessed online at http://www.ccel.org/ccel/edersheim/lifetimes.viii.xxv.html.

"I bear testimony . . .

Truman G. Madsen, *Christ and the Inner Life* (Salt Lake City: Bookcraft, 1988), 14.

"Restoring what you cannot restore . . .
>Boyd K. Packer, "The Brilliant Morning of Forgiveness," *Ensign*, November 1995, 19–20.

"In truth, it was only . . .
>Alfred Edersheim, *The Bible History: Old Testament* (Grand Rapids, MI: Wm. B. Eerdmans Publishing Co, 1956), 62.

"If anyone does not feel worthy . . .
>Jeffrey R. Holland, "'Sanctify Yourselves,'" *Ensign*, November 2000, 39.

No one promised this would be easy. . . .
>Nancy Sorensen, "Stretching," *New Era,* January 1987, 51.

"To get you from where you are . . .
>Richard G. Scott, "Trust in the Lord," *Ensign*, November 1995, 16–17.

"My call to you tonight . . .
>Jeffrey R. Holland, "'Sanctify Yourselves,'" *Ensign*, November 2000, 38–40.

"In the private sanctuary . . .
>Thomas S. Monson, "The Will Within," *Ensign*, May 1987, 69.

"In every block of marble . . .
>As quoted online at www.michelangelo-gallery.com/michelangelo-quotes.aspx.

"The artistry involved . . .
>Sterling W. Sill, *The Majesty of Books* (Salt Lake City: Deseret Book, 1974), 128–29.

"Hang on the walls of your mind . . .
>James McNeill Whistler, as quoted in Sterling W. Sill, "Great Experiences," *Ensign*, June 1971, 43.

"To every man there comes . . .
>Winston Churchill, as quoted in Jeffrey R. Holland, "'Sanctify Yourselves,'" *Ensign*, November 2000, 40.

The Fifth Month: Become Refined

Do not question too much . . .
>Myrtle Reed, *Old Rose and Silver* (New York: Grosset & Dunlap, 1909), 129.

"There may be times . . .
>Dieter F. Uchtdorf, "The Infinite Power of Hope," *Ensign*, November 2008, 23.

Have you come to the Red Sea place . . .

Annie Johnson Flint (1866–1932), accessed online at http://www.womenof
christianity.com/?p=2416

The Sixth Month: Become His Instrument

Our privilege and our responsibility . . .

Mary Ellen Smoot, "We Are Instruments in the Hands of God," *Ensign*, November
2000, 90.

"In the end . . .

Dieter F. Uchtdorf, "Happiness, Your Heritage," *Ensign*, November 2008, 120.

"told me never to arise . . .

John Taylor, *The Gospel Kingdom*, edited by G. Homer Durham (Salt Lake City:
Bookcraft, 1943).

"[The Holy Ghost] comes a little at a time . . .

Spencer W. Kimball, *Teachings of Spencer W. Kimball*, edited by Edward L.
Kimball (Salt Lake City: Bookcraft, 1982), 114.

"Is there yet more . . .

Richard G. Scott, "To Acquire Spiritual Guidance," *Ensign*, November 2009, 6–9.

"Truly, we may each be . . .

Mary Ellen Smoot, "We Are Instruments in the Hands of God," *Ensign*, November
2000, 89–92.

The Seventh Month: Become Drawn to Him

All that he had intellectually . . .

Tad R. Callister, *The Infinite Atonement* (Salt Lake City: Deseret Book, 2000), 153.

"He who reads it . . .

Joseph Smith, *Teachings of the Prophet Joseph Smith*, selected and arranged by
Joseph Fielding Smith (Salt Lake City: Deseret Book, 1976), 56.

"Whither the people followed him . . .

James E. Talmage, *Jesus the Christ* (Salt Lake City: Deseret Book, 1982), 181.

"I fear that many of us rush about . . .

Carlos E. Asay, "'Look to God and Live,'" *Ensign*, November 1978, 53–54.

THE EIGHTH MONTH: BECOME A TRUE FOLLOWER

True discipleship is for volunteers . . .

Neal A. Maxwell, *Not My Will, but Thine* (Salt Lake City: Bookcraft, 1988), 89.

"We become what we want to be . . .

Richard G. Scott, "The Transforming Power of Faith and Character," *Ensign*, November 2010, 43.

"I plead with you . . .

Thomas S. Monson, "Finding Joy in the Journey," *Ensign*, November 2008, 85–87.

"We must not give up hope . . .

Dallin H. Oaks, "The Challenge to Become," *Ensign*, November 2000, 34.

Eddie Aikau was a lifeguard . . .

See Burl Burlingame, "Eddie: Riding on the crest of the myth," *Honolulu Star-Bulletin,* March 6, 1998; available at http://archives.starbulletin.com/98/03/09/features/story1.html.

"We of this generation . . .

Gordon B. Hinckley, "The Dawning of a Brighter Day," *Ensign*, May 2004, 84.

THE NINTH MONTH: BECOME A SUCCORER OF MANY

I'm glad to think . . .

Myrtle Reed, *Old Rose and Silver* (New York: Grosset & Dunlap, 1909), 314.

"Most ministering opportunities . . .

Bonnie D. Parkin, "Personal Ministry," Brigham Young University Devotional address, February 13, 2007; available at http://speeches.byu.edu/reader/reader.php?id=11599.

"May I invite you . . .

Mary Ellen Smoot, "You and Your Essential Role Today," Brigham Young University Women's Conference address, 1999; available at http://ce.byu.edu/cw/womens conference/archive/1999/smoot_mary_ellen.htm.

"You could, this moment . . .

Henry B. Eyring, *To Draw Closer to God* (Salt Lake City: Deseret Book, 1997), 50; emphasis added.

When I went to the door . . .

Marguerite Stewart, "Forgiveness Flour," *Religious Studies Center Newsletter,* vol. 7, no. 3 (May 1993): 1.

"As thy days may demand . . .

"How Firm a Foundation," *Hymns* (Salt Lake City: The Church of Jesus Christ of Latter-day Saints, 1985), no. 85.

"The reason charity never fails . . .

Dallin H. Oaks, "The Challenge to Become," *Ensign,* November 2000, 32–34.

"My daughter-in-law's mother . . .

Bonnie D. Parkin, "Personal Ministry," Brigham Young University Devotional address, February 13, 2007; available at http://speeches.byu.edu/reader/reader .php?id=11599.

The Tenth Month: Become His Warrior

The kingdom of God

Martin Luther, as quoted in Jeffrey R. Holland and Patricia T. Holland, "Considering Covenants: Women, Men, Perspective, Promises," in *To Rejoice as Women: Talks from the 1994 Women's Conference* (Salt Lake City: Deseret Book, 1995), 105.

Thou art our rock . . .

"For All the Saints," *Hymns* (Salt Lake City: The Church of Jesus Christ of Latter-day Saints, 1985), no. 82.

"it is meant . . .

Boyd K. Packer, "Do Not Fear," *Ensign,* May 2004, 79.

"the man within . . .

James E. Talmage, *Jesus the Christ* (Salt Lake City: Deseret Book, 1982), 126–27.

"May I say once more . . .

Howard W. Hunter, "'Bind on Thy Sandals,'" *Ensign,* May 1978, 35.

O thou Rock of our salvation . . .

"O Thou Rock of Our Salvation," *Hymns* (Salt Lake City: The Church of Jesus Christ of Latter-day Saints, 1985), no. 258.

"Once there was a ship . . .

Myrtle Reed, *Old Rose and Silver* (New York: Grosset & Dunlap, 1909), 149, 154.

"The final outcome . . .

Ezra Taft Benson, "In His Steps," Brigham Young University fireside address, March 4, 1979, accessed online at http://speeches.byu.edu/reader/reader.php?id=6718.

THE ELEVENTH MONTH: BECOME HIS WITNESS

"Here then is a great truth . . .

James E. Faust, "The Refiner's Fire," *Ensign*, May 1979, 53.

"It is not even enough . . .

Dallin H. Oaks, "The Challenge to Become," *Ensign*, November 2000, 32.

THE TWELFTH MONTH: BECOME HOLY

Earth's crammed with heaven . . .

Elizabeth Barrett Browning, *Aurora Leigh: A Poem in Nine Books* (London: Smith, Elder, & Co., 1898), 286.

"Jesus recognized in the man . . .

James E. Talmage, *Jesus the Christ* (Salt Lake City: Deseret Book, 1982), 207; emphasis added.

"John R. Moyle lived in Alpine . . .

Jeffrey R. Holland, "As Doves to Our Windows," *Ensign*, May 2000, 76–77.

"were set apart . . .

Bible Dictionary, s.v. "Holiness," 703.

"Every moment of my life . . .

Brigham Young, *Deseret News,* April 2, 1862, 313.

"Consecration is not resignation . . .

Neal A. Maxwell, "'Swallowed Up in the Will of the Father,'" *Ensign*, November 1995, 24.

"the English word . . .

Bible Dictionary, s.v. "Anointed One," 609.